GAIA
&
GOD

GAIA
&
GOD

*An Ecofeminist Theology
of Earth Healing*

———

Rosemary Radford Ruether

HarperOne
An Imprint of HarperCollins Publishers

Grateful acknowledgment is made for the following:

The scripture quotations contained herein are from the New Revised Standard Version of the Bible, copyright © 1989, by the Division of Christian Education of the National Council of Churches of Christ in the United States of America, and are used by permission. All rights reserved.

Excerpt from "The Medical Consequences of Nuclear War" by Howard Hiatt in *Waging Peace: A Handbook for the Struggle to Abolish Nuclear Weapons.* Copyright © 1982. Reprinted by permission of HarperCollins Publishers, Inc.

"Poimandres" from *The Gnostic Religion* by Hans Jonas. Copyright © 1963. Reprinted by permission of Beacon Press.

Sermon by John Winthrop from *God's New Israel: Religious Interpretations of American Destiny* by Conrad Cherry. Copyright © 1971. Reprinted by permission of Simon & Schuster.

HarperCollins books may be purchased for educational, business, or sales promotional use. For information, please e-mail the Special Markets Department at SPsales@harpercollins.com.

HarperCollins Web site: http://www.harpercollins.com

HarperCollins®, ®, and HarperOne™ are trademarks of HarperCollins Publishers.

FIRST HARPERCOLLINS PAPERBACK EDITION PUBLISHED IN 1994

An Earlier Edition of This Book Was Cataloged As Follows:

Ruether, Rosemary Radford.
Gaia and God : an ecofeminist theology of earth healing
Rosemary Radford Ruether.
p. cm.
ISBN: 978-0-06-066967-6
Includes bibliographical references and index.
1. Human ecology—Religious aspects—Christianity.
2. Feminism—Religious aspects—Christianity.   3. Patriarchy—Religious aspects—Christianity.   4. Creation.   5. Violence—Religious aspects—Christianity.   I. Title.
BT695.5.R83   1992
261.8'362—dc20   91–58911

17 18 19 20 21 RRD(H) 30 29 28 27 26 25 24 23 22

*This book is dedicated to Adiba Khader and her
four daughters, Ghada (twenty-one), Abir (seventeen),
Ghalda (fourteen), and Ghana (twelve), and all the other
mothers and children who died in the early morning of
February 13, 1991, in a bomb shelter in Baghdad that
was shattered by two American "smart bombs."*

Contents

Acknowledgments

I wish to thank the many friends who have read parts or the whole of this manuscript and provided helpful feedback: Carol Adams, Richard Austin, John Cobb, Sarah Forth, Rich Hutchinson, Jay McDaniel, Don Moon, Wolfgang Roth, Herman Ruether, Brian Swimme, Susan Thistlethwaite, and Barbara Troxell.

Parts of this work were given as the Ferguson lectures at Manchester University in Manchester, England, and as the Willson lectures at the Earlham School of Religion in Richmond, Indiana, in March and April of 1992.

Introduction

Gaia and God, ecofeminism, and earth healing: these vast concepts point to the wide-ranging agenda that I seek to explore in this book. Are Gaia, the living and sacred earth, and God, the monotheistic deity of the biblical traditions, on speaking terms with each other? Ecology and feminism, brought together in the unified perspective of ecofeminism, provide the critical perspective from which I seek to evaluate the heritage of Western Christian culture. The goal of this quest is earth healing, a healed relationship between men and women, between classes and nations, and between humans and the earth. Such healing is possible only through recognition and transformation of the way in which Western culture, enshrined in part in Christianity, has justified such domination.

It would be useful to define the sense in which I use the terms *ecology, feminism,* and *ecofeminism.* The word *ecology* comes from the biological science of natural environmental communities. It examines how these natural communities function to sustain a healthy web of life and how they become disrupted, causing death to plant and animal life. Human intervention is the major cause of such disruption. Thus ecology, in the expanded sense of a combined socioeconomic and biological science, emerged in the last several decades to examine how human misuse of "nature" is causing pollution of soils, water, and air, and

the destruction of plant and animal communities, thereby threatening the base of life upon which the human species itself depends.[1]

Deep ecology took this study of ecology to another level. It
examined the symbolic, psychological, and ethical patterns of destructive relations of humans with nature. It particularly saw
Western culture, sanctified in Christianity, as a major cause of
this destructive culture. It explored ways to create a new, more
holistic consciousness and culture.[2]

Feminism also has many dimensions of meaning. As liberal
feminism, it seeks equality of women with men in liberal, democratic societies; as socialist feminism, it declares that such equality is not possible without a transformation of the social relations
of ownership of the means of production and reproduction. Radical feminism declared that the issue was deeper, that we had to
look at the patterns of culture and consciousness that sustain
male domination over and violence to women.

Ecofeminism brings together these two explorations of ecology and feminism, in their full, or deep forms, and explores how
male domination of women and domination of nature are interconnected, both in cultural ideology and in social structures.[3]

In this book I seek to assess the cultural and social roots that
have promoted destructive relations between men and women,
between ruling and subjugated human groups, and the destruction of the rest of the biotic community, of which humans are an
interdependent part. I also sift through the legacy of the Christian and Western cultural heritage to find usable ideas that might
nourish a healed relation to each other and to the earth.

If dominating and destructive relations to the earth are interrelated with gender, class, and racial domination, then a healed
relation to the earth cannot come about simply through technological "fixes." It demands a social reordering to bring about just
and loving interrelationship between men and women, between
races and nations, between groups presently stratified into social

classes, manifest in great disparities of access to the means of life. In short, it demands that we must speak of eco-justice, and not simply of domination of the earth as though that happened unrelated to social domination.

Classical Western cultural traditions, which were codified between 500 B.C.E. and 800 C.E., and of which Christianity is a major expression, have justified and sacralized these relationships of domination. Thus we inherit not only a legacy of systems of domination, but also cultures that teach us to see such relations as the "natural order" and as the will of God.

In particular, the way these cultures have construed the idea of the male monotheistic God, and the relation of this God to the cosmos as its Creator, have reinforced symbolically the relations of domination of men over women, masters over slaves, and (male ruling-class) humans over animals and over the earth. Domination of women has provided a key link, both socially and symbolically, to the domination of earth, hence the tendency in patriarchal cultures to link women with earth, matter, and nature, while identifying males with sky, intellect, and transcendent spirit.

But these classical traditions did not only sacralize patriarchal hierarchy over women, workers, and the earth. They also struggled with what they perceived to be injustice and sin and sought to create just and loving relations between people in their relation to the earth and to the divine. Some of this effort to name evil and struggle against it reinforced relations of domination and created victim-blaming spiritualities and ethics. But there are also glimpses in this heritage of transformative, biophilic relationships.

These glimpses are a precious legacy that needs to be separated from the toxic waste of sacralized domination. We do not need to and should not totalize negative judgment against past biblical and Christian cultures. It would be surprising indeed if there were no positive insights that could be reclaimed from three

thousand years of collective human struggle about the meaning
of life and the way to live justly and well. Ecofeminist critics of
classical culture are surely not the first humans to have positive
sensibilities.

A healed relation to each other and to the earth then calls for a
new consciousness, a new symbolic culture and spirituality. We
need to transform our inner psyches and the way we symbolize
the interrelations of men and women, humans and earth, humans
and the divine, the divine and the earth. Ecological healing is a
theological and psychic-spiritual process. Needless to say, spirituality or new consciousness will not transform deeply materialized
relations of domination by themselves. We must be wary of new
forms of privatized intrapsychic activity, divorced from social systems of power. Rather we must see the work of eco-justice and the
work of spirituality as interrelated, the inner and outer aspects of
one process of conversion and transformation.

I juxtapose the terms *Gaia* and *God* in the title of this book because all the issues that I wish to explore finally pose the question
of the relationship between the living planet, earth, and the concept of God as it has been shaped in the Western religious traditions. *Gaia* is the word for the Greek Earth Goddess, and it is also
a term adopted by a group of planetary biologists, such as James
Lovelock and Lynn Margulis, to refer to their thesis that the entire planet is a living system, behaving as a unified organism.[4]

The term *Gaia* has caught on among those seeking a new ecological spirituality as a religious vision. Gaia is seen as a person-
ified being, an immanent divinity. Some see the Jewish and
Christian male monotheistic God as a hostile concept that ratio-
nalizes alienation from and neglect of the earth. Gaia should replace God as our focus of worship.[5] I agree with much of this
critique, yet I believe that merely replacing a male transcendent
deity with an immanent female one is an insufficient answer to
the "god-problem."

We need a vision of a source of life that is "yet more" than what presently exists, continually bringing forth both new life and new visions of how life should be more just and more caring. The human capacity for ethical reason is not rootless in the universe, but expresses this deeper source of life "beyond" the biological. Consciousness and altruistic care are qualities that have some reflection in other animals, and indeed are often too poorly developed in our own species. To believe in divine being means to believe that those qualities in ourselves are rooted in and respond to the life power from which the universe itself arises.

A new ecological culture is often defined as rethinking the relationship of "man" and "nature," but both these terms are problematic. The male generic "man" conceals the Western ruling-class male context of the problem. But the word *nature* in Western thought is also part of the problem. The word *nature* is used in four distinct senses in Western culture: (1) as that which is "essential" to a being; (2) as the sum total of physical reality, including humans; (3) as the sum total of physical reality apart from humans; and (4) the "created" world apart from God and divine grace.

In this book I assume that earth forms a living system, of which humans are an inextricable part. We are latecomers to the earth, a very recent product of its evolutionary life. Yet we, particularly in the West, have constructed our concept of ourselves as humans over against all that is nonhuman, and thereby constructed our concept of "nature" as both the nonhuman and the non-divine.

In our social and cultural construction of "nature," humans, from the outset of hunting and agriculture, have modified and changed the earth systems themselves, reshaping plants, animals, air, water, and soil. Nature, in the sense of the earth system apart from human influence, is in its own constant process of adaptation and change. Human reshaping of nonhuman nature is itself a phase of this process of continuous adaptation. In this book I will use the term *nature* within this framework of understanding. I use quotation marks when the term is being used in a questionably static, unrelational, or essentialist sense, or in contrast to "grace."

This work is organized into four sections, under the headings of Creation, Destruction, Domination and Deceit, and Healing. These four sections correspond in some ways to the more familiar categories of Christian theology of creation, judgment, sin and fallenness, and redemption. But in this book, each of these four categories are examined for their ideological biases, which have contributed to distorted relationships. Each section both critiques these categories in their traditional understanding and suggests a more holistic meaning of these concepts.

The first section, Creation, has two parallel chapters. In the first chapter, I review three classical creation stories that have shaped the biblical and Christian tradition: the Babylonian story, the Hebrew story, and the Greek (Platonic) story. I show how these stories, shaped as the classical systems of patriarchy were being codified, functioned to sacralize relations of domination.

The second chapter looks at the breakdown of classical cosmology and the shaping of a post-Newtonian cosmology and earth history. I ask, is this scientific account a new and potentially global creation story for humanity today? Are there elements in it of ethics and spirituality that can relate our story of earth and the cosmos to a holistic culture? How can we heal the modern split between "fact" and "value," which has separated religion and science into noncommunicating compartments of ourselves?

The section on Destruction also has two parallel chapters. In the third chapter, I review the development of scenarios of world destruction in the biblical and Christian tradition. Why have so many Christians (and others) spent so much time imagining the fiery end of the cosmos? Why have we imagined a God who destroys the earth and most living things on it as a justified expression of his wrath and angry judgment on human evil? How have these stories shaped our relations to other people and to the earth and cosmos?

The fourth chapter looks at the interrelated, contemporary crises of ecological devastation, poverty, and militarism, and asks, is this the new apocalypse, the new story of impending world destruction? How is the way we tell the story of these impending threats and dangers shaped by the heritage of biblical/Christian apocalyptic? Does this heritage tend to inform certain story patterns: angry judgment juxtaposed with utopian hope? How can we speak of the urgency of global crises without inducing either passivity and hopelessness or unrealistic escapism?

The third section, Domination and Deceit, has three chapters. The theme of all three is an exploration of the meaning of evil in relation to "nature," both in the sense of human "nature" and in the sense of the "material" world generally. The fifth chapter reviews the classical heritage of Jewish, Greek, and Christian understandings of evil. To what extent have these constructions of the relation of evil to "nature" been victim-blaming deceit, misnaming evil in ways that reinforce dominating relations to women and subjugated people, and negation of the earth? Are there recoverable elements in this heritage for ecofeminist theology and ethics?

The sixth chapter outlines contemporary versions of the story of the "fall from paradise" in ecofeminism, deep ecology, and creation spirituality. This story, found in contemporary radical culture, tells of a time of innocence and goodness before the "rise" of patriarchal "civilization," locating this fall into patriarchy sometime between the beginnings of agriculture and the consolidation of early urban cultures, that is, between 6000 B.C.E. and 2000 B.C.E. The chapter also explores some of the efforts of contemporary paleoanthropologists to reconstruct early human patterns, asking whether the story of the "fall into patriarchy" is corroborated in this literature.

There is some historical basis for seeing this era as a time when a critical shift took place in human relations and in human relations to the earth. But I also see a problem in the way history and myth are confused in many ecofeminist accounts of this transition. "Myths," in the sense of exemplary stories, are not illegitimate. Moreover, history is never completely objective, but is always a selection and interpretation of the past to make meaning for the present. But this does not mean that there can be no historical knowledge apart from subjective wishes, nor that myth does not need to be examined for its spiritual and ethical values.

The danger of the story of the prepatriarchal paradise and the fall into patriarchy is that it too easily allows somewhat marginalized Euro-American women and men to identify themselves with a lost innocence and to fail to take responsibility for their own complicity in the evils they excoriate. This "fall story" has great mythic power, but it is too simplistic. It is both too total in its negativity toward classical cultures and too naive about early tribal people. Without more careful evaluation, this "story" can mislead us about how we understand ourselves as Western people and our capacities for both good and evil.

The seventh chapter outlines the patterns of patriarchal societies, as those evolved from early Near Eastern urban configurations through the Greek and Roman empires, the shaping of Christianity, and their breakdown and transformation in Western scientific and colonial systems of modernity. The purpose of this chapter is to demonstrate the interconnection of domination and deceit, the social systems of power over women, workers, animals, and land, and how this domination is justified and sacralized in symbolic culture. The conclusion of the chapter also seeks to clarify the operating understanding of the relation of "evil" to "nature" in this work.

The final section of the book is called Healing. Here I trace two lines of biblical and Christian tradition that I seek to reclaim for an ecofeminist theology and spirituality, the covenantal tradition and the sacramental tradition. These two traditions seem to me to be complementary rather than alternatives to each other. The one tradition shapes our relation to nature and each other in terms of law and ethical responsibility. The other tradition ecstatically experiences the divine bodying forth in the cosmos, and beckons us into communion.

Neither of these traditions can be accepted simply in its traditional form, however. Both traditions were shaped in patriarchal, slave-holding societies and also reflect ancient geocentric cosmologies. Christians need to reshape these ideas in ways that free them from patriarchal constructions. We also need to bring these modes of relating to nature into dialogue with contemporary scientific knowledge and global realities.

The concluding chapter seeks to envision a healed society, in the sense of nondominating relations between humans beings in interrelation with the rest of nature. It suggests, in practical ways, how we, as affluent Western people, can begin to move from patterns of production, consumption, and waste that destroy the earth, to ecologically sustainable ones. But it also emphasizes that such shifts cannot be done only on the level of technological "fixes" without reshaping patterns of social domination between men and women, and between rich and poor classes and nations. For these are the social underpinnings that promote and allow such profligate and wasteful exploitation of the biosphere.

The chapter concludes by suggesting ways of moving forward in this work of transformative eco-justice through base communities of spirituality and resistance. In such base communities, groups of people can find local support, both for personal *metanoia,* or change of consciousness, and for sustaining a long struggle against systems of domination. Those who profit from such systems will not readily yield to new, more just social organization of human life within the biosphere.

Why do I construct the cultural line of this discussion around the Western Christian tradition, with its roots in the Babylonian, Hebrew, and Greek cultures? I do this for two reasons. First, because this is my tradition and therefore it is the culture for which I must be accountable. Second, it is a culture that has shaped and continues to shape (particularly in its secularized, scientific form) the rest of the world, through imperialist colonialism and neocolonialism. It is the major culture and system of domination that has pressed humans and the earth into the crises of ecological unsustainability, poverty, and militarism we now experience.

This does not mean that other cultures, such as the diverse Asian cultures, are simply innocent and good. They also have classic patriarchal, hierarchical, and militarist patterns. Their elites often have cooperated with Western hegemony, especially when this reinforced their local dominance. Asian spiritualities and cultures, such as Hinduism, Buddhism, Taoism, and Confucianism, also have countervailing traditions of harmony of humanity and nature that need to be reclaimed. These are not simply duplicates of Western patterns, but are distinct and different resources for ecological spirituality.

I have been influenced throughout my life by what creation theologian Matthew Fox calls "deep ecumenism."[6] Growing up in a combined Protestant and Roman Catholic family, with extended family that included Jews, Mexicans, Unitarians, Quakers, and Russian Orthodox, a multiplicity of perspectives living together has always seemed normal. Early in my education I entered into a dialogue with preclassical religions and cultures that lie behind the Hebrew world of the Ancient Near East, and also with the classical Greek world, acknowledging these "pagan" cultures as genuine theophanies or encounters with the divine. I decided that the three monotheistic faiths of Judaism, Christianity, and

Islam were incorrect in rejecting polytheistic "nature" religions as simply false and evil.

This attraction to and positive evaluation of the ancient non-biblical religions of the Near Eastern and Greek worlds has also disposed me to a similar openness to the non-biblical religions and cultures of other areas of the world: the Mayan, Incan, and Mexican cultures that underlie colonized and Christianized Latin America. In other parts of the world I have visited, such as South Africa, the Philippines, Korea, and India, there also are the heritages of indigenous, non-Christian cultures. Those creating feminist, ecological, and liberation spiritualities today seek to synthesize these heritages: Western, Eastern, and indigenous.[7] I have also been involved in dialogues between "classical" religions: between Christianity and Judaism, Islam, and Buddhism.

However, I have not sought to write this book as a "world religions" ecofeminist theology. I believe that a plurality of ecofeminist perspectives must arise from many cultural backgrounds and enter into dialogue with each other. No one person can do it all. My primary task is to speak from that broad configuration of culture that has shaped me and my context. This is a Western Christianity, which looks back to the ancient Near Eastern, Hebrew, and Greek worlds and stands in the post-Christian world of secularity. This is the context for which I feel called to take responsibility, without making any privileged truth or value claims for this culture.

I believe, with Jeremy Rifkin, that there is something like a new global consciousness arising from the union of these concerns and movements for a new society and spirituality.[8] But we need to allow "every voice to be lifted,"[9] to gather together in mutual interaction and transformation the many cultural heritages of humanity, some that have been unjustly dominant and yet do not lack precious resources, and others that have been deeply silenced and rightly claim space to flower again.

I wish to play my part in that new consciousness and social vision in this book, but not to preempt a conversation that is still
very far from fruition. Deep repentance needs to happen among
the powerful of the earth, to whose community I mostly belong.
We need to bring the mad bombers out of the sky and make them
stand before the rubble, the charred bodies of the dead, the sufferings of the living, and call them to account. We who belong to
this community, however, also have to take responsibility for
these mad bombers as our brothers (and sometimes sisters!).

We also need to bring from our heritage the language to critique violence to other people and to the earth and to envision an
alternative world of healing and wholeness. In this book I hope
to make a contribution to this process of calling the Western,
Christian, and American worlds to account for their profligate
violence. I also hope to contribute something to generating hope
for a saner world, as the ground of resistance to this violence.

PART ONE

Creation

1

Three Classical Creation Stories

Creation stories not only reflect current science, that is, the assumptions about the nature of the world, physical processes, and their relationships; but they are also blueprints for society. They reflect the assumptions about how the divine and the mortal, the mental and the physical, humans and other humans, male and female, humans, plants, animals, land, waters, and stars are related to each other. They both reflect the worldview of the culture and mandate that worldview to its ongoing heirs.

Three classical creation stories have particularly shaped the Christian world. Its normative creation story is the one found in the first chapters of Genesis, which the Christian church incorporated through its selective takeover of the Hebrew Bible from Judaism.[1] Behind this Hebrew creation story lies a more ancient one, the *Enuma Elish,* or Babylonian creation story, which was read yearly on the fourth day of the New Year Festival to assure the renewal of the cosmos. The epic in its Babylonian form was probably composed in the early part of the second millennium B.C.E.[2] The priestly authors of the Hebrew creation stories, composed in the sixth or fifth century B.C.E., originally in Babylonia, were well aware of this Babylonian story, and composed their own story both to reflect their own cultic system and in selective appropriation and correction of this earlier story.[3]

The third creation story discussed here is Plato's *Timaeus*. Composed in the early fourth century B.C.E., it reflects both Plato's own cosmology and the cosmology that would be regarded as "scientific" for the rest of classical antiquity, as well as for the Middle Ages, until it was challenged by the heliocentric model of Copernicus and Galileo in the sixteenth and seventeenth centuries. Although Christians took the Hebrew story as theologically normative, for 1,500 years they read it with the cosmology of the *Timaeus* in the back of their minds.[4]

THE BABYLONIAN CREATION STORY

The Babylonian creation story was itself rooted in earlier stories from the Sumerian world. These stories begin with a primal Mother who is the origin of both the cosmos and the gods. The story is thus both cosmogonic (generation of the cosmos) and theogonic (generation of the deities). The deities emerge in successive generations, representing the successive stages of the generation of the cosmos. First there emerges from her body the primal parents, Heaven and Earth; then the primal cosmic forces, water, air, and vegetation; and then the anthropomorphic gods and goddesses who represent the ruling classes of the city states.

The Babylonian story also assumes an intergenerational struggle between the older and younger deities, a struggle that represents both the political conquests of younger states over older states and villages, and also the struggle to harness and organize the machinery of political control and control of land and water against the "chaotic" social and natural forces that erupted periodically against this order. Droughts and floods threatened the agricultural system, which had been brought under the control of the urban elites of priestesses and priests, kings and queens. Social eruptions from the serfs and slaves who did the manual work and invasions from rival states and migrating nomads from outside all threatened the fragile order they had imposed on their "world."[5]

The *Enuma Elish* was reworked from earlier creation stories to celebrate the ascendancy of the city of Babylonia and its deity, Marduk, over other cities during the first Babylonian dynasty (nineteenth to sixteenth centuries B.C.E.). In this reworking the ancient Mother Goddess, Tiamat, and her subordinate consorts, Apsu and Kingu, are made to stand for these forces of "chaos" that threaten the control of the new dynasty. Tiamat's consort Apsu is described as planning to kill the younger gods because their noise disturbs his peace. But Ea, their son, protects the younger gods by subduing Apsu. Ea rips off Apsu's tiara and puts it on his own head and then kills him. Ea assumes ascendancy over the cosmos and gods, establishes his cult, and with his wife, Damkina, creates his son, Marduk.

Tiamat then prepares to intervene to avenge Apsu's death, fashioning an army of monstrous beings and placing them under the command of Kingu, whom she elevates as her new consort. The gods are thrown into consternation, turning first to the god Anu and then to the god Ea to protect them from Tiamat, but both fail to be able to face her. Finally they turn to the young champion, Marduk. Marduk meets Tiamat in hand-to-hand combat. Catching her in a net, he kills her with an arrow through her heart. Extinguishing her life, he casts her down and treads upon her lifeless carcass.

Marduk then splits Tiamat's body in half "like a shellfish." He raises one half upward as the sky, to seal off the waters above. He then fashions the stars and planetary abodes of the heavens in the underside of her body. Marduk then imagines an even more daring work. He summons Kingu, Tiamat's conquered consort, judges him guilty of supporting her, and kills him. He then fashions the humans out of Kingu's blood mixed with clay. Imposing servitude on these mortal creatures, he frees the gods for leisure.

What are some of the social messages we can surmise from this story? First, the lords of the newly ascendant city-state of Babylonia, and its god, Marduk, did not assume they preexisted the world. They knew they arose as a recent generation of power out of earlier stages of development, out of earlier states, and behind those, a pre-city-state world less under human control and more under the control of nonhuman forces.

Second, this earliest world is seen as matriarchal. The female is dominant, with subordinate male consorts. This world has been replaced in the generation of Marduk's father, Ea, by one of dominant male powers, with subordinate female consorts. Third, the earliest model of generation is parthenogenetic gestation. Apsu, the primordial begetter of all things, commingles in a single body with Tiamat, who bears all things. The gods and goddesses gestate within this commingled male-female union.

However, with Marduk, the new model of power becomes military and architectonic. Marduk extinguishes the life from Tiamat's body, reducing it to dead "stuff" from which he then fashions the cosmos. From the dead body of Kingu, he takes the blood to make the enslaved humans. This transition from reproductive to artisan metaphors for cosmogenesis indicates a deeper confidence in the appropriation of "matter" by the new ruling class. Life begotten and gestated has its own autonomous principle of life. Dead matter, fashioned into artifacts, makes the cosmos the private possession of its "creators." Even though the new lords remember that they once were gestated out of the living body of the mother, they now stand astride her dead body and take possession of it as an object of their ownership and control.

Finally the story mandates the basic class hierarchy of rulers and slaves. The gods who are given their ease through the creation of humans, "charged to the service of the gods," are the immortal counterparts of the leisured aristocracy of temple and palace who expropriate the product of the labor of the serfs who toil in their fields and workshops. The hieratic power of ritual and law and the military power of armies and weapons are the spheres of these two aristocracies, whose wealth and ease are built upon the bowed backs of enslaved workers. Leisure, based on the expropriated labor, marks this aristocracy off from the lower ranks of serfs/slaves and identifies them with the gods.

THE HEBREW CREATION STORY

The Hebrew creation story has both continuities with and important differences from the Babylonian story. In the Hebrew story the Creator coexists with the primal "stuff" of the cosmos and is in serene control of the process. Strife between Creator and the primal Mother has been eliminated. Instead the Mother has already been reduced to formless but also malleable "stuff" that responds instantly to the Creator's command.

Modeling their creation story on the work week they wished to enshrine in sacred law, the Hebrew authors describe the shaping of the cosmos as proceeding majestically through the six days of the Creator's work. The Creator first creates light, separating it from darkness. On the second day he, like Marduk, creates the vault of the sky to separate the waters above from those below. On the third day, the dry land emerges from the lower waters, and the seed-bearing plants appear. On the fourth day the Creator shapes the stars, the sun, and the moon, to govern night and day. On the fifth day, he creates the fish and birds. On the sixth day, he creates the land animals, cattle, reptiles, and wild animals, followed by humans.

Humans are distinguished from the animals by being made "in the image of God." They are given the rulership over all the animals of the earth, fish, birds, and land animals. All seed- and fruit-bearing plants are given to humans for food, while green plants are given as food to wild animals, birds, and reptiles. At the completion of each day's work, the handicraft of the Creator is blessed by being pronounced "good." On the seventh day, the Creator rests, hallowing this day as the day of rest.

What are the social messages of this story? Although in other places in Hebrew Scripture God is modeled after the king-warriors, who control others through military force,[6] in this story God is modeled after the intellectual power of the priestly class, who call all things into being through ritual naming. The commanding "let there be" is the mode of God's creative work.

Second, the division between rulers and workers, between leisure and labor, is eliminated. God both works and rests and makes this the pattern for all humans, and even for (domesticated) animals. They too belong to the covenant and are to be given rest on the seventh day.[7] (The context of sabbatical rest is that of the household, and hence has limited application outside that context.) Humans, although understood as servants of God, possess the servanthood of royalty rather than of slaves. As the collective bearer of God's "image," Adam is the representative of divine rule on earth over the other animals of land, sky, and water.[8]

Was there then no male domination or class domination in the original work of God in the minds of these writers? On the surface the story mandates no hierarchy of one class of humans over another, in the manner validated by the Babylonian story. Humans are thought of as a unified corporate entity, made in God's image, to be the representative of divine sovereignty. Hebrew law allowed slavery, but it is thought of as an inappropriate temporary state between Jews, although allowed over gentiles.[9] The foundational story of God's liberation of the people of Israel from slavery sets limits to the enslavement of Jews by other Jews. They are to be treated with kindness as hired servants, not with the harshness of slaves, and they are to be set free at the time of the Jubilee (every fifty years).[10]

While the text leaves open the equality of male and female "in the image" of God, the maleness of the pronouns for God and for Adam already suggests that males are the appropriate collective representatives of this God, females sharing in the benefits of corporate "human" sovereignty, but also falling under the rule of the male head of family.[11] Lest there be any doubt about this, the priestly authors appropriated an earlier folk story about the creation of male and female, and attached it to their account of creation.

In this story, which appears in Genesis 2, the male is described as created first and the female second, extracted from his rib. This account is specifically intended to mandate the patriarchal relationship of husband and wife. The husband is the primal and collective person. The woman is derivative, made to serve him. Husband to wife as master to servant is thus explicitly mandated. The Lordship of God over the (Jewish patriarchal) male, as God's royal servant, is reduplicated in the lordship of husband over wife.[12]

Environmentalists have criticized the idea of "dominion" given this collective Adam over the rest of creation as the prototype of both anthropocentric and exploitative use of the animals and plants by "man."[13] There is no doubt that the account is anthropocentric. Although created last, the human is the crown of creation, given sovereignty over it. However, an exploitative or destructive rule over earth is certainly not intended. Humans are not given ownership or possession of the earth, which remains "the Lord's." God, finally, is the one who possesses the earth as his creation. Humans are given usufruct of it. Their rule is the secondary one of care for it as a royal steward, not as an owner who can do with it what he wills.[14]

This obviously means that humans are to take good care of earth, not to exploit or destroy it, which would make them bad stewards. The inclusion of domesticated animals in sabbatical rest, the forbidding of many animals for human consumption, restrictions on the use of the flesh of those mammals humans can eat, all limit human rights to the lives of other earth beings. The word for human, *Adam* (from *adamah,* earth), assumes a deep kinship of humans and earth. Humans also share a common warm blood with mammals, which is why they are forbidden to eat the meat of these animals without removing this blood.[15]

Other Hebrew texts also show a keen sense that human control over earth is limited. In storms and droughts, wild animals, and wild places, a world of nature is manifest that is still directly under divine sovereignty, not given over to human stewardship. God appears as judge and punisher of human misdeeds in this realm of uncontrolled nature. Whereas Babylonian thought saw the primal power of Tiamat in this realm of chaotic nature, of droughts and storms, Hebrew thought would interpret this violent nature, which brought human "order" to naught, as God's punishing wrath for human wrongdoing.[16]

THE GREEK CREATION STORY

Plato's creation story, the *Timaeus,* is yet more abstract and philosophical, and less in the mode of mythic personification, than the Hebrew priestly story. Plato starts by defining the primal dualism that underlies reality; its division into two realms, the invisible, eternal realm of thought and the visible realm of corporeality. The invisible realm of thought is primal and original. In the beginning there existed alongside it the unshaped matrix of visible being, which Plato calls "space" or "the nurse."[17]

In between the two was the Creator or Demiurgos, the cosmic artisan. Like the work of the Babylonian Marduk and of the Hebrew Creator, the Demiurgos creates by "making." The metaphor for cosmogenesis is taken from the work of the artisan, who shapes things from dead stuff, not from the reproductive process of begetting and gestating. This concept of the cosmos as "made" and not "begotten" will appear in Christian theology as the primary means of distinguishing between the generation of the divine in the Trinity, and God's creation of the world.[18] Having been "made" rather than "begotten" (gestation no longer appears, even as an option),[19] demotes the cosmos to the status of a possessed object, and distinguishes it from the self-subsistent life of the divine.

The Demiurgos first shapes the space into the primal elements of fire, air, water, and earth, and then shapes these into the spheric body of the cosmos. This cosmos is assumed to be geocentric and hierarchic. The earth at the center is ringed by the seven planetary spheres and the realm of the stars in ascending order. The supralunary world of the planets and stars is made of the more "spiritual" element of fire, the sublunar realm of water and earth, with air standing in between. The Creator then shapes the world soul and infuses it into the cosmic body as its principle of life and motion. Appropriate beings are placed in each realm: the gods in the planets and stars; birds, who communicate with the gods, in the air; fish in the watery realm; and animals on earth.

The Demiurgos then proceeds to shape human souls from the same elements from which he had mixed the world soul, but in a more diluted form. This soul mixture he divides up into parts and places in the stars, where they receive a celestial education in the eternal nature of reality. Creating the bodies of these beings is too low a task for the Demiurgos and is assigned to the planetary gods. Once the souls have received their celestial infusion of truth, they are incarnated into the male bodies. There their task is to control the chaotic sensations that arise from the body.

If the souls succeed in this task, they will shed the body and return at death to their "native" star, there to have a "blessed and congenial existence" (like the gods). But if one fails to attain this control over the body and its sensations, the soul will be reincarnated and pass in a second birth into a woman. If in that state he[20] doesn't desist from evil, he will be reincarnated as a "brute" who resembles the "evil" nature into which he has fallen. This round of incarnation will continue until the soul masters the body and returns to his "first and better state," that is, as a (ruling-class) male human, winning finally his return to his original disincarnate state in his star above.

What are the messages of this story? First, Plato thinks of reality as divided between mind and body. Mind or consciousness is primal, eternal, and good. Body or visible corporeality is secondary, derivative, and the source of evil, in the form of physical sensations to be mastered by the mind. Consciousness or mind is also immortal and godlike, and humans share in the divine nature through the possession of the mind, while the body is the source of mortality and mutability. The soul, mind, or consciousness is alien to earth and body. Its true home is the pure and eternal world of the stars, while incarnation in a body is a preparatory "testing place" or purgatory.

Second, this hierarchy of mind over body is duplicated in the hierarchy of male over female, human over animals. It is also duplicated in the class hierarchy of rulers over workers, but that is not made explicit in the *Timaeus*. It comes out in Plato's *Republic*, where the just and ordered society corresponds to the hierarchy of the well-ordered self, with mind in control, the will under the lead of reason, and the appetites controlled by both. This hierarchy of the self corresponds, for Plato, with the three social castes of philosopher-rulers, guardian-warriors, and manual laborers.[21] In this text women are seen as belonging to all three castes, but as secondary and inferior members of each.[22]

These three creation stories were shaped in the patriarchal, slave-holding world of early urban civilization in the eastern Mediterranean of the second and first millennia B.C.E. In the Babylonian story that urban world is still new and precarious. Another world, not under male/human control, stands as the earlier beginning, ruled by a huge theriomorphic Great Mother, who gestated all things, gods and cosmic beings, in the mingled waters of her womb. The story mandates her dethronement, and with it a demotion of the female from primal power to secondary consort.

Slavery is a central institution mandated by this story. Slaves are the human tools by whom wealth is extracted through exploited labor, allowing aristocratic leisure to the rulers. Leisure versus work, rule versus servitude, are the primary metaphors for the divine-human relation.

The Hebrew priests also inhabit this patriarchal, slave-holding world; but remembering their roots in a nomadic, simpler, and more egalitarian patriarchal society, they seek to modify it.[23] They reject the work-leisure line between divine and human, which mandates the master-slave hierarchy. This is an inappropriate relation, at least between males of God's chosen people. The community of Israelite male heads of family is to be more egalitarian, all sharing equally in God's mandate to care for the land, extending their covenantal rest to those under their care, including animals.

But this equality is not intended for the male-female relation. And lest wives not understand their place as secondary, derivative, and of service to their husbands, the second story of the creation of Eve from Adam's "rib" is appended to the first story of the creation of all humans collectively "in God's image."

In Plato's story male domination, class hierarchy, and inferiorization of animals are all part of the accepted social order, manifesting the primal division of reality into consciousness over body. In this story not only are ruling-class males at the top of the hierarchy of embodied beings, but they mirror in their consciousness the higher world of the eternal ideas and the gods and share in the animating principle of the universe itself, the world soul.

However, Plato adds to this mandate for social domination an additional cultural attitude, that of alienation from the body and earth. The earth itself is seen as the lowest level of a cosmic hierarchy of planetary spheres that mount above it. Like the body, "prisonhouse" of the soul, earth is the collective prison of incarnated souls, which must work their way out of this fallen state to return to their "true home" in the starry heavens. Earth and body, once dominated and made inferior, are now fled from altogether in the quest of the male mind to free itself from the "contamination" of mortality and to secure immortal life.

THE CHRISTIAN COSMOLOGICAL SYNTHESIS

Western Christianity accepted the Genesis 1 account as its official "revealed" story of creation, which shaped its understanding of the God-cosmos relationship. But it read this account through the eyes of Greek science of the sort reflected in Plato's *Timaeus,* and it also made its own synthesis of ancient Near Eastern, Hebrew, Greek, and Christian ideas. The result was a view that contained ideas not strictly present in the Hebraic account.

One such view was an understanding of God, who not only eternally preexists the visible cosmos, but also creates the cosmos "out of nothing." Neither the Genesis nor the Platonic stories contain this dogma of *creatio ex nihilo,* since both assume some kind of chaotic "stuff" that was "there" in the beginning. In both stories God shaped this chaotic material into the cosmos. But Christian philosophical theology objected to this possibility of the eternal coexistence of "matter," since it suggests a source of being parallel to God. This challenged God's absolute sovereignty.

To avoid this conclusion, God was seen as creating the original matter itself, as well as shaping it into the cosmos. This doctrine leaves Christianity with an unresolved ambiguity about the ontological status of "matter." If it comes from God, then in some sense it is seen as an emanation from divine being, grounded in divine being. Yet its status as "creation" identifies it as a kind of "being" outside of God, non-divine and mortal by nature, having no self-subsistent principle of existence of its own.[24]

Christianity developed the Jewish understanding of the male monotheistic God into a Trinity of "three persons." The role of this pluralism in God is to span the divide between divine transcendence "outside" of creation and immanence or divine presence "in" creation, grounding its existence and being revealed in history, and finally bringing creation itself to transformed communion with God. The concepts of divine "Word" and "Spirit" perform these roles of creational, revelational, and perfecting immanence.[25]

Yet these immanent principles in God also raised the question of the God-cosmos division. If the Word and Spirit of God are the "ground of being" of creation, are they themselves "created"? This was the view of Arianism. Orthodox Trinitarianism rejected this view for a belief that they are wholly divine, equal to the "Father." It also rejected suggestions of several early Christian groups that saw male and female elements in God as the symbols of divine movement from transcendence to immanence.[26]

Yet if the Word and Spirit of God are equally male and transcendent, alongside the Father, then how are they also "within" creation? Again the Christian view seems to want to span two concepts of the divine-cosmos relation, seeing God as a totally distinct, eternal, and self-subsistent Being, over against the non-divine, dependent status of created being; and yet also, in some sense, seeing creation as welling up out of and being sustained in existence through the being of God.[27]

Christian cosmology also inherited certain problematics from the Platonic tradition. One of these is a geocentric and hierarchical world picture. The cosmos is seen as spherical, with the earth at the center. But this position of earth is also seen as the lowest point in a series of hierarchical levels. The earth and the region of air between the earth and the moon is seen as the realm of mortality, while the supralunar region of the planetary spheres and "fixed stars" is seen as composed of immortal "matter."

Beyond the fixed stars is the "eternal space," where God dwells with the angels and saints. The location of the opposite realm of "hell" is unclear in this picture, perhaps outside but "below" the cosmos. This meshing of the Greek world picture with Christian eschatology would bring Christian theology into conflict with science when this world picture was challenged in the seventeenth century, as we will see in the following chapter.

Platonism also believed that the human soul was inherently immortal, preexisting its incarnation into a body, and originally dwelling in the stars in the upper regions of the cosmos. For Hebrew thought the soul is the life principle of the body, and future life takes the form of a resurrection of the body on a renovated earth. Christianity would attempt various syntheses of these two views. Christian Orthodoxy rejected a preexistent soul, but Greek Christianity saw humans as having been created with immortal, "spiritual" bodies, which then "fell" into "gross" mortal forms of bodiliness with sin. Augustine retained a version of this idea of original immortality prior to sin.[28]

Although Christianity retained the symbolism of the rational soul as "masculine," and the body and its passions as "feminine," it rejected the solution of reincarnation to explain social hierarchy. There is no place in Christianity for a series of reincarnations of the soul from male to female and even to animal, and from ruling class to lower class, reflecting the failure of the soul to control the irrational body. Each soul is created uniquely by God and with equal capacity for holiness and redemption.

Thus there arises in Christianity an unexplained division between equality of souls in relation to God, and yet inequality of bodies and status in society across gender and class hierarchy.

Female subordination is explained both as "natural," reflecting the inferiority of the female body and personality, and also as punishment for causing original sin. At the same time, women are equal before God in regard to redemption. Thus God seems to will different principles in creation and redemption. In creation women are inferior and under male subordination, yet this inferiority is abolished in their equal capacity to transcend creation and be transformed by grace.[29]

How souls are related to their bodies also fuses divergent views. Latin Christianity accepted a Hebraic view, together with an Aristotelian concept of the soul as the life principle of the body itself. Yet it also accepted a Platonic view of the soul as capable of being "detached" from the body and existing in a disembodied form after death, although its eschatological fulfillment comes only when this immortal soul is rejoined with a "spiritual" body at the resurrection. Thus the soul-body relation remains ambiguous, divided between a concept of the soul as capable of existing apart from the body, and a concept of the soul as the life principle of the body. This ambiguity mirrors the ambiguity of the God-cosmos division.

This notion of the soul as created but nevertheless capable of immortal, transcendent life apart from the body reaffirmed in Christianity a sharp division between humans and other forms of life, animals and plants. Humans have a "rational" soul, destined for immortal life. Animals and plants have "lower life," or what was traditionally called "animal and vegetable souls," but lack this higher soul, which is rational and immortal.

This human-animal split is reinforced by the soul-body split. These splits reinforce a view of the essential human as a transcendent, disembodied, immortal "soul" that can kick aside the physical world of bodily life. Its destiny is not an integral part of this bodily world. Thus despite the official continuation in Christianity of certain Hebraic concepts of the resurrected body and redeemed earth, operative Christian eschatology for the most part is one of an immortal soul that escapes from and is not limited by the mortal fate of earth's creatures.

Despite these views of the rest of life on earth as mortal, lacking the distinct human destiny of immortal life, Christianity nevertheless harbors a view of the original earth as paradisal. God originally created not only humans but the whole creation as "very good," lacking any evil. This posed a dilemma for understanding how evil came about, not only in the sense of human meanness to each other, but also "natural evils," death, and the violence that is observed in other animals, as well as in humans.

The Christian solution has been to see all these evils as the consequence of human sin. Through sin comes death, not only to humans but also to the entire created world, which has "fallen" through human sin. Humans are rescued from this state of sin and death through Christ. But this leaves the fallen and mortal state of the cosmos in doubt. The classical Christian solution was to see the whole cosmos as eventually to be redeemed and immortalized in the final redemption. But this was only applied to planetary structures, not to animal and plant life.

Thus the Christian world picture remains ambiguous, unable to close the loop between its vision of original goodness as a paradisaical state without rapaciousness or death, its sharp division between animals and plants, who lack "by nature" the capacity for immortality, and humans, who transcend this mortal fate. This imbues Christianity with two oddly conflicting stances toward the rest of life.

On the one hand, humans are said to be guilty for the inadequacies of the rest of nature. Human mortality and all rapaciousness mirror and are a consequence of human sin. On the other hand, humans bear no ultimate responsibility for the rest of creation. Animal and plant life can be exploited at will by humans as our possessions. They have no personhood of their own that need be respected, and we share no common fate with them.

These ambiguities in the Christian world picture, and the extent to which aspects of this world picture have contributed to ecological irresponsibility, will be the themes of this volume. My underlying assumptions can be summarized here as follows. Nature, in the sense of the sum of cosmic life, was not originally paradisaical (benign for us) and is not capable of completely fulfilling human hopes for the good, in the sense of benign regard for individual and communal life, which is the human ideal.

Human consciousness and impulses to loving care of others as individuals and communities give us the experience of standing out from our mortal limits, and also a demand for greater kindness than that found in most inter-animal or even inter-human relations. These human thinking and caring impulses are not, however, rootless and meaningless, but point to an aspect of the source of life that is also an impulse to consciousness and increased kindness that is still imperfectly realized.

We humans are the evolutionary growing edge of this imperfectly realized impulse to consciousness and kindness. But this does not separate us from the common fate we share, of organisms that grow and then die. An ecological ethic must be based on acceptance of both sides of this dilemma of humanness, both the way we represent the growing edge of what is "not yet" of greater awareness and benignity, and also our organic mortality, which we share with the plants and animals.

We pass on our ideals to the future not by escaping personal death, but by partly reshaping "nature" to reflect these human ideals. But this reshaping is finally governed by the finite limits of the interdependence of all life in the living system that is Gaia. Ecological ethics is an uneasy synthesis of both these "laws": the law of consciousness and kindness, which causes us to strain beyond what "is," and the laws of Gaia, which regulate what kinds of changes in "nature" are sustainable in the life system of which we are an inextricable part.

2

Does Science Have a New Creation Story?

THE BREAKDOWN OF THE CHRISTIAN CREATION STORY

Creation stories, as we have seen, traditionally have mandated not only a view of (nonhuman) "nature," but also a view of the relation of humans to the rest of nature, their relation to each other in society, and their relation to the ultimate foundational source of life (the divine). They have been blueprints for what today we would call a combined scientific, social-ethical, and theological-spiritual worldview.

In the sixteenth and early seventeenth centuries, this unifying worldview began to break down for Western Christian/post-Christian people. The new physical and biological sciences began to pioneer a scientific account of the nature of external reality that was radically at variance with the combined biblical-Classical view that Christians had inherited from Christianized Greco-Roman antiquity.

For several centuries church leaders dueled with the new leaders of science, trying to censor and repress the legitimacy of their new knowledge. There were several stages of this struggle. The first stage had to do with the model of the cosmos, the relation of the planet earth to the sun, stars, and other planets. In the early sixteenth century, Nicolaus Copernicus had put forth the heliocentric view of the solar system, but his full theory, published at the time of his death in 1543, bore a preface by the hand of Protestant theologian Andreas Osiander, that described his theory as only hypothetical.[1]

When Galileo took up Copernicus's theory and taught it more directly in 1613 as the correct view, over against the classical Ptolemaic view, it was condemned by the Holy Office (Sacred Congregation of the Roman and Universal Inquisition). Copernicus's treatise was put on the Index of Forbidden Books of the Inquisition in 1616, and remained there until the mid-eighteenth century (1757). When Galileo broke this imposed silence and disputed the condemnation of the Copernican theory in 1632, he was handed over to the Inquisition, imprisoned, and forced to recant under threat of torture.[2]

For those today who can hardly comprehend why the Christian church leaders would remain so opposed to a heliocentric universe for so long, it is well to remember what was at stake. Not only did the heliocentric view shift the entire focus of reality from an earth-centered world to one where earth was a minor planet circling around the sun, but it also destroyed a whole moral and spiritual system that had been built on this earth-centered view. No longer was it possible to view earth in relation to the "heavens" as the bottom of a cosmic hierarchy, in which the "upper" levels defined the realm of the angels and finally of God.

The heliocentric view also destroyed the notion of different types of "matter"—sublunar, mortal "dense" matter, and supralunar, immortal, "fiery," "spiritual" matter—on which Christian eschatology had been based. This concept of two kinds of body allowed theology to explain the immortality of the "risen body," as the doffing of the mortal body for the immortal, "spiritual" body.[3] If all matter is equally "material" and mortal, and there is no longer a heavenly realm spatially located at the top of the cosmic system, then this world picture of where God dwells and the soul, with its transfigured body, "goes" at death disappears.

A second critical blow was dealt to the Christian view of creation in the third quarter of the nineteenth century, with the development of the Darwinian science of evolution. The pieces of this view had been coming together among biological scientists for more than a hundred years, but it was given new clarity and public recognition in Darwin's *On the Origin of Species* (1859) and *The Descent of Man* (1871). Evolution shattered the concept of distinct species that were separately "created." It showed that all species of plants and animals evolved one from the other over a long process of mutation.

For most Christians the most threatening part of this idea was the inclusion of humans in the evolutionary history. The distinctiveness of humans from animals was broken down. Humans were shown to be a part of the animal world, descended from apes, who in turn evolved from earlier mammal forms, which arose from reptiles, fish, and insects, in a long regress that led back even to prebiotic forms. With this breakdown of the lines of separation of species, that between human and animal particularly, the whole notion that human consciousness was the manifestation of a separate and immortal soul, which decisively distinguished humans from animals, was thrown into question.[4]

In addition to this question of the distinctiveness of humans from animals, evolution increasingly suggested a much longer time span for earth history than that which had been mandated by calculations from the Bible.[5] Far from earth having appeared a mere four thousand years before the birth of Christ, it began to appear that the earth was millions and even billions of years old.

Although liberal Christians gradually adjusted to this concept of evolution, the duel between more conservative Christians and scientists over a separate creation, particularly of humans, is hardly finished. A state law in Tennessee forbade the teaching of evolution in public schools, and John Scopes, a high school biology teacher, was convicted of violating this law in a famous trial in 1925. This law was repealed in 1967, and a similar law struck down in Arkansas in 1967.

In the 1970s and 1980s in the United States, fundamentalist Christians took a new approach. No longer seeking to ban the teaching of evolution altogether, they sought rather to declare evolution to be only an unconfirmed theory, and to make the biblical view of distinct and separate creations a "scientific" hypothesis of equal status to be taught in schools. This view was struck down by the Supreme Court in 1987, on the grounds of promoting a specific religious belief and hence as violating the separation of church and state. But the assumed incompatibility of religion and science was all the more reinforced by this ruling.[6]

In the last one hundred years, the duel between the Christian biblical view of the world and that of the physical and biological sciences has lessened, not so much by the creation of a new synthesis between the two, but rather by the tacit agreement of each to demarcate for themselves separate and nonoverlapping spheres of authority. This separation of the spheres of science and religion followed the dualist lines presumed by mechanistic science. The Baconian scientific method defined only that which can be empirically observed and measured as scientific, while all subjective matters of inward experience and value judgment, the ethical, the aesthetic, and the spiritual, belong to a realm outside of scientifically verifiable truth.

Scientists, influenced by the mechanical objectivism of the scientific method, increasingly came to regard these subjective matters as "unreal." Yet it was precisely this "unreal" realm that became the sphere of religion, and even of the "humanities" in general. Insulated from scientific questioning by the demarcations set by the scientific method itself, religion could then establish its own separate reality in the subjective sphere. Using the split between "fact" and "value" laid out by Albrecht Ritschl (d.1889), twentieth-century theologians adjusted to the view that "faith" had to do solely with the subjective sphere of personal value stances, not with outward "facts."[7]

Even the historical sciences could not penetrate and challenge this subjective realm. For example, faith in the bodily resurrection of Christ could neither be proved or disproved by historical investigation, because it belonged to the separate realm of a subjective faith stance toward the meaning of Jesus' life and death. In effect, religion and science, particularly the physical sciences, coexisted by tacitly agreeing not to communicate with each other.

However, for several reasons, from the 1960s onward this mutual insulation of religion (Christianity) and science began to break down. One reason was that the triumphalistic assumption of science that religion was an obsolete superstition, destined to fade away as science established its sure results, became tempered. The nuclear bomb shattered naive faith in science as a tool for inevitable good, and the growing evidence that technology was perhaps doing irreparable damage to the environment eroded that faith still more. It seemed more and more likely that the tools created by science might result in the destruction of the earth, rather than its decisive establishment on the road to prosperity and happiness for all.

Although modern science had claimed that its method was "value-free," and therefore capable of establishing certain truth, uncontaminated by subjective desires, in reality it had always made value claims over its religious rivals. It had claimed that its objective truth would also lay the basis for a more enlightened world, a world where "fair-mindedness" could deliver both a more prosperous world, where human survival needs would be satisfied, and also a more just one, where this prosperity would be gradually distributed to all.[8]

It was these claims to be able to create a "good" world, in all these senses of the word, that was being challenged by the specter of terminal evils facilitated by science. Even though scientists might claim that they could not be held responsible for the evil ways their "truths" were wrongly applied, science itself could not avoid the onus of moral failure, in the light of the use of scientific knowledge to embark on a frighteningly destructive global society.

Moreover, scientific reductionism proved incapable of satisfying the longings of the human spirit for aesthetic, ethical, and spiritual dimensions of reality. These were implicitly, if not explicitly, rejected as unreal by the strict scientific worldview. Marxist states, which had attempted to substitute such a concept of science for religion as the comprehensive and solely legitimate source of culture, proved unable to eradicate religion despite decades of persecution. Religion not only failed to fade away in the face of the definitive establishment of science as the sole official perspective, but even young people raised entirely in the "scientific" perspective were turning to religion to fill this felt need.[9]

Equally important was the changing paradigm of scientific knowledge itself, created by Albert Einstein, Wolfgang Pauli, Niels Bohr, and others, focusing on both the macro-level of astrophysics and the micro-level of subatomic physics. Just as science had broken down the Christian separation of spheres between earth and planetary matter and between humans and animals, so the new physics itself began to break down the distinction of spheres on which the separation of science from religion (and the humanities) had been based. It no longer seemed possible to distinguish so clearly between matter and energy, as had Newtonian physics. Nor was it so clear that science could demarcate an objective realm of "facts," distinct from subjective perspectives.

Newtonian physics had assumed that matter could be reduced to hard entities, atomic particles that remained inert until external force was applied to them to make them "move." This mechanical system resided in a fixed, static framework of space and time.[10] Under the influence of relativity and quantum theory, this concept of matter, with its fixed framework of time and space, began to dissolve. Einstein's famous formula $E=mc^2$ (energy equals mass times the square of the speed of light) encapsulated the new view, in which the atomic and subatomic world lost its fixity. Like light, matter could be seen either as particles of energy or as waves of energy, depending on the context in which it acted and the methods of measurement of the human researcher.

For physicists after Einstein, even the distinction between existing or not existing became fluid. Wavelike patterns in interdependent relation showed probable "tendencies to exist" as events or particles. Instead of decomposing the world into ultimate entities as "building blocks," scientists arrived at a voidlike web of relationships in which events arise in interconnection with each other. This relational web is coterminal with the entire cosmos, in which everything is connected with everything, not only across space, but across time as well.[11]

The line between the observer's perceptions and external "facts" became hard to delineate. Not only were the answers given by observed phenomena relative to the standpoint of the observer, and his or her processes of observation and measurement, but also the underlying distinction between consciousness and object began to flow together, as two aspects of one reality. Biology also could no longer dissolve "living stuff" into building blocks of "dead stuff."

Rather, underneath the appearance of ultimate entities, or subatomic "particles," was simply the "dance" of movement itself, a dance without dancers, engaged in restless, continual motion. Subatomic matter had become dynamic and "lifelike." It is this ultimate dance without dancers from which the "appearances" of nuclear, atomic, and molecular structures are built up and are in turn the basis of those visible entities that humans experience as rocks or plants or other humans.

called unimaginatively "the Big Bang." Physicists envision a time of intense concentration of all matter-energy in a single unity, a single cosmic nucleus (cosmic egg?). In one rapid "explosion," this concentration of intensely charged, radiant light-waves expanded, not into "empty space," but created space and time itself by its expansion. This is seen as taking place some 18 billion years ago.[13]

In the first stage of the expansion of this radiant energy as a unitary center, the various forms of force, from the gravitational force that will arrange the relation of the galaxies to the stars to the planets to the electromagnetic, nuclear, and subnuclear forces that will arrange the atomic nuclei and atoms, were differentiated. The first atomic structures of hydrogen and helium were formed. Gravity then began to gather the expanding gases into clouds, forming stars and galaxies. As these first stars were formed, burned, and eventually exploded, the rest of the basic atomic elements were formed. Except for the even older hydrogen and helium atoms, all of the atomic elements that make up earth, from rocks to the human body, are ultimately "stardust."

As the stars exploded, new stars and planets were formed, now enriched by these heavier atomic elements. The sun of our solar system is one such later star, with its orbiting planets. Earth, one of the smaller planets of our solar system, condensed from a whirling cloud of gases and dust, along with the sun and its sister planets, about 4.6 billion years ago, some 13.4 billion years after the beginning of the universe.

As scientists envision the origins of the universe, they also begin to imagine its end. For 18 billion years, the original explosion of radiant energy has continued to expand, shaping billions of galaxies, each with billions of stars and planets. As the universe continues to expand, it is possible that it will reach a point where it will start to collapse back on itself. Perhaps over many more billions of years, it will be sucked back into its center, forming a vortex from which a new explosion from a cosmic nucleus and a new universe will be generated. This view is called the "closed system" of the universe.[14]

But some evidence suggests a different scenario, an open system of the universe. According to this view, the force of gravity will not curb the expanding force of the universe. It will continue to expand indefinitely. New stars and planets will continue forming, burning, and expiring in the galaxies. But eventually, after unimaginable billions of years, the resources of gas forming the galaxies will be exhausted, and stars will explode or fade away without replacement. The lights of the universe will gradually go out, leaving only dead stars and black holes in skeletal galaxies still hurtling through space. Thus, to use the popular phrase, the universe will end, not with a "bang" (and a new creation), but with a terminal "whimper."[15]

Are these the only two options? Given that no scientists could have predicted the wondrous cosmos if they had been around at the time of the Big Bang, perhaps we should leave room for a mystery of cosmic creativity that we can hardly imagine from our present vantage point! In any case, many billions of years before any cosmic denouement, the sun that powers our solar system may have become exhausted, ending the power source of life on earth. Yet even our sun has such enormous reservoirs of energy that it is estimated it will continue to burn for several billion years more.

Although the planet earth seems even more unpretentious in the light of this vastly expanded picture of the universe than when it first was displaced from its centrality in the geocentric universe of Ptolemy in the seventeenth century, in another way the present world picture renews the sense of earth's uniqueness in the universe. Despite continued efforts to discover other planets where life has developed, first in our solar system and then in other galaxies, these explorations so far have failed. It seems puzzling that, in the myriad assemblies of billions of planets in billions of galaxies, the particular conditions for life would not have happened on some other planets.

Yet, in the absence of evidence for this, earth continues to be the one planet in all the universe where life is known to have developed. Not only does this mean that only on this one small planet have the varieties of plants and animals developed in a biosphere, but also that only on this one planet does there exist the capacity to imagine, visualize, and know the universe. The thinking mind or "noosphere" that is privileged to contemplate the cosmic process beams outward from this one planet, and perhaps from this one planet alone. In the form of humans, earth is where the whole cosmic process becomes conscious of itself.[16]

For its first billion years or more, earth would have seemed inhospitable to the life that later evolved on its surface. Its atmosphere was nearly devoid of oxygen. The planet was bathed in poisonous ultraviolet radiation, was continually bombarded by meteors, and had a molten surface of exploding volcanic activity. Yet all the atomic elements that would combine to create life were already present in its molten seas. As the planet cooled, a thin surface crust began to form, allowing the oceans to condense out of the water vapor in the atmosphere. The sections of earth's outer crust, formed over its molten interior, were mobile, and even today continue to shift, forming new sea floors, raising up new land from volcanic activity, and causing earthquakes along the edges of the tectonic plates.[17]

One hypothesis holds that the chemistry of life began in the seas and continued to grow there for the first 4 billion years of the earth's 4.5-billion-year history. The carbon atom would provide the building block for the organic molecules. Sometime about 1.3 billion years after earth was formed (a little over 3 billion years ago), complex organic molecules began to form, which developed a primitive form of photosynthesis. It is this process that is the key to life on the planet. Through photosynthesis, these precursors of green plants would be able to take in the sun's radiant energy, convert it to carbohydrates, and expire oxygen through cellular combustion. This process created the carbohydrates that are the basis of food for all organic life, as well as the oxygen in the seas and in the atmosphere that allowed these organisms to breathe.[18]

Another 2 billion years saw the gradual creation of multicelled bacteria, and then the evolution of aquatic animals and plants in the seas. These are the ancestors of all the animals and plants that emerged from the seas about 500 million years ago to colonize the barren land. The first plants to begin to emerge from the sea were algae that gathered in coastal ponds, followed by insects that fed on them. This took place about 4.1 billion years after the creation of earth. Gradually, over the next 200 million years, these algae developed into large fern trees and the fish into amphibians, which in turn became egg-laying reptiles and birds.

About 225 million years ago, some of these reptiles and birds grew to giant proportions as dinosaurs, which ruled the earth for 160 million years. Mammals also began to develop during this period, but they remained small and inconspicuous. Most dinosaurs were plant-eaters. Seed-bearing and then flowering plants also developed. The extinction of the dinosaurs some 65 million years ago remains a mystery, whether it was a slow dying off or the result of a sudden catastrophe. One suggestion is that the earth was hit by an asteroid, creating a dust storm that temporarily cut off the sun's rays and shut down photosynthesis, decimating earth's flora and fauna.[19]

The disappearance of the dinosaurs left the stage free for the proliferation of mammals for the most recent 50 million years of earth history. This evolution of mammals led to the first proto-humans, which began to differentiate themselves from the great apes some 4 million years ago. The species of hominid that can be called *Homo sapiens*, however, appeared only about 400,000 years ago. Without fur to keep them warm or fangs and claws to tear apart their food or protect themselves, these early "naked apes" would have seemed very vulnerable, banding together in small groups and living off what they could gather of plants, insects, and animals. But their dexterous hands and capacity to envision and plan would eventually more than compensate for these deficiencies.

Some 10,000 or 12,000 years ago, humans made a breakthrough in the search for a secure food supply with the development of agriculture. As will be discussed later, this breakthrough to agriculture was probably made by females, as their plant-gathering activity led them to observe the growth of plants from seeds and hence to the idea of planting such seeds themselves and tending the growing plants.[20] With this development humans began to alter their environment in a new way, and a new stage of earth's history began.

As we contemplate this history of biogenesis on earth, one of its striking features is its stepped-up tempo. Each stage of biotic development leads more rapidly to the next stage. It took about 3.9 billion years, some eight-ninths of earth's history, simply to generate photosynthesizing bacteria. The entire evolution of land plants and animals has taken place in the last one-ninth of earth's history. Within that history of land animals, humans occupy a fraction of time, a mere 400,000 years, or less than one-tenth of 1 percent of earth's history.

The first human efforts at "control" over their environment, in the form of precarious garden plots, began a still smaller fraction of that fraction of time occupied by human development, a mere 12,000 years ago, some 2 percent of human history. Clearly the anthropocentric claims to have been given "dominion" over the earth, and over all its plants and animals, appears absurd in the light of the 4,599,600,000 years in which earth got along without humans at all!

Yet, in that short period of time in which humans began to cultivate the earth and control their own food supply, the human population has proliferated at a startling rate. At the beginning of the agricultural revolution, some 12,000 years ago, the human population of earth is estimated at about 5 million. By 1650 C.E., the beginning of the scientific revolution in Europe, the human population had multiplied a hundredfold to 500 million.

It look only another two hundred years to add another 500 million to make 1 billion. By 1930, a mere eighty years later, human numbers had expanded as much as they had during the whole previous evolution of humans, to 2 billion. By 1975 that 2 billion had doubled to 4 billion, thus adding in forty-five years as many humans as from the beginning of human evolution.[21] By the end of the second millennium, human population is expected to exceed 6 billion.[22]

This accelerating human population has been accompanied by an accelerating human colonization of the entire planet, paving its surface with buildings, streets, and parking lots, pushing back its primordial forests to plant food or graze animals. The proliferation of human numbers today presses every other animal species into increasingly constricted habitats, making any regions outside of humanly managed zones where genuine "wild life" exists increasingly rare. As forests disappear, more and more animals and plants face extinction, threatening the biotic diversity that is the legacy of earth's entire evolutionary history.[23]

Even the atmospheric oxygen balance, painstakingly created during 4 billion years of plant photosynthesis, is today threatened with destruction after less than one hundred years of expanding use of fossil fuels. The fossil fuels of petroleum and coal are themselves the product of many millions of years in which decaying primeval forests stored carbon under the surface of the earth. And yet at least one of these fuels, petroleum, the major fuel of modern industrialism, may be exhausted in less than 150 years of human use.[24]

One latecomer species, humans, seems to be rapidly outrunning their sustainable place in earth's biosphere, consuming both the basis of their own life and that of the rest of earth's biota. Like the dinosaurs, only in a much shorter period of time (a mere 400,000 years, all but the last few thousand years spent as a nondominant species, rather than the dinosaurs' 160 million years), humans face the possibility of their own extinction, with ramifications that threaten the whole biosphere. The challenge that humans face in the last decade of the twentieth century is whether they will be able to visualize and organize their own reproduction, production, and consumption in such a way as to stabilize their relationship to the rest of the ecosphere and so avert massive social and planetary ecocide.

NATURE'S LAWS AND HUMAN ETHICS

Ecology is the biological science of biotic communities that demonstrates the laws by which nature, unaided by humans, has generated and sustained life. In addition, its study also suggests guidelines for how humans must learn to live as a sustaining, rather than destructive, member of such biotic communities. Thus, unlike those modern physical and biological sciences that have claimed to be only descriptive, ecology suggests some restoration of the classical role of science as normative or as ethically prescriptive.

In what way can ecological ethics arise from the description of how nature works? As I have suggested in the previous chapter, human ethics can neither be reduced to a description of physical and biological processes, nor regarded as simply a negation of those processes derived from "higher" truths. Since human conscience and consciousness arise from natural evolution, we should regard these capacities in ourselves as reflecting the "growing edge" of nature itself. Yet consciousness also allows us an element of volitional power that seeks to rearrange patterns in nature to suit human demands. In so doing we are constrained by nature's ecologic system, but we can also find in that system echoes of our ethical and spiritual aspirations.[25]

One of the most basic "lessons" of ecology for ethics and spirituality is the interrelation of all things. Both earth science and astrophysics give us extraordinary and powerfully compelling messages about our kinship, not only with all living things on earth, but even with distant stars and galaxies. A profound spirituality would arise if we would attempt to experience this kinship and make it present in our consciousness. Such meditation would parallel the ancient contemplative philosophies, which saw in the human soul a fragment of the cosmic soul that moved the universe, and which saw the body as the microcosm.

Astrophysics tells us that all the elements that make up both our own human bodies and those of all things on earth were generated in the alchemy of exploding stars and came to us from the galaxies as stardust. Earth science tells us that all the elements that make up our present bodies have been circulated billions of times through other biotic and abiotic beings throughout the 4.5 billion years history of earth's evolution.

The elements of our bodies were once part bacteria that floated in the primal seas, rocks that were crumbled by wind, rain, and plants to make soil, insects that ate the algae of primal coastal pools, reptiles and birds that ate the algae, giant ferns nibbled by dinosaurs, as well as the bodies of those dinosaurs themselves, myriad plants, animals, and their decaying bodies that found their way back to the earth and waters as nutrients, or were cycled through the air to descend as life-giving rain.

Recognition of this profound kinship must bridge the arrogant barriers that humans have erected to wall themselves off, not only from other sentient animals, but also from simpler animals, plants, and the abiotic matrix of life in rocks and soils, air, and water. Like the great nature mystic, Francis of Assisi, we may learn to greet as our brothers and sisters the wolf and the lamb, trees and grasses, fire and water, and even "holy death," the means by which all living things are returned to earth to be regenerated as new organisms.

Another compelling message that is revealed in earth history is the coevolution of plants, air, water, soil, and animals. Nature lovers of Christian culture have a tendency to imagine that in the beginning of earth's history, there was Eden, a paradise of flashing lakes, luxuriant trees, and gamboling animals, without humans to spoil the picture. It is a startling shift to imagine a molten earth with a poisonous atmosphere, bathed in ultraviolet radiation. Our utter dependency on green plants is made evident when we realize that plants are the creators, not only of the food chain that supports all animals, but also for the generation of a breathable atmosphere. The sun and green plants together have been the major creators of the conditions for life on earth as we know it.

Yet, oddly enough, the very earliest organisms found oxygen itself poisonous and generated energy from fermentation, as yeasts do today.[26] Thus the slow buildup of oxygen in the seas and then in the atmosphere, through early photosynthesis, itself coevolved with the development of organisms that took in oxygen, transforming it into energy through cellular respiration and expiring carbon dioxide and water. Carbon is also returned to the atmosphere through the agency of bacteria and fungi that cause decay and through the weathering of limestone rocks. These byproducts of organic respiration, decay, and weathering are, in turn, taken in by plants to be transformed into carbohydrates, expiring oxygen as a byproduct. Thus is established the basic codependency of the carbon cycle, which sustains organic life processes.

The nitrogen cycle is another example of coevolutionary interdependency. Nitrogen is an essential component of proteins. Long protein molecules or enzymes serve as the biological catalysts inside living cells that regulate the chemical processes of life.

But most organisms cannot take in the gaseous nitrogen of the atmosphere. So, along with photosynthesis, the ability of certain bacteria to transform gaseous nitrogen into the nitrogen in protein enzymes is crucial. This ability in some bacteria seems to have developed early, perhaps even before photosynthesis.[27]

Today these nitrogen-fixing bacteria live in the soils and sea algae. The nitrogen compounds thus formed are taken in by plants as an essential nutrient, and the plants are, in turn, consumed by animals to provide this essential component. Through animal excretion and the decay of dead plants and animals, nitrogen is returned to the soil as ammonia, where it is broken down by nitrate bacteria into a form that can then be utilized by plants. Some nitrogen is returned to the atmosphere in this process. Thus the loop of the nitrogen cycle is completed through this interdependency of bacteria, plants, and animals.[28]

The coevolution of life-sustaining air, water, and soil is as much a part of the cycle of life as the interdependency of plants and animals. The evolution of soils that sustain plant life is itself a wonder of earth history. The combined weathering of rocks by winds and the breakdown by bacteria of decaying plant and animal bodies generate a teeming life system of fertile soils, which can be transformed by plants into nutrients for growth.[29]

Water is another essential ingredient in the sustaining of life. But most land plants and animals cannot tolerate the salty water that exists in abundance in the oceans. Water is made usable to land plants through evaporation by the sun's energy, by which it is taken up into the atmosphere and returned to the surface as precipitation in rain and snow. Snow and ice accumulate in mountains, and some melts slowly in summer, feeding streams and lakes. Some rainwater runs directly into rivers and lakes and finds its way back to oceans.

Some of this water is used by plants. Over the centuries much unused groundwater has seeped deeply into the soils to be stored in underground aquifers, or natural underground reservoirs between rock formations. Thus vast reserves of fresh water lie under islands and continents, indeed much more than fills lakes and rivers. These aquifers are the source of springs and wells tapped by animals and humans for much of their water supply.[30]

Forests play an essential role in this cycle of evaporation and precipitation. An abundant growth of green plants is not only fed by water through their roots, but also respire water vapor through the pores in their leaves. This water vapor creates clouds that moderate the climate by blocking and reflecting the sun's rays, insulating the earth from excesses of cold and heat. The water vapor stored in clouds is returned to earth in precipitation.

The continued stripping of the earth's forests is thus one of the components contributing to desertification of the land, both through loss of rain and excessive heat. The buildup of excessive carbon dioxide in the atmosphere through the burning of fossil fuels, which may be leading to the "greenhouse effect" of global warming, is also accelerated by deforestation, which has removed much of the forests that might otherwise absorb and use this carbon dioxide.[31]

Other aspects of our interdependency are food chains and the cycle of production, consumption, and decomposition. Again the sun and green plants are the foundational basis of the nourishment consumed as food by animals. Through photosynthesis plants capture solar energy and transform it into organic molecules. Animals in turn sustain their life and growth by consuming the carbohydrates (sugars, starches, and cellulose) and proteins of plants. Most animals are herbivores, but some eat other animals. Fish and birds eat insects and worms. A few large animals are primarily carnivores, but many large animals, such as elephants and giraffes, are also herbivores.

As energy is transformed from one stage of transfer to another, much of it is dispersed and lost as usable energy. Plants can only take in and use about 1 percent of the sunlight that falls on them. Animals who eat plants can only convert about 10 percent of the energy stored in plants as food. And carnivores, in turn, can only use as food about 10 percent of the energy in the bodies of other animals. This means that each stage of the food chain must be roughly only one-tenth the size of the one on which it depends in order to create a sustainable relation.

Excessive meat-eating, which has evolved as the elite Western diet, threatens this entire food chain. Western anthropology has falsely presented our preagricultural ancestors as primarily hunters, when humans, for most of their history, have actually been omnivores, who ate mostly the leaves, roots, and fruits of plants, as well as insects. The flesh of small or large animals has been the occasional food of festivals, not the staple diet.[32]

Medieval aristocracies made meat-eating the privilege of the wealthy, who could monopolize domesticated animals and game.[33] This elite "beefeater" diet of the British aristocracy has become the American ideal. American cultural and business imperialism has been disseminating this diet around the world to peoples such as Asians, who historically ate very little meat and that mostly as garnish for a grain and vegetable diet.

One result of this expansion of the meat, especially beef, diet is excessive grazing of animals, which is destroying forests and polluting streams through failure to recycle animal excrement. A large segment of humans today is starving or malnourished, and this is partly related to the fact that a Western elite is eating high off the food chain, not only consuming much meat, but feeding the animals it eats with grain and fish proteins. Both inter-human justice and a sustainable relation to the rest of nature demands that humans return to feeding themselves primarily from the first stage of the food chain, from the food produced by plants.

A third essential aspect of the food chain, in addition to the production of food by plants and consumption of this food as plants and animals by animals, is decomposition. The bodies of dead plants, and the bodies and excrement of animals, are broken down into their constituent parts by decomposers: bacteria, fungi, and insects, as well as some larger carrion-eaters. These derive their energy by consumption of dead plants and animals, fallen leaves, and body wastes. Through these bacteria and fungi, the nutrients in decomposing bodies are returned to the earth to construct fertile soil and to be taken up again by growing plants.[34]

This cycle of production, consumption, and decomposition in nature prevents waste from accumulating. Nonhuman nature has developed a system of recycling that prevents the accumulation of waste as pollution. The crisis of pollution that afflicts modern civilization results, in large part, from its failure to imitate nature in this system of recycling. By failing to develop co-industries that break down and recycle technological wastes of production and consumption, as well as the natural wastes of food and excrement, these wastes are allowed to accumulate in concentrated forms that poison the soils, air, and waters.

In nature death is not an enemy, but a friend of the life process. The death side of the life cycle is an essential component of that renewal of life by which dead organisms are broken down and become the nutrients of new organic growth. Cultural avoidance of death, then, may be an essential root of the inability of some human cultures to create sustainable ecosystems and the turning of waste into pollution, a topic to which we will return later in this book.

In addition to recycling, sustainable ecosystems demand diversity and a balance of interdependency. This demands, as we have seen, that plants exist in much larger numbers (at least tenfold) than animals, and herbivores in much large numbers than carnivores. It also demands versatility. Most herbivores survive best when they can feed off a variety of plants. Carnivores survive better if they are not too specialized in their food supply and can eat plants and various types of animals. The more diversified the plant and animal life, the more various and hence sustainable the interdependency.

Oversimplification of ecosystems—created, for example, by farming, which strips the lands of all plants but one kind—tend to cause infestations of worms or insects that feed on this one type of plant. These species would be controlled in a more diverse ecosystem, with a variety of plants and with other insects and birds that would feed on this particular population. Thus the creation of what is called "pests" that plague the farmer is a direct result of the destruction of complex, balanced ecosystems. The more an ecosystem is simplified, that is, vast plains of just one crop, rather than diversified gardening, the more it is prone to this collapse by cogenerating an excessive population of one type of insect that will feed on this one plant.

Biotic diversity creates a complex feedback system that keeps each population of plants and animals in controllable limits through their interdependency on each other. If one kills all the birds and insects that eat a particular insect, that insect population will proliferate out of control. If one removes the predator of an animal, its population will proliferate. Eventually any escalating population will destroy its food supply and die off, sometimes in a precipitous fashion. But, in the process, it may strip the environment for other members of the biotic community.

The escalating human population represents an extreme case of such a proliferation of one population, which threatens to strip the planet of its life basis and thus eventually to destroy itself. Humans are a species who have no other predators. Although occasionally a trapped and enraged animal may kill a human, it does not do so for food. Humans are the primary predators of other humans. At least since the agricultural and urban revolutions, they have continually slaughtered one another.[35] Although a few human groups have been cannibals, they have done so more as an extension of war than as food supply.[36] Generally humans have killed each other not for food, but to express social hostility and competition for resources.

Until a few hundred years ago, human population was kept relatively small by war, lack of food, and disease. Women, the reproducers of the human population, died early through childbearing; many of their children died because of malnutrition and disease. Improved sanitation, disease control, and food production have allowed the human population to proliferate, first in the Western world and then in Asia, Africa, and Latin America, despite war and poverty. However, cultural hostilities toward women's agency as decision-makers in reproduction still continues to retard efforts to spread the use of birth control and thus to bring the human population under control in relation to its life-support matrix.[37]

Social philosophers have long debated whether competition or cooperation is the main "natural" impulse. The popular presentation of "wild" nature, particularly under the influence of social Darwinist views of evolution, has tended to present nature as "red in tooth and claw," the world of carnivore animals killing other animals. This has carried the social message that the strong have a right to prevail over the weak and that, in the competitive struggle for existence, might makes right. The evolutionary slogan of the "survival of the fittest" has suggested that the lion slaying and eating the plant-eating deer is the model for those who should prevail in human society as well.

This is a vastly distorted picture of nature. It greatly exaggerates the place of meat-eating in nature, in relation to the total food chain of nature, where most food is provided by plants. It fails to recognize that all the diverse animal and plant populations in an ecosystem are kept in healthy and life-giving balance by interdependency. Competition, that is, the control of each population in relation to the others by a pattern in which some populations feed others, works to sustain the total life of a biotic community only because it is set within a larger pattern of mutual limits. If a particular plant-eater strips all of the plants, it will starve itself. Most small animals elude their predators, and so the numbers of large carnivores are kept in check.

The diversity of nature has evolved through patterns of interdependency. Plants have evolved a variety of protective devices, such as unpleasant tastes, thorns, and nettles, to discourage eating by herbivores. Different colors of fur camouflage animals in different environments. All of the plants and animals in a biotic community, including those animals that eat high off the food chain, depend ultimately on the humble fungi and bacteria, who break down dead plants and animal bodies and recycle the nutrients into the soil, allowing for the renewal of food production from its primary producers, the plants. No one type of being is "king of the forest."

Within and between populations, there are many patterns of cooperation, as well as interdependent competition. A particular bird may be allowed to ride on the back of a large bison because it picks off and eats the insects that plague this animal. Animal groups form families of mutual help that care for the young, protect, and share food with each other. Cooperation and interdependency are the primary principles of ecosystems, within which competition between populations stands as a subcategory that serves to maintain this interdependency in a way that sustains the balanced relation of each population in relation to the whole.

Some biologists, such as Lynn Margulis and James Lovelock, have given us a new vision of earth as Gaia, a living organism of complex interdependencies and biofeedback, linking biota and its "environment" of soil, air, and water. In this system of interdependency, any absolutization of competition that causes one side to be wiped out means that the other sides of the relation thereby destroy themselves as well. The falsity of the human cultural concept of "competition" is that it is mutually exclusive. It imagines the other side as an "enemy" to be "annihilated," rather than an essential component of an interrelationship upon which it itself interdepends.

Human ethics should be a more refined and conscious version of this natural interdependency, mandating humans to imagine and feel the suffering of others, and to find ways in which interrelation becomes cooperative and mutually life-enhancing for both sides. Too often, however, human culture has moved in the other direction: imagining the "other," whether other humans, animals, or forests and swamps, as "enemies" to be annihilated, rather than as members of a biotic community upon which we depend for our own life. In this false ethic of competition, interdependency shows its negative face as mutual destruction.

If the new cosmic stories of astral and atomic physics and ecology are to provide a new and shared planetary "myth" for ethics and spirituality, as well as scientific understanding, it is necessary to heal the splits between "fact" and "value," theory and practice, private and social, that have been created in Western thought. Brian Swimme, a proponent of "remything" the scientific story, has spoken of the mechanistic mind-set of science as like a lobotomy. The components of awe and wonder, which are the roots of reverence for life, are split off from scientific consciousness.[38]

Mechanistic thought is reductionist. It reduces the complex and living interconnection of nature to its component parts. Its language prefers nonliving parts to living and dynamic wholes. This bias disposes scientists to describe the extraordinary mystery of life's origins as the Big Bang, a term that suggests a loud explosion, rather than choosing a term, such as the "cosmic egg" or the "superabundant nucleus," that might put us in touch with the wonder of the very story that they themselves have uncovered. The masculinist bias undoubtedly also operates here in the choice of a metaphor of destructive violence, rather than of gestation and birth.

Even ecologists have mostly ignored the spiritual and ethical import of ecology. Paul Ehrlich, for example, has used mechanistic language for the life processes he describes, such as the "machinery

of nature," thus implicitly denying the self-organizing capacity
that is the characteristic of living beings. Westernized consciousness must heal itself of its split-off divisions that have separated
knowledge from wonder, reverence, and love before we can learn
how to tell the cosmic story in a way that will rekindle an ethic
and spirituality capable of calling us to the tasks of healing and
sustaining the earth. We need scientist-poets who can retell the
story I have alluded to in this chapter, the story of the cosmos and
the earth's history, in a way that can call us to wonder, to reverence for life, and to the vision of humanity living in community
with all its sister and brother beings.

PART TWO

Destruction

3

Religious Narratives of World Destruction

Why have narratives of world destruction played such a large part in religious consciousness? What role does apocalyptic narrative play today, as humans face the destructive possibilities of their own power on an unprecedented scale? In this chapter I trace the development of apocalyptic narrative from its ancient Near Eastern prototypes to its contemporary uses.

The prototypes of such narratives lie in ancient experiences of real destruction, both from nature and from other human groups. Extremes of drought, searing heat, and torrential rains characterized the Tigris and Euphrates river valley. Large-scale agriculture was built on separating the "sweet" from the salty waters in systems of irrigation. Periodically torrential rains broke down these irrigation ditches, flooding fields and houses.

One particularly great flood that destroyed everything was long remembered in the ancient Near East. The earliest version of this flood story goes back to Sumerian times (c. 3000 B.C.E.), preserved in a fragment of a tablet from the library at the city of Nippur.[1] In this story the assembly of the gods decided to destroy "the seed of mankind." But some of the gods, among them Nintu and Inanna, regretted the cruel decision. They chose a pious king, Ziusudra, distinguished by his obedient reverence for the rites of the gods and his receptivity to divine revelation in dreams, and instructed him to build a great boat.

Although the fragmentary nature of the text doesn't make clear what Ziusudra put in the boat, he becomes the one through whom human life begins anew after the flood.

> After, for seven days and seven nights, the flood had swept over the land, and the huge boat had been tossed about by the windstorms on the great waters, Utu [the sun] came forth, who sheds light on heaven and earth. Ziusudra opened a window on the huge boat. The hero Utu brought his rays into the giant boat.[2]

Ziusudra performs rites of thanksgiving to Utu, slaughtering an ox and a sheep. The waters receded and vegetation comes up out of the earth. Ziusudra himself is raised to the status of a god, "the preserver of the name of vegetation and of the seed of mankind."

This ancient flood story, the prototype of the Hebrew flood story, has been so domesticated in Christianity as a children's story that we have become oblivious to the horror that lay behind this remembrance. The Sumerians recalled five cities that were wiped out by this flood. Immense destruction of human life must have taken place, together with the wiping out of all the animal and plant life in the great flood plain of the Tigris-Euphrates Valley. In remembering this story, we should spend less time on the cute animals that went into the boat, two by two, and more time reflecting on the stark meaning of the phrase "and all flesh died that moved on the earth" (Genesis 7:21).

Ancient Near Eastern societies faced many disasters. In addition to floods, marauding bands of nomads and then more organized armies periodically assaulted the urban settlements with their surrounding villages, trampling fields, burning houses, slaughtering humans and animals, and carrying away booty in the form of slaves, as well as other portable wealth. War would provide another key image in the narratives of world destruction.

The searing heat and drought of summer were eventually followed by the rains that allowed the new planting, the renewal of life to parched fields and hills. Yet the drought seemed interminable as the people waited for the new rain. When it finally came, there was rejoicing, dancing, and celebration. Around this yearly cycle of drought and rain, ancient Near Eastern religion built a year cycle of cult and story. With the drought a deity was imagined to have died and sunk into the underworld, to be restored to life with the new rains.

The Sumerian story of Inanna's descent into the underworld[3] and the punishment of her male consort Dumuzi;[4] the Greek story of the abduction of Persephone, the daughter of Demeter (the Earth Mother), into the underworld by Hades;[5] the Egyptian story of the death and resurrection of Osiris aided by his Queen Isis;[6] and the Canaanite story of Anath and Ba'al[7] are versions of this basic myth of the death of nature through yearly drought. Through the enacted myths of the defeat of a god by the powers of death, the human community participated in the yearly death of nature, experiencing the devastation of the god's death, but also rejoicing with the yearly restoration of the powers of life.

In the hymn of joy at the resurrection of Ba'al, the Canaanite community sang exultantly:

> The heavens fat did rain,
> The wadies flow with honey
> So I knew that alive was Puissant Baal!
> Existent the Prince, Lord of earth![8]

In these stories of yearly drought and death of vegetation, destruction and new creation, death and resurrection, are two sides of the same story. Through participating in the rites of death, mourning the goddess who has descended to the underworld or the god-king who has been killed, the human community assures the passage of nature from death to life, the renewal of the powers of fertility.

The Hebrew world took over these prototypes but revised them in accordance with their own view of God as one and transcendent to the cycles of nature and the changing fortunes of history. In their hands the stories are moralized and placed in the context of the historical fortunes of Israel. World destruction, through floods, drought, and trampling armies, becomes punishment by God, retribution for failure to obey the laws of one God, who controls nature and history from above.

In the Hebrew version of the flood story, Noah was born in the tenth generation from Adam. In this period human wickedness began to proliferate, and God regretted that he had created them. God decided to "blot out from the earth the human beings I have created—people together with animals and creeping things and birds of the air, for I am sorry that I have made them" (Genesis 6:7). Noah alone finds favor with God as a righteous man. So God makes a covenant with Noah and instructs him to build a great boat, taking into it his wife and his three sons, together with their wives, and a male-female pair of all the animals, birds, and reptiles, together with all kinds of food.

Rains fell on the earth for forty days and nights, and the waters of the flood mounted until they covered the highest mountain. "And all flesh died that moved on the earth, birds, domestic animals, wild animals, all swarming creatures that swarm on the earth, and all human beings" (Genesis 7:21). The waters continued to swell for another one hundred and fifty days and then began to abate, until land reappeared. Finally, almost a year after the flood began, Noah, his family, and the animals were able to come out of the ark.

Noah's first act is to build an altar to God and to offer to God burnt offerings of all the clean animals and birds. God, pleased by these offerings, promised never again to destroy the earth, even though the evil tendency continues in the human heart. Yet "as long as the earth endures, seedtime and harvest, cold and heat, summer and winter, day and night, shall not cease" (Genesis 8:22). God made a covenant with Noah and his descendants, and with all the animals that were in the ark, never again to destroy the earth by flood, sealing this promise with the sign of the rainbow in the rainclouds.

Yet life on earth is not as good after the flood as before. Enmity between human and animals, human and human, worsens. In the first covenant with Adam, God gave humans only the green plants for food. The animals are put under human care, but not given as food. But after the flood:

> The fear and dread of you shall rest on every animal of the earth, and on every bird of the air, on everything that creeps on the ground, and on all the fish of the sea; into your hand they are delivered. Every moving thing that lives shall be food for you; and just as I gave you the green plants, I give you everything. (Genesis 9:2–3, New Revised Standard Version)

The limit that is set to this eating of flesh is that humans should not eat the warm blood of animals, for this is the same blood that runs in human veins. God also will require a reckoning from every animal who sheds human blood and from every human who sheds the blood of another human (Genesis 9:4–6).

Although the Hebrew God promises never again to destroy the world by water, the searing heat of the summer sun and the trampling of armies continue as images of divine retribution through world destruction. The pages of Hebrew scripture abound with images of destruction meted out by God to his chosen people, Israel, in particular, for its failure to obey God's commandments.

Drought and war, sword, pestilence, and famine will sweep over the land in the day of divine wrath. Conquering armies will devastate their cities, slaughtering them or carrying them off as slaves into exile. In the language of the prophet Ezekiel 7:1–4:

> You, O mortal, thus says the Lord God to the land of Israel: An end! The end has come upon the four corners of the land. Now the end is upon you, I will let loose my anger upon you. I will judge you according to your ways; I will punish you for all your abominations. My eye will not spare you. I will have no pity. I will punish you for your ways, while your abominations are among you. Then you will know that I am the Lord.

In Isaiah, the description of divine retribution draws dramatically on the language of the devastation of the land by yearly droughts and flood, with its yearly cultic lamentations:

> Now the Lord is about to lay waste the earth and make it desolate, and he will twist its surface and scatter its inhabitants . . . The earth shall be utterly laid waste and utterly despoiled; for the Lord has spoken this word. The earth dries up and withers, the world languishes and withers; the heavens languish together with the earth. The earth lies polluted under its inhabitants; for they have transgressed laws, violated the statutes, broken the everlasting covenant. Therefore a curse devours the earth, and its inhabitants suffer for their guilt; therefore the inhabitants of the earth dwindled, and few people are left. (Isaiah 24:1, 3–6)

For those who have survived the droughts there come the floods:

> For the windows of heaven are opened, and the foundations of the earth tremble. The earth is utterly broken, the earth is torn asunder, the earth is violently shaken. The earth lies heavy upon it, and it falls and will not rise again. (Isaiah 18–20)

Despite such notes of finality, these acts of divine destruction envisioned by the prophets are not terminal. They act as warnings, calling Israel to repentance. Once Israel has repented of its infidelity to God's commandments and returned to the right path, God will restore its fortunes. Then the land will flourish with abundant rain and bountiful harvests. The people will return from exile to its lands and restore its ancient cities. It will prevail over its enemies and reduce them to servitude, or, in a more universalist vision, the other nations will stream to Zion, be converted to its God, and peace and justice will prevail throughout the earth.[9]

As Israel fell under the control of one imperial power after another, Assyria, Babylonia, Persia, Hellenistic Greece, and then Rome, the prophetic imagination turned increasingly to the vision of divine punishment directed against these enemies of God's people. The vision of world history becomes extended. Instead of local changes of fortune, it becomes a perspective on the whole history of the world. This vision sweeps from creation through millennial stages of history, until a final drama of culminating destruction and transformation.

In these apocalyptic stories, Israel is envisioned as languishing under a reign of evil brought about by its own sins. God allows the evil nations and demonic powers to triumph over them. In due time, however, God will bring an end to this reign of evil. He will intervene, judge, and destroy the wicked nations and vindicate the righteous in a renovated earth, where peace and good times will prevail.

These Jewish apocalyptic writings, which began to be written in the second century B.C.E., were probably influenced by Persian religious thought. The Zoroastrian picture of world history was based on a cosmic conflict between the good God, Ahura Mazda, and the spirit of evil, Angra-Mainyu. The history of the world was divided into four periods, each of three thousand years, reflecting the conflict between these two cosmic powers for the possession of humans and the earth.

In the first three thousand years, these two powers remain apart, producing their own creatures. In the second period, the

material creation appears and the two spirits war over its possession. In the third period, the evil power establishes his ascen-
dency over the earth. The final era of world history begins with
the birth of Zoroaster. With the spread of the true religion, there
is to be a progressive triumph of good over evil.

Three good rulers or Saoshyants (saviors) reign over the three
millennia of progressive triumph of good over evil. Not only personal moral evil, but social and natural evils, misery, hunger, and
disease, will be gradually defeated. Humanity will reach a state
of near perfection. Then the final savior will appear and inaugurate the "last things." The savior will raise the dead, beginning
with Gayomard (the first man or Persian Adam). All humanity,
past and present, will assemble and be judged for their good and
evil deeds. Then the righteous are separated from the unright-
eous; the sinners are punished for three days in hell and weep for
their sins, while the righteous in heaven weep for the the sins and
sufferings of the wicked.

This period of purgation is followed by one of cosmic transformation. The mountains will be melted down and flow like a
molten river. All humans will pass through this river of fire, being
purified thereby of the impulse to evil. The Savior then slaughters
the cosmic beast, Hadhayos, and prepares a sacrament that is fed
to these purified humans, making them immortal. As a final act
of world redemption, the good spirit, Ahura Mazda, seizes the
evil spirit and destroys it, purifying hell itself, and bringing it
back "for the enlargement of the world." Thus the world itself is
purged of both evil and mortality, and "the world becomes immortal and everlasting."[10]

In the Hebrew versions of world redemption through fire, the
story becomes both more militaristic and punitive, and less universal. The dead rise to be judged for their sins, but the separation
of the righteous from the wicked is permanent. The righteous are
vindicated and triumph in a renovated earth, while the evil ones

are punished. There is glee rather than compassion among the righteous at the sight of the sufferings inflicted upon the sinners. They are destroyed forever, rather than being restored through purgation.

Although one second-century church father, Origen, suggested that all fallen spirits, including the Devil and his demons, would eventually be converted and the entire cosmos restored to unity with God, this generous vision was rejected by Christian orthodoxy.[11] In Christian eschatology hell remains as the permanent place for eternal punishment of the wicked, parallel to the eternal happiness of the saints.

Jewish apocalyptic writings flourished during the period of struggle against the Greek and Roman empires, from the period of the Maccabean Revolution (166–5 B.C.E.) to the Jewish wars against Rome in 66–73 C.E. and 133–36 C.E. The only apocalypse in Hebrew scripture, the book of Daniel, actually was written by an anti-Hellenizing Hasidist during the period of the Maccabean revolt against the Seleucid king, Antiochus Epiphanes. But the author read the timeframe of the book back into the period of the Babylonian captivity of the Jews under Nebuchadnezzar (600 B.C.E.). From this vantage point, he could survey the unfolding of history up to his own time.

In the last half of the book, the unfolding of Persian history is recounted in a series of apocalyptic visions. The visions tell of the defeat of the Persian king by Alexander the Great and the rise of the rival Hellenistic kingdoms, which divided up the vast regions conquered by Alexander. This sequence of evil kingdoms, under which Israel has suffered, culminates with the worst of evil kings, Antiochus Epiphanes (176–164 B.C.E.) against whom Judas Maccabaeus and his sons had raised their standards of revolt in the name of fidelity to the true God of Israel.

But the power of this evil king and his ability to "wear out the Holy Ones of the Most High" is nearing its end. Soon, however:

his dominion shall be taken away to be consumed and totally destroyed. The kingship and dominion and the greatness of the
kingdoms under the whole heaven shall be given to the people of
the holy ones of the Most High; their kingdom shall be an everlasting kingdom, and all dominions shall serve and obey them.
(Daniel 8:26–27)

In a previous vision, Daniel sees the scene of divine judgment
in which the Ancient One (God) takes his seat upon the fiery
throne with burning wheels. The books of judgment are opened,
and the evil kings judged and destroyed. Then there descends
from heaven a figure in human likeness. This "Human One" is
presented to the Ancient One. This figure is understood as representing both Israel collectively and a righteous king (Messiah)
that will rule over it.[12] His kingdom will be everlasting:

> To him was given dominion and glory and kingship that all
> peoples, nations, and language should serve him. His dominion
> is an everlasting dominion that shall not pass away and his king-
> ship is one that shall never be destroyed. (Daniel 7:14)

These visions of the reversal of Israel's fortunes, overthrowing
evil empires and putting Israel in world dominion, were elabo-
rated over the next two centuries. Although their central message
remains religio-political, other religious issues are dealt with in
them, such as the purging of the evil impulse from God's people
themselves, the settlement of accounts with the dead of past times,
and the overcoming of mortality in both humans and nature.

The theme of resurrection of past dead is suggested in Daniel
12:3–4:

> Many of those who sleep in the dust of the earth shall awake,
> some to everlasting life and some to shame and everlasting con-
> tempt. Those who are wise shall shine like the brightness of the
> sky, and those who lead many to righteousness, like the stars for-
> ever and ever.

But this eschatology seems to be added from a source other than that of the apocalyptic visions of judgment, where such resurrection of the past dead is absent.[13] Moreover, in the passage above, there is no general resurrection, but only a limited awakening of the specially righteous and specially wicked, to receive their respective vindication and punishment.

In the early apocalypses, resurrection functions as a way to settle the accounts of past unrequited injustice and unrewarded righteousness, not to overcome human mortality. Hebrew religion, before the Greek period, saw mortality as natural rather than a problem to be overcome. Its vision of blessedness had focused on a healthy and prosperous life in a full term of years, not escape from mortality altogether.[14]

However, in the apocalypses of the first centuries B.C.E. and C.E., while the settling of the accounts of justice remains important, there is a new focus on immortality. Not only are the past dead to rise, but finally the whole cosmos is imagined to undergo a process of destruction and re-creation, overcoming its mortality and making it the bearer of the immortal life of the resurrected. This process of development reaches its fullest form in the Christian Book of Revelation, written during the persecution of Christians by the Roman emperor Domitian (c. 95 C.E.).

CHRISTIAN APOCALYPTIC

In the Book of Revelation, the Christian saints are seen as suffering under the power of successive evil emperors, but the time of their delivery is at hand. God is about to pour out the seven bowls of divine wrath, inflicting plagues on those who have worshiped the Roman emperor and the power of Satan that stands behind him. The sea and rivers will be turned to blood, and every fish will die. After these plagues, divine judgment is pronounced against the seat of the evil empire, Babylon (representing Rome).

Fallen, fallen is Babylon the Great! It has become a dwelling
place of demons, a haunt of every foul and hateful bird, a haunt
of every foul and hateful beast. (Revelation 18:2)

The saints are called to exit from the evil city:

Come out of her, my people, so that you do not take part in
her sins, and so that you do not share in her plagues. (18:4)

All the kings and merchants of the earth, who had subjected
themselves to the power of the (Roman) empire, paid tributes to
it, and brought it their rich cargoes of merchandise, are pictured
as mourning and weeping as they envision their own demise,
along with the demise of the great city. Then an angel takes up a
great millstone and throws it into the sea to signal the decisive
overthrow of the imperial power. The angels and saints set up
great hallelujahs of rejoicing in this expected destruction.

There then unfolds the final battle between the Messiah-
warrior, who appears from heaven, leading the angelic armies,
and Satan with the armies of the evil kings. The evil armies are
defeated, and their flesh left to be devoured by carrion birds. The
demonic cosmic power behind the armies, the Devil, is seized and
locked in a pit for a thousand years. There is then a resurrection
of the saints, who reign with Christ over the earth for a thousand
years.

After this millennial period, Satan is again released from his
prison, and there is a final battle between God and Satan, with
his followers. Fire comes down from heaven and destroys these
armies. Satan, together with other evil powers, is thrown into a
lake of fire, to be "tormented day and night forever and ever."
This destruction of the power of evil is followed by a general resurrection. All the dead, great and small, stand before the throne
of God. The record books are opened, and all are judged according to their deeds. A second book, the book of life, then is
opened, and any whose name is not found in the book of life is
thrown into the lake of fire.

After this judgment there is a general renovation of creation itself. The first heaven and earth passes away, and the New Jerusalem comes down from heaven. Not only evil, but also mortality will be banished. All things are made new, with God dwelling as a direct, unmediated presence in the midst of the saints.

> And God himself will be with them; he will wipe every tear from their eyes. Death will be no more; mourning and crying and pain will be no more, for the first things have passed away. (Revelation 21:3–4)

This apocalyptic vision appealed to those Christians who saw themselves as persecuted outsiders to the Roman empire, set in deadly conflict with its political power, its cultural sway, and its gods. However, already by the early second century, Christianity began to attract persons of Greek culture and middle-class social status who wished to convince the Roman authorities that the Christian church nurtured loyal citizens, not subversives committed to its overthrow. Although these Hellenized Christians continue to be confident that Christianity is the true religion, worshiping the one true God, this is seen more as the full disclosure of intimations of truth found in their earlier culture, including Greek philosophy, rather than a total contradiction of this culture.

For these converts from Greek culture, apocalyptic became distasteful, and they would have been happy to drop the Book of Revelation from the Christian canon altogether. Only a compromise between Greek and Latin church traditions saved this book from exclusion from the final Christian canon.[15] But its importance was downplayed in the philosophical, mystical Christianity that came to flourish in the eastern Mediterranean. For Latin Christianity it remained a formal part of the vision of the historical future, but speculations about the nearness of such events was discouraged.

Thus apocalyptic thought, rooted in intense reading of the books of Daniel and Revelation, became the characteristic of marginalized Christians. These groups saw themselves as pitted, not only against evil pagan empires, but also against Christianized empires and against those imperial churches that had merged with such Christian empires. Already in the second century, Montanism revived the apocalyptic perspective of early Christianity that was fading among more Hellenized Christians. They also revived the participation of women in prophetic leadership, which was being rejected by a patriarchalized church.[16]

In the fourth century, the North African Donatists kept alive an apocalyptic Christianity, linked with hostility to the power of the Roman empire, a hostility that was being softened by imperial Christians such as St. Augustine. Rigid rejection of all political and cultural amalgamation with the empire, and readiness for the martyr's death, were the hallmarks of the Donatist way.[17] Augustine's own vast treatise on world history, *The City of God,* incorporated the apocalyptic dramas of the Hebrew and Christian scriptures and thus assured their continued importance in the medieval church.[18]

Although all medieval Christians continued to assume that this drama of world destruction and re-creation would be the culmination of history in the not too distant future, a new era of intense apocalyptic speculation arose in the late medieval period and continued on through the period of the Wars of Religion of the seventeenth century. During this period the Latin Catholic church was becoming discredited as a representative of God and an instrument of good order. Instead it came to be seen through the lens of the corrupt Whore of Babylon, whose reign was about to be overthrown by the righteous Warrior-Messiah. Once again Christians studied the signs of the "last things" in the books of Daniel and Revelation, and saw in them the events of their own times.

The period of the English Civil War and Protectorate, which pitted Anglican supporters of the Stuart kings against Puritan supporters of Parliament (1640–60), was one such period of intense apocalyptic fervor. The left wing of the Puritan movement proliferated radical groups, most of whom had access to small independent presses to distribute their visionary tracts. The anti-establishment character of these movements often allowed women and working-class men to find their voices in them.[19]

One such female prophet of the Civil War period was Mary Cary, who wrote her apocalyptic interpretation of British political history in the 1640s and 1650s. Her extant writings include "A Word in Season to the Kingdom of England" (1647), "The Resurrection of the Witnesses and England's Fall from the Mystical Babylon, Rome" (1648; enlarged edition, 1653), and "The Little Horn's Doom and Downfall," containing a section entitled, "A New and More Exact Mappe of New Jerusalem's Glory" (1651).[20]

In her "Word in Season," addressed to rulers on all levels—King, Parliament, synod, and city and county officials—Cary calls these authorities to account before the bar of scripture and its God. They are to cease oppressing the poor and failing to punish evildoers. They should accept the sovereignty of Christ over them, and stop repressing the saints and stopping the mouths of prophets and preachers of the gospel. God, she says, has delivered this kingdom (of England) from its enemies, and now expects it to bear fruit in just and godly behavior.

Cary's primary purpose in this tract is to declare the rights of the free prophetic spirit to proclaim its message throughout the land, unhindered by church or political authorities. This prophetic spirit is fundamentally egalitarian. It is not channeled or controlled by social hierarchies. It blows where it will, and it is given to women as well as men without regard to education or status. The free flowing of this prophetic spirit, moreover, signals that the last days of world history are dawning. These are the days in which God is fulfilling his promise to "pour out my Spirit upon all flesh, and your sons and your daughters shall prophecy" (Acts 2:17).

In the "Resurrection of the Witnesses," Cary correlates the story of the prophetic career, death, and resurrection of the two witnesses of Revelation 11 with English history. These witnesses are the prophets who proclaimed in the period of 1641–45, who were slain, and now have risen in the form of a new wave of prophets in the seven years of 1645–52.[21] These events prove that the time when the Great Babylon made war on the saints, and when the Beast prevailed over them, has run its course, and the time of the reign of Jesus Christ is about to dawn.

Finally, in "The Little Horn's Doom and Downfall," with the "New and More Exact Mappe of New Jerusalem's Glory," Cary maps out the sequence of world destruction and transformation. England is God's elect nation, and thus it is to be here that these events will unfold. Papal Rome represents the continuation of the evil Babylon of the Roman empire, which has sprouted the ten horns of the kings of Europe and England. Charles I of England was that king of whom scripture predicted that he would put down three kings (reign over the three kingdoms of England, Scotland, and Wales), and would "wear out the saints of the Most High" (Daniel 7:24–25).

The overthrow of Charles I indicates that the time of affliction has come to an end, his dominion is to be taken away and given to the saints (Daniel 7:25–27). Over the next fifty years (1651–1701), Cary calculates that the saints will establish their rule over the whole earth. They will execute divine vengeance on the heathen (both "pagans" and Christian "apostates") and destroy them. The Jews, however, will be converted (to Christianity) and will return to their ancient land (of Palestine). After this fifty-year war period is over, the saints will enter upon the thousand years of peace. The saints of the past will rise to join them, and Satan will be bound.

This millennial reign of the saints will be filled with material blessings. There will be good weather, abundant rain and sun. The barns of the saints will be filled with wheat, and they will have nice houses and gardens. But, being restored to primal innocence, they will not be corrupted by this material abundance. At the end of this millennial period, Satan again will be loosed, there will be the final battle between good and evil; the final judgment, the destruction of the mortal heaven and earth, followed by its immortal recreation. Thus did one English prophetess confidently survey the future from the years immediately after the execution of King Charles by the Puritan army.

This apocalyptic tradition was inherited by American popular Protestantism, along with the confident belief that America was God's elect nation and promised land. Revivalism kept these visions alive, with their continual calls for vast rectification, not only in personal lives, but in the life of the nation as well. In nineteenth-century America, two quite different lines of futurism established themselves in different religious and social sectors of American life, one progressive and the other catastrophic.

Progressivism, represented by Christian liberals and socialists of the Social Gospel tradition, believed that democracy had already established itself in American political institutions. There remained only to extend this democratic tradition of equal rights and popular government to the economic sphere.[22] The Spirit of God was seen as immanent in history, leading it on to higher and higher development, until world peace would be established; and a virtual millennium of peace and prosperity would dawn on earth, with America at the forefront of this march to perfection.[23]

The catastrophic school of American Christianity cultivated quite a different vision and saw these progressives as apostates. Catastrophic apocalypticism typically has come from sects, such as Seventh Day Adventists and Jehovah's Witnesses, who gather people who have not been included in the benefits of the American "dream." One such movement was represented by the Millerite tradition. In the 1840s a New England Baptist preacher, William Miller (1782–1849), began to draw large crowds as he traveled about proclaiming that the end of the world would come "about 1843." Miller had calculated from Daniel 8:14 that 2,300 years were predicted to elapse between the rebuilding of the city of Jerusalem in 457 B.C.E. and the Second Coming.

When the time of fulfillment failed to come by March 1844, the date was recalculated for October 1844, but still the crowds awaiting the end were disappointed. Most followers of Miller drifted away at this point, but a small remnant gathered around the reinterpretation of these predictions by one Millerite, Hiram Edson. Edson explained that what had taken place on October 22, 1844, was an event in heaven, rather than earth, and thus invisible to material eyes. On that date Christ had entered the inner Sanctuary of the heavenly temple to cleanse it. This act was preliminary to his final coming. Although the end was not yet, the world was indeed in its last days, and true believers should prepare themselves and others for the world's destruction and transformation.[24]

Among the core leaders of this remnant of Millerites was Ellen White, who distinguished herself by her revelatory visions that confirmed these reinterpretations. She became accepted as the prophetess of the Adventists, teaching not only on heavenly matters, but offering a variety of instructions on child care, education, and diet. White saw God as calling the Adventists to a strict observance of Hebrew law, including the Saturday Sabbath and avoidance of pork. Eventually all meat and stimulants, such as alcohol, coffee, and tea, were also to be avoided. Adventists would come to distinguish themselves by their ardent support of missions, which typically featured educational and medical institutions.[25]

Despite these ventures into world reconstruction, the core of the Adventist message was the nearness of the end and the need to prepare oneself and others for this day. Ellen White's monumental apocalyptic work, *The Great Controversy* (1880), detailed this history from scriptural times into nineteenth-century America. For White, like many Protestant millennialists, the papacy and the Roman Catholic church remained the anti-Christ, the continuation of the Beast and the Great Babylon of the Book of Revelation. Not only Catholic nations, but also those Protestant nations that continued to have established state churches, represented the continuation of this Satanic empire.

America was initially an exception to this demonic character of government. It was that second beast that arose out of the earth (Revelation 13:11) with horns like a lamb and speaking like a dragon. The lamb's horns indicated that the character of America corresponded to that of Christ. Its defense of democratic government and freedom of religion made it the apt bearer of God's people. But its speaking like a dragon indicated its liability to corruption. In fact, in White's view, it had been corrupted by the Protestant church establishment, which had allowed the institutionalization of Sunday observance in America. It thereby sold out to the changes of God's law brought about by Satan's church, Catholicism, and disobeyed God's true law, in which the Saturday observance of the Sabbath remains unchanged.[26]

White envisions the unfolding of the last things, beginning with the persecution of the true Sabbatarian believers. When this persecution reaches its worst point, Christ will return and call the persecuted together. They will be taken up into heaven to enjoy a thousand years of felicity. Meanwhile the earth will be handed over to desolation and destruction. It will be utterly laid waste (drawing on Isaiah 24). The binding of Satan for one thousand years actually signifies the turning of the whole earth into a desolate wilderness for Satan and his demons. Only at the end of this thousand-year period will there be the final battle between God

and Satan. Satan will then be utterly destroyed, and the earth itself purged by fire.

This fiery purgation of earth will be the means by which God
will purify it of evil and then recreate it on a new and immortal
basis. The saints can then descend from heaven to earth to inhabit this renovated earth forever. Although this tract was published over one hundred years ago, its currency even today is not
confined to Seventh Day Adventists. Reprinted in 1988, it is cur-
rently distributed by groups such as the Fountain of Life, Inc., of
Evanston, Illinois, under the title *America in Prophecy*.

The Cold War and the threat of nuclear war from the 1950s
to the 1980s have proved fertile ground for new apocalyptic
speculations. The founding of the state of Israel in 1948, and its
expansion to the West Bank and Gaza Strip in 1967, have been
new grist for these premillennialist apocalypticists. Jewish
restorationism had been a feature of Protestant apocalyptic since
the seventeenth century, as we have seen in the writings of Mary
Cary.[27] In this Protestant interpretation, Jewish conversion to
Christianity in the last days is linked to their return from exile.[28]
They would then reestablish their state in Palestine and would rebuild the Jewish temple on its ancient site in Jerusalem (since 685
C.E. the site of the revered Islamic Shrine of the Dome of the
Rock).

When Jews began to emigrate to Palestine under the inspiration of Zionism in the late nineteenth century, and established a
Jewish state in 1948, many Christian premillennialists saw these
predictions being fulfilled. However, since these Zionist Jews
were not becoming Christians, this aspect of the apocalyptic
timetable had to be revised. It was now said that the Jews must
return to the Promised Land in an "unbelieving" state (that is,
unconverted to Christianity).

When this ingathering was completed, the final events of redemption would unfold. One hundred and forty-four thousand
Jews would be converted to true (that is, fundamentalist

Protestant) Christianity, the Temple would be rebuilt, and the war of Armageddon between God and Satan would wipe out all unbelievers: false Christians as well as Jews, Muslims, pagans, and Communists. The true believers would be raptured up to heaven and thus kept safe during this war.

Twentieth-century apocalypticists readily identified this war with nuclear war. They have imagined that, after this purgation of the earth by nuclear fire, the saints would be returned to a renovated earth to live in millennial bliss. In this fashion twentieth-century realities, such as nuclear war, pro-Zionist politics, and Cold War antagonisms, are incorporated into apocalyptic tracts, such as Hal Lindsay's *The Late Great Planet Earth* and *The 1980s, Countdown to Armageddon,* which were popular with fundamentalist American Christians in the 1970s and 1980s. The 1990 Persian Gulf crisis saw a retooling of these speculations to incorporate Saddam Hussein into the apocalyptic scenario in John Walvoord's best-selling *Armageddon, Oil and the Middle East Crisis.*[29]

CONCLUDING REFLECTIONS

It is easy for religious liberals and secularists to dismiss these apocalyptic visions as the fanaticism of a dwindling and insignificant group. But this would be to misunderstand the perennial attraction of these visions as a way of coping with incomprehensible and seemingly unmanageable social chaos. The end of the twentieth century, with its extremes of poverty and wealth, stockpiles of weapons, and threats of disaster from nuclear war and ecological collapse, is ripe for such magical shortcuts to problem solving, which claim to assure the victory of total good over total evil. In the Reagan administration, several officials, including the President himself, appeared prone to such apocalyptic thinking.[30]

Apocalyptic is the offspring of prophetic thought. As such it has often carried messages of protest against the dominant system

of political and religious power. Classes of people silenced by
these dominant institutions have been empowered to speak and
speak boldly against these systems. The belief that prophecy will
be restored in the last days, and that "upon my slaves, both men
and women, in those days I will pour out my Spirit" (Acts 2:18),
has been a continuing mandate in radical Christian movements
for both class and gender role rebellion. Those at the bottom of
the social hierarchy, women and oppressed men, have felt mandated to speak critically over against the world that had marginalized them.

But this empowerment to prophetic protest has been fatally
corrupted by apocalyptic because of its dualistic mode of
thought. "Us and them" as absolute good against absolute evil,
God against Satan, have been the hallmarks of its thinking. This
does not mean that there is no such thing as good and evil, but
this distinction should be defined in quite a different way. Good
and evil need to be seen as different kinds of relationships, rather
than different kinds of "beings" (a distinction that will be developed further in a later section of this book).

Fundamentalists, however, typically reify good and evil. They
treat good and evil as though these were opposite substances, ultimately embodied in opposite cosmic principles, God and Satan.
They imagine that it is possible, through some combination of
right belief and behavior, to align oneself absolutely on the one
side, disassociated from and purified of all contact with the
other.[31]

Moreover, this reified dualism of good and evil is identified with
sectarian and tribal-national hostilities. God's people are a particular ethno-religious group, Israel, or a particular religious group,
Christians. The English Reformation renewed the identification of
God's chosen people with a particular nation. England, and then
America, was identified as that elect nation. Within these elect nations, there are seen to be the "saints," those who are the true believers. It is this specific group of people who will be vindicated and

victorious in the final victory of good over evil, while their adversaries are punished and exterminated.

The extermination of evil is thereby tribalized, identified with absolutized enmity against other racial, ethnic, and religious groups. The impulse to apocalyptic thus becomes genocidal, the extermination of those people who are seen as "Satan's people." This also means that the God of apocalyptic is a tribal-warrior God, a God whose extermination of evil is pictured in terms of military force on behalf of "his people." Massacres of the enemy through military weapons, ranging from the sword to nuclear bombs, are fantasized by apocalypticists as instruments of righteousness.

The projection of absolutized evil upon enemies to be slain shuts off the wellsprings of compassion. This is the basic characteristic of the war mentality, one inculcated in every exercise in "basic training," which prepares young men to be killers. The war ideology also prepares societies to rejoice in the slaughter of others by imagining that, with each life snuffed out of the bodies of those defined as "enemies," one has progressed another step to the elimination of "evil" and the establishment of "good" in the world.

Apocalypticism, like Platonic eschatology, is based on the fantasy of escape from mortality. Death itself is the "last enemy" to be overcome. The very nature of the life of the biosphere, rooted in mortality and renewal through disintegration, is denied. Instead life and death are absolutized as opposites. One imagines that through destruction not only of the "enemy" humans, but the earth itself, one side, death, can be finally eliminated, and the other side, life, can be immortalized.

The foundation of this fantasy of escape from the body, earth, and evil is a certain model of God, a God unrelated to earth, body, or mortality. A God who is absolute good against absolute evil in a way that is unrelational. It is this kind of concept of a transcendent, unrelational God, and the identification of themselves with this God, which allows apocalypticists to imagine themselves to be safe from world destruction. Their own security and escape from this destruction is assured. Indeed world destruction is the means by which they can escape.

Thus the apocalypticist, far from being concerned about the evidences of destruction, is immensely cheered by them. Violence directed against others with whom they do not identify is evidence of divine punishment, while violence against themselves is persecution of the righteous. Both forms of violence are proofs that the "last things" are happening and one's own deliverance is at hand. The apocalypticist may even oppose efforts to ameliorate poverty, prevent war, or clean up ecological damage, for this is to oppose God's will and retard the final deliverance.

Yet some militant environmentalists have not been immune to their own forms of apocalypticism. As they envision the enormous damage presently being done to nature by modern industrialism, they are tempted to imagine "Mother Earth" rising up like a chthonic Jehovah to topple the human empires and return the earth to precivilized simplicity when humans, in small hunter-gatherer tribes, lived lightly off the land. The fact that most human beings would die in the process seems to them a justified revenge of "nature" against "civilization."[32]

It seems unlikely that any ecological disaster that would destroy most humans, together with the superstructures of civilization, would restore a paradisaical earth. Yet, if we are to prevent recourse to these despairing "shortcuts" to salvation, we must acknowledge the deep fears and desperate hopes on which they are based. We must seek to shape an alternative spirituality and ethic that channels these fears and hopes more realistically and more lovingly. This is particularly important in the last decade of the twentieth century, when the extreme images of impending disaster offered by the "prophets" of the ecological movement will too readily lend themselves to such escapes into paranoid and magical thinking.

4

New Narratives of World Destruction

The narratives of world destruction we have surveyed, from the religious traditions that have shaped Judaism and Christianity, function as warnings, as threats of punishment for the wicked, but ultimately as assurances of salvation. Israel may be punished for her sins, but if she turns and repents, God will inaugurate a time of harmony between humans and between humans and nature. In the apocalyptic narratives, punishment is turned against enemy nations and unbelieving communities. Through cosmic destruction, their annihilation, and the annihilation of the cosmic powers of evil they represent, is assured. But a renovated earth will rise on the other side of this destruction.

The narratives of world destruction that are arising from ecologists in the last decades of the twentieth century carry no such assurance of subsequent renewal. Ecological apocalyptic conveys a message that would have seemed unbelievable in an earlier period, and one that most humans today still have difficulty comprehending. The ecological message is that humans have usurped such power over the foundational life forces of the planet itself, and this power has been used so unwisely, that we are facing at the end of the twentieth century the real possibility of irreparable destruction to a biosphere that nature took 4.5 billion years to develop.

Scientific culture no longer has a God that is independent of nature. It cannot expect any life force unconnected with the biosphere to intervene and renovate the earth after we have destroyed it. Nor is there another world in the sky to which we can escape. We have no home outside the earth. And so our destruction of this home is the permanent destruction of ourselves as well. Human power has assumed a frighteningly new responsibility. The capacity to be the agents of destruction of the earth also means that we must learn how to be its cocreators *before* such destruction becomes terminal. This cannot be done by an adversarial or dominating relation toward nature. For nature, even in its destruction, is following its basic laws of energy. We can construct our existence within these energy patterns constructively or destructively, but we cannot change these basic laws themselves. Only by understanding how the web of life works can we also learn to sustain it rather than destroy it. This is not simply a task of intellectual understanding, but of *metanoia*, in the fullest sense of the word: of conversion of our spirit and culture, of our technology and social relations, so that the human species exists within nature in a life-sustaining way.

Moreover, we must effect this *metanoia* quickly. We do not have thousands of years to unlearn the wrong patterns that were established over thousands of years. The exponential speed-up of these culminative patterns of destruction means we have to both learn new patterns and put them into practice on a global scale within the next generation. By 2030 C.E. it may be too late, or at least too late to save much of the life-capacity of the biosphere that could be saved now. Instead we will find ourselves operating on the other side of global catastrophes, with much narrower options.

Human psychophysiology and culture have not prepared us for such foresight. We have been accustomed to responding to limited disasters after they have happened, sometimes learning to avoid repeating the same mistakes, but too often reacting in ways that assure that the disaster will be repeated in new forms. To anticipate disasters on a global scale, disasters that reach into the very foundations of the biosphere, to plan and act before disaster strikes, is something for which all human societies seem ill-prepared by our various histories and cultures.

Many aspects of Western culture, in particular, mitigate against such foresight and effective change on a global scale: our adversarial political divisions; our class, gender, and race antagonisms, which suggest to the powerful that they can ride out the crisis, transferring the costs to a growing number of victims; and finally, the disinformation and fragmentation of our communication systems, long misshaped to distract people from reality, rather than to inform them intelligently. Thus the prophets of ecological catastrophe may well be like Cassandra of Greek tragedy, who knows that the true prophecy she bears is doomed to be disbelieved, to be ignored until it is too late.

In this chapter I will trace several of the major trajectories of the accumulating crisis and point to the likely results within the next forty years. I will follow the information and analysis available from well-established sources, such as the Worldwatch Institute, funded in part by the United Nations Environmental Program, which since the mid-1970s has issued its *Worldwatch Papers*, and since 1984 its annual *State of the World* report.[1]

This pattern of accumulating crises will be detailed under the categories of population, food, energy, pollution, extinctions of species, and war. The issue of poverty, of the growing global division between misery and affluence, will thread through this whole account. It is important to be clear at the outset that these are interconnected aspects of one picture. Population is not separate from food, nor from energy; pollution from poverty or war; extinction of species from toxic wastes and expanding populations.

The crisis that I wish to describe is the multiplication of all these factors in their interconnection with each other.

POPULATION AND POVERTY

The exponential growth of human population in the last several centuries; that is to say, the doubling of the human population on the earth in shorter and shorter periods of time, is one of the major factors threatening the carrying capacity of the earth. Yet the net environmental impact of population growth must be seen in its interconnection with the level of human consumption and the use of technology. This is expressed by the formula that population × consumption × technology = environmental impact.[2]

This means that the same size population that primarily uses the human body for labor and transportation, that has a subsistence economy (producing or gathering its own food, using only local, natural materials for its clothes, building materials, and fuel, and reusing or recycling all its wastes), will make much less of an environmental impact than the same number of people who consume a great variety of foods and goods transported from great distances, using petroleum, gas, and electricity for transportation, production, heating, and cooking, and discarding toxic waste products of each stage of production and consumption.

If we imagine the first group as having an environmental impact of one, and the second group as consuming ten times more than the first, and employing technology that uses ten times more energy, then the environmental impact of the second group would be one hundred times that of the first group. This is, in fact, approximately the ratio of difference between the environmental impact made by the average American and that of poor third-world people. It has been established that an American of average income has one hundred times the environmental impact as the poor third-world person, while the affluent American has several hundred times the impact of a poor third-world person.[3]

Yet such an analysis of the multiplication of factors in the overall environmental equation does not allow us to regard the proliferation of poor populations as unproblematic. Even poor people, living at a low level of consumption and technology, make an environmental impact. The destruction of wild habitats and the confiscation of land by the wealthy means that few human populations today can live as self-subsistent gathering and gardening societies. Poor populations are poor because they lack access to sufficient land for their traditional life-styles, but their work is not needed in the new productive systems of affluence. And so they must scavenge the scraps of work and waste from the tables of the wealthy.

Crowded on marginal lands by those who have monopolized the best land, the farming and animal grazing of such people will erode the thin soils, and their wood gathering for fuel will strip the remaining forests, causing floods and desertification of the land. Their crowded conditions probably also mean that their water supply is polluted by being mixed with human and animal feces, and their children are dying in great numbers from malnutrition and intestinal parasites.

The extreme maldistribution of access to land, jobs, services, and education today means that populations with low consumption and technology will most likely not be living in a healthy simplicity, but in misery and degradation. Thus the high consumption of the wealthy few and the low consumption of the many are not separate, but interdependent, realities. The same systems of power that allow a small percentage of the world's population to monopolize most of its resources also throws the growing masses into conditions of misery and into an environmentally destructive relation to their habitat.

It is this pattern of environmental destruction on both ends of the wealth-poverty scale that must be kept in mind when the facts of expanding population numbers are cited. As mentioned in chapter 2, human population has been growing at an exponential rate since the development of agriculture allowed humans to store food. At the beginning of the agricultural revolution about 10,000 years ago, humans numbered only 5 million. By 1991 they had multiplied a thousandfold to 5.3 billion.

Population growth has not taken place evenly over the globe. The seventeenth to the nineteenth centuries saw a rapid population expansion in western Europe due to increased wealth from colonial trade, which also allowed improved sanitation and expanded food and industrial production. This was the same period that saw the conquest of much of the Americas, Africa, and Asia by European colonialism. Western Europe exported millions of its expanding numbers as settlers in this colonial venture. At the same time, it stripped Central and South America of its precious metals, laying the capital basis of its industrial revolution.[4]

While western Europe exported its surplus population, vast numbers of indigenous people died, due to war, displacement, or enslavement, and diseases brought by these European colonialists. In Central and South America, it is estimated that of the 80 million indigenous people present when the Spanish and Portuguese colonialists arrived in 1550, only 10 million remained one hundred years later.[5] Displacement, war, and disease also devastated the indigenous population of North America, as the white settlers arrived.[6] The same pattern was repeated among indigenous populations in the Pacific islands. In some areas, such as Tasmania and the Caribbean islands, the entire indigenous population was wiped out.[7]

Where the indigenous population was not destroyed, they were either enslaved or else driven into marginal areas in the mountains and forests, thus laying the basis for the monopolization of the best agricultural land in plantation-style agro-export economies that still shape the relation of wealth and poverty in the colonized regions of the globe. With their expanded wealth and land, European populations continued to grow. In the twentieth century, third-world populations began to expand dramatically.

The most rapid expansion of population in history has taken place in the twentieth century. The 1991 figure of 5.384 billion may expand to 6.25 billion by 2000 C.E. Even with major efforts at population control through family planning, it may reach 10 billion sometime in the mid-twenty-first century, before it begins to level off.[8] However, much of this "leveling off" may be due, not to lowered numbers of those born, but to their rapid death from starvation and disease after birth. In 1989, 40,000 infants were dying each day due to such causes, or 14.6 million a year.[9]

In the second half of the twentieth century, much of the rapid population expansion has taken place in the third world, the regions of former colonization. Birth rates in the industrialized regions of western Europe and North America began to fall from the late nineteenth century, and have continued to fall. As more children survived, as fewer families needed child labor on the farm, as educational expectations for each child grew, most parents in these regions began to have families of three children rather than of eight or ten. At the same time, life expectancy in these regions almost doubled, with an average lifespan of seventy-five years rather than the average of forty-five years found in earlier centuries, and still found today among the third-world poor.[10]

The burgeoning population in the third world reflects the fact that enough medical control of disease and infant mortality, enough sanitation and expansion in food and industrial production has taken place to create the condition for more and more of those born to survive. But this "death control" has not been matched by a corresponding birth control, especially among the poorest and most uneducated populations.

The disproportionate growth of population between the third world and the first world is reflected, for example, in the fact that in North America and in Latin America in 1950, the population was roughly equal, with 163 million in North America and 168 million in Latin America. Twenty-five years later, the North American population had added 73 million for a total of 236 million, while Latin America had added 182 million for a total of over 350 million.[11]

Yet even these figures are not proper comparisons between the two situations of population growth. Among whites in North America, parents of two or three children can assume that almost all of these children will grow up and enjoy a life expectancy into their mid-seventies. In Latin America, Asia, and Africa, out of every three children born, one will die before the age of twenty, and those who live into adulthood can expect a shorter and less healthy life. As long as children are likely to die in infancy and childhood, parents will continue to have more children. Thus the voluntary use of family planning is closely interconnected with the health and security of families, as well as the education of mothers.[12]

Population growth in regions of poverty presses all the other indices of decent human living conditions. More and more of this growing population will be illiterate, malnourished, lacking potable water, chronically ill and without medical services, underemployed or unemployed, and living in crowded and substandard housing in urban shantytowns. They are also likely to be subjected to additional stress from noise, crime, and police repression. Thus, for example, in the third world, 80 percent of the population lives in crowded urban areas; 30 percent of the population in these countries is underemployed or unemployed, and 50 percent or more lack access to basic medical services.[13] Illiteracy is also growing throughout the world, as nations lose the race to add more schools and teachers for the growing population of children. Two-thirds of the illiterate are female.[14]

FEEDING THE WORLD'S HUMAN POPULATION

In the 1960s and 1970s, there was great optimism about the ability of new seeds and new technology to greatly expand the world's harvests of basic grains. World grain harvests between

1950 and 1984 expanded 2.6 times, an effort that dwarfed all previous world agricultural production. World population almost doubled during that same period, so expanding harvests were ahead of expanding population. In 1950 grain production was about 245 kilograms per person (per year). In 1984 it had expanded to 345 kilograms per person. But this increase began dropping in the late 1980s due to major droughts in China and the United States, bringing production levels back to about 290 kilograms per person per year. Reserve stocks of grain have also dropped to a dangerous low, and grain prices rose 48 percent between 1987 and 1989,[15] making food even more inaccessible to the poor.

Much of the confidence in expanding food production in the 1960s was based on the Green Revolution, which provided new, high-yield grains to farmers in Asia, the Middle East, and Latin America. But these new grains demanded high inputs of petroleum-based fertilizers and pesticides, and mechanized farm equipment. China, with its large-scale cooperative system of agriculture, made extensive use of these new grains, but in most of the third world wealthy farmers with large areas of land were the only ones who could afford the new technology. Some 36 percent of farmers adopted the new grains in Asia and the Middle East, only 22 percent in Latin America, and only 1 percent in Africa.[16]

The Green Revolution further biased world agriculture toward large mechanized farms and away from the small farmers. Moreover, at the beginning of the Green Revolution, the price of oil from the oil producers was $2 a barrel. But oil producers began to realize that with finite limits to oil reserves, production must be slowed and the price raised to conserve supplies. In 1973 the price went up to $12, and in 1979 to $34. Conservation resulting from this rapid price rise caused a temporary glut of petroleum, bringing the price down again to as low as $10 a barrel. The 1990–91 Persian Gulf crisis sent oil prices on a roller coaster of changes, rising to as high as $43 and falling as low as $13.

The result of rising oil prices was an escalation in the cost of all petroleum-based products, putting the costs of fuel, fertilizer, and pesticides out of the reach of many smaller farmers. Other costs of high-energy farming also have become evident. Mechanized farm equipment adds to air pollution. Petroleum-based pesticides and fertilizers build up the toxicity in the soils and in the runoff of irrigation water into rivers and lakes. Air pollution also descends on cropland in the form of acid rain. These effects of soil, air, and water pollution begin to take their toll in reduced yields per acre.

Soil erosion is also affecting world food production. Each year some 24 billion tons of topsoil are lost from crop land. This is equivalent to the loss of one inch of topsoil each year on 150 million acres of cropland.[17] In addition to soil erosion, soils are being degraded in other ways. Continual irrigation on intensively farmed land without adequate drainage builds up the salt level in the soil, eventually destroying its fertility and causing it to be abandoned. In addition to soil erosion, more and more fertile cropland is withdrawn from production each year by the spread of houses, roads, and parking lots. In the United States, 5.2 million acres of prime cropland was converted to nonagricultural use between 1967 and 1975.[18]

Wood gathering and overgrazing of land by cattle strips the foliage, and causes erosion and eventual desertification. Creeping deserts have claimed large areas in the Middle East and Africa that once were farmland. The Dust Bowl that wiped out farms in the central and western United States in the 1930s was caused by such overcultivation and overgrazing. Farmland is also threatened by global climatic changes that may come about as a result of the buildup of carbon dioxide and other gases in the air. If there is a pattern of global warming—with 5° F to 10° F increases in summer temperatures, together with drought—much of the grain farming in the moderate zones of the planet could be devastated.

All of these factors of soil degradation, loss of farmland, and changing climate point to finite limits of the ability of world agriculture to increase its harvests to meet an expanding population. Yet in the 1980s, most of world famine was caused, not by lack of sufficient food, but rather the way that food was used and distributed. Much grain and other crops, as well as food from the sea, was used to feed animals to be slaughtered for meat rather than to feed people directly. The elite British and American pattern of meat-eating, spread to the affluent of the rest of the world, contributes to the malnourishment of the poor.[19]

The urbanization of the world's population, with fewer and fewer people living on the land and involved in food production, means that more and more people must buy food rather than being able to eat food that they have produced. The local, national, and global structures of marketing food make a vast array of food available to a wealthy elite, but put most of these foods out of the reach of the poor.

The food that is produced is lost to those who need it most. For example, 10 percent of the food produced is lost to rats and insects in initial stages of storage. The longer the transportation chain from land to table, the more food spoiled in the process, and the more energy expended in moving it along the chain. American supermarket shoppers eat off the longest food transportation chain in human history, with meat, fruits, and vegetables from around the globe. To keep prices affordable in the supermarket, the laborers in the field are paid starvation wages. This means that many farm workers who harvest the world's food cannot afford to buy the food they pick. The snow peas produced by small farmers in Guatemala for the American supermarket will not appear on the dinner tables of Guatemalan peasants.[20]

The intensive use of energy to produce food—from the petroleum for farm equipment, fertilizers, and pesticides, to the transportation, handling, and packaging of it, to the cars used to buy it—mean that as much as 1.5 calories of energy may be expended to produce 1 calorie of food. Globalization of food production often means that prices for food in farm areas do not differ much from prices in urban areas. Underemployment and unemployment deprive a large part of the world's population of the money to buy an adequate amount of food to feed their families. The results of these inequitable patterns of food production and distribution means that chronic undernourishment affects some 20 percent of the population of the world (1 billion people).[21] It is not uncommon for nations who have large numbers of starving people to also be exporters of food.

ENERGY, CLIMATE, AND POLLUTION

Energy is needed for every aspect of human life: to produce food and consumer products, and for the transportation and packaging of these products, as well as for transporting humans themselves and for heating and cooling homes, offices, and workplaces. The sun is the ultimate energy source of the planet, and every other form of energy that we use derives from the energy of the sun. Much of this solar energy has been transmitted through the photosynthesis of green plants to produce wood and other biomass fuels, as well as the stores of fossil fuels from ancient forests from which petroleum, coal, and peat have come.

The energy crisis of advanced industrial societies is twofold: first, the rapid depletion of these stores of fossil fuels, and second, the filling of the atmosphere with the gaseous byproducts of burning these fossil fuels. The petroleum age is less than one hundred years old. Historically human civilization has used the energy of the bodies of humans and animals for work and travel; wood, tallows, and vegetable oils for heat and lighting; wind and water to move ships and grind grain. Peat bogs have provided fuel for heating for centuries in Ireland and elsewhere. Coal became a major fuel for factories, railroads, and home heating in the nineteenth century.

With the invention of the automobile and then the airplane, petroleum became the major fuel of modern industrialism. Today it accounts for over 33 percent of the total fuel use (coal is 27 percent and natural gas, 18 percent). At present use there are enough supplies of coal to last several hundred years. The end of the supplies of petroleum, however, is already in sight. At present rate of use, readily accessible petroleum would be used up in the second decade of the twenty-first century.[22] This process, however, could be prolonged in several ways.

In the last fifteen years, rising oil prices have already created a considerable conservation of the use of oil. As supplies dwindle, the costs of oil-based products will become inaccessible to more and more people. New ways of using it more efficiently will be created. Fewer people will be able to afford cars and plane rides, and alternative fuels will be developed. Yet it is hard to imagine major aspects of modern industry and transportation running without petroleum, and planning for substitutes has been rudimentary and inadequate. As the petroleum age sputters to an end, major changes in the modern life-style, perhaps accompanied by great crises and hardships, are likely, particularly if there is not organized transitional planning to alternative energy.

The burning of petroleum in cars, planes, houses, and factories emits gaseous byproducts into the air. This is not only true of petroleum. Coal burning emits sulphur-dioxide and other gases. Carbon dioxide in the earth's atmosphere is now 25 percent higher than in preindustrial times, nitrous oxide is 19 percent higher. Other gases, such as methane, previously present only in trace amounts, are growing in the atmosphere. A gas new to earth's atmosphere, chlorofluorocarbons, emitted by refrigerators and aerosol cans, play a role in the depleting of the ozone layer of the stratosphere, which deflects harmful ultraviolet rays from the sun. This protective ozone layer has been depleted by 2 percent worldwide and much more over the Antarctic icecap.

These gases allow the sunlight to pass through, but trap heat. World climate depends on a delicate balance of these gases in the atmosphere, and the likely result of an increase of this "greenhouse effect" of atmospheric gases is a global warming of between 5° F and 10° F over the next century. The difference between 90° F and 100° F weather in the summer in temperate zones could be devastating for agriculture, as we mentioned above. But global warming could bring other devastating effects. One possibility is a melting of polar icecaps, causing a rise in sea level in coastal areas.

Many of the world's most populous cities are located close to sea level in coastal areas or along rivers. The flooding of these cities could destroy enormous regions of human, animal, and plant life. Flooding could also destroy wetlands that are precious habitats for fish and birds, and flood croplands. Some countries may try to invest in high dikes in an effort to hold back the sea, but some of the poorest nations could not afford such projects. Their cities and low-lying areas would be abandoned in a scramble for higher ground. Plague, famine, violence, and mass death of humans and animals, caused by such flooding of huge urban areas, would be a scene that would far surpass the ancient flood story that wiped out the cities of the ancient Near East in the fourth millennium B.C.E.

Climate changes are also being caused by the rapid destruction of the world's forests, particularly the rain forests in tropical zones, such as Brazil, Central America, and tropical Asia. This deforestation is caused primarily by clearing land for lumber and cattle. In the process an enormous and largely unstudied wealth of biotic diversity is being destroyed. The thin soils of such rain forests are quickly eroded when stripped of their foliage. But even more dangerous is the removal of one of the major sources of regulation of global climate. The tropical forests generate the great rain clouds that keep the areas moist. Without them, drought and desertification take place.

Air pollution is taking its toll on the forests in Europe and North America in the form of acid rain. West German studies in 1988 showed that 52 percent of the forests that cover 18 million acres of the nation's land had been damaged by acid rain. Similar levels of damage to forests exist in other central European nations.[23] Acid rain doesn't only damage forests. It also descends on lakes and croplands, raising the acidity of soil and water. Acid rain also is eroding the surface of historic buildings throughout the world, destroying major monuments of the legacy of human history.

Air pollution has been a health hazard to humans in industrial cities since the beginning of the industrial revolution. As late as 1952, four thousand people died and tens of thousands became ill as a result of a London "black fog." Although controls on auto emissions in many Western cities have improved air quality, air quality continues to be poor in many of these cities and has grown to catastrophic levels in some third-world cities. For example, air quality in Mexico City has grown so bad that seven out of ten newborn infants have lead levels in their blood in excess of World Health Organization standards.[24]

Toxic wastes in the soil, water, and air can cycle through the global food chain, killing animals as well as eventually ending up in human food. Many of these poisons are caused by the failure to recycle wastes that are reusable. For example, manure from animals in feedlots is a major source of pollution in the Great Lakes, causing eutrophication or overfertilization that depletes the water of oxygen and kills off the plant and animal life. Yet this manure, when properly treated, is valuable fertilizer for agriculture. Metals, paper, and glass, as well as organic materials that are mummified in landfills, are all valuable materials that can be reused.

Some industrial chemicals, such as chlorinated hydrocarbons in pesticides such as DDT, and the polychlorinated biphenyls, are not broken down by biological decomposition. Rather they bioamplify when discarded. Diluted in water, they work their way up the food chain from microscopic creatures to large fish and birds, magnifying their concentration ten to one hundred times with each stage of the food chain, to lethal levels for animals and humans. These substances can be carried worldwide by wind and water, showing up even in remote regions of the globe.

Nuclear wastes are another byproduct that is causing long-term damage to the biosphere. A 1,000-megawatt nuclear reactor produces about 375 kilograms of plutonium a year. Discarded in the reactor fuel wastes, plutonium has a radioactive half-life of 25,000 years. No safe way has been found to store this toxic and carcinogenic element that will not leak into seas and soils long before its negative potency has disappeared. While most of the wastes that cause pollution could be handled by recycling and reuse, some of these toxic chemicals are new human fabrications that cannot be readily broken down by nature. They need to be handed by ceasing to produce them altogether.[25]

EXTINCTION

Another effect of expanding population, deforestation, and toxic wastes polluting the air, water, and soil, is the dwindling biotic diversity of the planet. The last 350 years, and particularly the last forty years, have seen the extinction of tens of thousands of species of flora and fauna. By the year 2000, as many as a million different species of plants and animals may have disappeared entirely in this period, a figure representing perhaps as much as 20 percent of the species of the earth.[26] Extinctions of species happen slowly throughout evolutionary history. There have also been several periods of mass extinction. For example, at the end of the Cretaceous Period, some 65 million years ago, the dinosaurs and a variety of other organisms disappeared for reasons that remain obscure. But today seems to be the first time when so much of the diversity of evolutionary development has been destroyed primarily by the expansion of one species, humans, at the expense of the whole.

The expansion of humans is destroying the rest of life in several ways. Many animals have been exterminated by being hunted for food, pelts, tusks, or simply for recreation. Air and water pollution, with the effects we have already described in acid rain and ozone depletion, are not only reducing, but are destroying some plant species altogether. Toxic chemicals such as DDT bioamplify, causing, among other things, the thinning of birds' eggshells, thereby threatening the reproduction of whole species. Toxic wastes in oceans are destroying marine flora and fauna in some regions, such as coral reefs.

The major cause of destruction of species comes simply from the expanding human population, which is steadily destroying the habitats that support free animal and plant life. This is particularly true in tropical rain forests, which also contain the largest number of as yet unstudied plants and animals. Many pages of the book of life are being ripped out before we have even had a chance to read them. These regions are also among the economically poorest in the world, whose governments have the least money to spend for conservation. Population in these regions is expanding quickly, and the pressure of wealthy people to clear forests for profit, or of poor people simply to expand into forests because of land hunger and the need to raise crops for food, make it difficult to defend the preservation of unexploited areas for their "wildlife."

Of what great concern should it be if, in the year 2000, there are only 4 million species of plants, animals, and insects rather than 5 million? There are two levels of answer to this question, one anthropocentric and another biocentric. That is, we can point out how much humans stand to lose from extinction of species, but we can also insist that species have their own intrinsic value in themselves and as members of biotic communities.

Each species that is extinguished represents a unique mode of biological life closed off forever, never again to be restored. The closing of so many chapters of biological evolution in such a short period of time threatens the biological diversity that sustains the mutual sustainability of the whole biosphere. Many plants potentially useful for food and medicine will have disappeared, and with them the complexity of the types of life that can renew local ecological communities.

When species are extinguished, not just one species, but whole communities of interdependent plants, animals, and insects are being wiped out. The result is a degraded whole. The many species, with their great capacity for creative interaction, are replaced by a few hardy species that thrive under adverse conditions, of the kind we usually call "weeds" and "pests." Cockroaches and crabgrass replace more complex biotic communities. Such hardy plants and insects tend to multiply and prevent the restoration of the more delicate tissues of life.

Not least among the losses of such environmental degradation may be the aesthetic imagination that can sustain human biophilia, and with it the moral urge to value life itself. It may not be accidental that so much of the art, music, and poetry of modern urban environments is nihilistic. Without the rich beauty of the natural environment, humans may also have been losing that which has nurtured their moral-aesthetic "soul," their sensitivity to complex and subtle realities, their capacity to imagine ecstatically and to care deeply about life.[27]

MILITARISM AND WAR

Militarism also has to been seen as a major ecological hazard today. Human mass destruction of other humans, together with their towns, animals, and crops, through war, has a long history. But the twentieth century has seen a sharp escalation in the level of such destructive violence between humans in forms of war that obliterate any distinction between combatants and noncombatants. Modern military technology has enormously expanded this capacity to kill and destroy.[28] The end of World War II ushered in the Nuclear Age, with the first use of atomic bombs capable of wiping out entire populations of cities at one blow. Nuclear weapons also leave behind the legacy of slow death from radiation for generations to come.

Although the forty-five years between 1946 and 1991 has been without a "major" war, this period has seen an unprecedented level of global militarization of almost all nation-states in all the regions of the world, the developing nations, as well as those of the NATO and Warsaw Pacts. In 1987 global expenditures for armaments topped 1 trillion dollars, some 5.5 percent of the aggregate economic product of all the nations of the world.[29] In 1972, when the U.S. Arms Control and Disarmament Agency began its research on world armaments, the figure was $197 billion (in 1972 dollars).[30]

In the forty years between 1950 and 1990, the United States expanded its military spending from $13 billion to $300 billion. Total American military spending over the forty-five years since 1945 has topped $4,400 billion; $1,500 billion from 1945 to 1975; $1,500 billion from 1976 to 1985 and $1,400 billion from 1986 to 1990. In 1990 the U.S. Federal deficit topped $3,000 billion, with a large piece of the budget taken up with paying interest on this debt.[31]

Military expenditures worldwide have expanded continually in the last twenty years. The United States expanded its share of world armaments in this period from 22.8 percent to 30 percent. The biggest arms spenders by far continued to be the USSR, spending $303 billion, and the United States, which spent $296.2 billion in 1987. Such spending, however, represented a much larger part of the Soviet GNP: 12.3 percent, compared with 6.5 percent of the U.S. GNP. The next largest spenders were France, with $34.8 billion, West Germany, with $34.1 billion, and the

United Kingdom, with $31.6 billion. Japan, which spent almost nothing on arms in 1972, was spending $24.3 billion in 1987 (all these figures in 1987 constant dollars).

In the developing world, the largest share of world armaments has gone to the Middle East: 43 percent. Iran, Iraq, and Saudi Arabia have spent between $10 billion and $20 billion each on arms. Arms expenditures represent 11 percent of the GNP of Middle Eastern nations. Although black African nations have far less money for arms, arms spending represents an expanding sector of their GNP: 4.3 percent of the GNP of African nations in 1987 compared to 3.6 percent in 1978. By contrast NATO western European nations were spending somewhat less on arms in 1987: 3.3 percent of their GNP compared to 3.6 percent in 1978. The other Warsaw Pact nations spent about the same percentage of their GNP on arms as the United States: 6.8 percent.[32] Such expenditures for the military have drained all nations of the world of the funds that might have been more than adequate for solving many of the social problems of hunger, illiteracy, lack of adequate housing, medicine, and potable water.

What has this vast amount of money for the military, not only from the United States, but from nations all over the world, been used for over these last four decades? Nations in the "nuclear club" have used it to buy these enormously expensive weapons, which fortunately have not been used, but that have also been continually renewed and refurbished for possible use. In addition, there has been continual development of the destructive power of "conventional weapons."

Western intervention to prevent third-world revolutions from succeeding has fueled many regional wars, with devastating death tolls and environmental destruction, typically followed by more military buildup. The Lentz Peace Research Laboratory estimates that in the nine years between 1980 and 1989, there were twenty different wars going on that took a total of 4 million lives.

The post-Vietnam U.S. policy of "low-intensity warfare" assured that most of the bodies would be brown, and hence this vast carnage did not arouse domestic protest.[33]

Much of the weaponry of the second half of the twentieth century has not been directed to defense against outside nations, but rather has been turned by governments against their own people. The militarism of this period reflects three interlocked levels: the global East-West competition between the capitalist and Communist blocks; regional conflicts, such as the Arab-Israeli and Iran-Iraq wars; and internal civil wars, such as those in Southeast Asia, Central America, and southern Africa. The 1991 Persian Gulf War may set a dangerous new precedent, the potential for turning regional disputes into world wars.

These regional conflicts have seldom been purely "internal," but have been fueled by superpower—especially United States—intervention. Civil wars also have a global dimension with arms sales and the transfer of aid from all over the world. For example, Iran and Iraq, in their devastating 1979–88 stalemate war with each other, went on a huge military spending spree. The two countries received arms and military aid from forty-one different countries. Twenty-eight of these countries, which provided 93 percent of the arms, sold arms to both sides of the conflict.[34]

Chronic wars, supported from outside, rage in the impoverished, formerly colonized regions of the world, where guerrillas, seeking a new, more just social and economic order, battle existing oligarchies and their armies. In some areas, such as Cuba and Nicaragua in the Caribbean/Central American region, in Angola, Mozambique, and Zimbabwe, and in southern Africa, where nationalist revolutionary regimes had taken control, economic boycotts and "contra" armies were organized and funded by outside countries in an effort to sabotage the economic development of these new regimes and thereby bring them back under the hegemony of their powerful neighbors.

For example, in 1954 the United States government sponsored a coup that overthrew the reform government of Jacobo Arbenz in Guatemala. The democratic constitution developed by this regime was repealed, and violently repressive military regimes, with American support, have ruled the region ever since.[35] Guatemala was the first country to see the development of government-sponsored "death squads," which murdered peasant and labor leaders and other reformers. They either disappeared without a trace, or else their mutilated bodies were dumped in public view to terrorize others.

Between 1979 and 1984, some 441 Guatemalan villages were totally destroyed, and a million indigenous peasants displaced, in a scorched-earth policy aimed at "draining the sea" in which the small, but persistent Guatemalan guerrilla armies moved. Tactics developed in Vietnam, such as defoliants, were and continue to be sprayed on Guatemalan mountain forests.[36] The same tragic patterns of destruction have been repeated in third-world countries around the globe, as the United States, South Africa, and other neocolonial powers have sponsored the destruction of national liberation movements.

In the vast panoply of modern weapons, nuclear weapons are at the top of the system. Over the last four and a half decades since the United State dropped the first atom bombs on Japan, larger and more powerful bombs, with many times the destructive capacity of the Hiroshima bomb, have been constructed. At the same time, tactical nuclear weapons have grown lighter and more mobile, allowing nuclear missiles to be carried around on the back of a truck or even in the backpack of a soldier.

In 1986 the United States had the deployed nuclear capacity of 1,010 intercontinental ballistic missiles and 656 submarine-based ballistic missiles, while the Soviet Union had 951 ICBM and 1,336 submarine-based missiles. The Soviet nuclear arms had a lesser force than those of the Americans: 448 of the Soviets' most powerful ICBMs carried a 1-megaton force, while 450 of the American ICBMs carried a 1- to 2-megaton force, and ten Titan ICBMs carried a 9-megaton force.[37] One megaton is the equivalent of 1 million tons of TNT, fifty times the force of the Hiroshima bomb, which carried a force of 20,000 tons of TNT.

However, in today's military world, megatonnage has become less important than accuracy. The United States leads the world in the development of the kind of "smart bombs" that can pinpoint targets, decapitating the war-making (and economic) infrastructure of a country. It is this new level of accuracy that is allowing the United States to reduce its nuclear arsenal, while keeping in place and even expanding its overall strategy of world military hegemony.

Despite peace treaties between the United States and the former Soviet Union to reduce nuclear armaments and the political disarray of Eastern Europe, the basic U.S. plan for first-strike destruction of the military infrastructure of the former Soviet Union, SIOP (Single Integrated Operating Plan), signed by President Bush in 1989, still remains in place.[38] Nuclear disarmament is pursued one-sidedly: for example, strict efforts to assure that Iraq is prevented from developing such weapons, while looking the other way at the three hundred nuclear weapons possessed by Israel.[39] The threat of a war in which nuclear weapons are used even on a country without such weapons remains a real possibility.

Since the peace movements have recently shelved concern about nuclear war, it is important to remember what it would mean if such a bomb fell on a city. The U.S. Arms Control and Disarmament Agency estimates the following effects of the explosion of a 1-megaton bomb over New York City above the Empire State Building:

> The area of total destruction, the circle within which even the most heavily reinforced concrete structures do not survive, has a radius of 1.5 miles. That circle extends from the Brooklyn Bridge to Central Park Lake and from Long Island City to Hoboken. Included within it are the Empire State Building, Lincoln Center

and the Stock Exchange. Within this circle almost all the population is killed.

At a distance of three miles from the center of the blast, past Jersey City and Elmhurst, past the Brooklyn Museum in the south and 145th Street in the north, concrete buildings are destroyed. The heat from the explosion and the spontaneous ignition of clothing cause third-degree burns over much of the body, killing most of the people in this area.

More than four miles from the center, brick and wood-frame buildings are destroyed and fire caused by the intense heat are fanned by 160-mile-per-hour winds. In a circle extending to Hastings on Hudson, Livingston, New Jersey, and beyond Far Rockaway to the sea, brick and wood-frame buildings sustain heavy damage. The heat exceeds 12 calories per square centimeter, and all individuals with exposed skin suffer severe third-degree burns. At the outer limits of this circle brick and wood-frame structures sustain moderate damage.

Miles beyond this last ring, people suffer second-degree burns on all exposed skin and additional burns from flammable clothing and environmental materials. Retinal burns resulting from looking at the fireball may cause blindness. As high winds spread the fires caused by the initial blast and thermal radiation, the number of causalities grow.

If we assume a population for the metropolitan area of 16 million, more than 1,600,000 are killed. There are 2,800,000 injured. Many of the survivors are badly burned, blinded, and otherwise seriously wounded. Many are disoriented. These are the short-term effects. The problem of radiation sickness, including intractable nausea, vomiting, bleeding, hair loss, severe infection, and often death will grow in the days and weeks ahead. Fallout from the bomb will spread well beyond the area of impact.[40]

Medical or other relief for these victims would be difficult to come by, since the cities where they had lived have virtually ceased to exist as either physical or social entities. Government, hospitals and medical supplies, transportation, food supplies, and clean water all would be largely destroyed as well. In any major exchange of nuclear weapons, that is, 1,000 megatons on each side, the effects of blast, firestorm, and radiation would interact with each other in incalculable ways. Even a 1-megaton bomb might blow out electrical equipment, on which much food preservation, medicine, heat, lighting, and communication depend, over a range extending across the continental United States, Canada, and Mexico.[41]

Radioactive fallout would circulate throughout the global ecosystem, penetrating the tissues, bones, and fibers of all animal and plant life and detonating there indefinitely. The dust lifted into the stratosphere by such a collection of explosions might destroy much of the ozone layer, letting in deadly ultraviolet radiation. Thus there is a good chance that any such major nuclear exchange might not only destroy human life, with its social and physical infrastructures, but destroy the very conditions that make the planet earth habitable to life.[42]

Militarism must be seen as the ultimate polluter of the earth. Even without warfare, the world's armies cause immense environmental damage. Through confiscation of large amounts of land for training and weapons testing, they remove this land from farming and other peaceful uses. They tear up the soil through troop maneuvers and litter it with dangerous materials. Nuclear testing, done primarily in regions of native or colonized peoples, such as the Pacific Islands, contaminate entire regions. The burial of nuclear wastes presents a danger of radioactive leakage indefinitely. Armies are enormous users of petroleum and emit a large share of air pollutants.[43]

Actual warfare today is total warfare, waged not only against the entire human population, but against the environment as well. Defoliants, bomb craters, and unexploded bombs make the area a dangerous wasteland. Air war against guerrilla armies has been waged in such a way as to destroy the forests where guerrillas might take refuge, and to wipe out the crops and animals of the peasantry on which they might depend. Releasing oil into the Persian Gulf and setting oil wells alight to pollute the air is a new expression of this general pattern of total war. In the 1991 air war against Iraq, not only were some 200,000 Iraqis killed, but the entire infrastructure of the country was devastated. In the words of a member of the UNICEF team that investigated the health aspects of the damage, "Iraq has been bombed back to the preindustrial era."[44]

From 1946 to 1990, the rationale for the continued buildup of weapons by the superpowers was the East-West antagonism and the assumption that each side was restrained from actual war by the possession of such weapons by the other. In 1990, however, the Communist parties of Eastern Europe came rapidly unglued. The leader of the former Soviet Union, Mikhail Gorbachev, displayed great restraint in intervention against these changes and a strong desire to scale down both nuclear and "conventional" armaments on its side, so that the USSR could turn its resources to economic and environmental redevelopment.

Suddenly the whole rationale of the Cold War came tumbling down. As the whole region of the former Soviet Union fell into chaos, it was no longer possible to think of the Soviet Union as poised on the brink of throwing tens of megatons of nuclear weapons at the United States, risking planetary holocaust. This shift in eastern Europe has also allowed President Bush to plan some cuts in military forces, with a planned 25 percent cut in military expenditure by 1991.

Yet the 1991 Federal budget proposed by the Bush administration contained items such $5.5 billion for five new Stealth bombers, $4.7 billion for continued Star Wars research and development, $2.8 billion for twelve new MX missiles, $54.1 million for one hundred new advanced cruise missiles, $1.5 billion for another Trident nuclear submarine, $1.7 billion for 52 additional Trident II submarine-based missiles, and $112 million for the Lance missile slated for European deployment.[45]

The U.S. government and corporate establishment seem to regard the collapse of the Cold War as a "victory" for "our side," rather than a real opportunity for a shift in priorities from military power to peacetime development. American military policy seems to be that of a smaller, but higher accurate military firepower that can back up threatened Western economic hegemony around the world.

This new face of warfare saw its dress rehearsal in the 1991 Persian Gulf War. When Saddam Hussein seized the oil-rich mini-state of Kuwait, President Bush immediately reciprocated by a rapid buildup for a major military response. Although the declared purpose of this war during January and February of 1991 was only the removal of Saddam Hussein from Kuwait, the larger goals clearly were the destruction of Iraq as a potential military rival to Israel in the region and the securing of a permanent U.S. military base off Kuwait for the control of Gulf oil.[46] In 1992, Pentagon planners listed several other potential enemies, among them North Korea, that might be the targets of similar high-tech "middle intensity" warfare. [47]

Thus, on the eve of the twenty-first century, the human experiment and the biosphere that has sustained it stand in profound jeopardy. The "four horsemen" of destruction—human population explosion at the expense of the plants and animals of earth; environmental damage to air, water, and soil; the misery of growing masses of the poor; and a global militarization aimed at retaining unjust advantage over the earth's resources for a wealthy elite—create a combined set of catastrophic scenarios. Those with the greatest power seem determined to refuse to take these danger signs seriously and instead plan to keep "business as usual" in place, even as the capacity of the planet to sustain such "business" erodes. Yet our task is not to indulge in apocalyptic despair, but to continue the struggle to reconcile justice in human relations with a sustainable life community on earth.

Domination and Deceit

PART THREE

Domination and Deceit

5

Classical Narratives of Sin and Evil

In the previous two chapters, we have looked both at the heritage of fantasies of world destruction as divine judgment on human evil and at some realities of our actual destructiveness of the earth and its beings. What understandings of the nature of human capacity for evil do Christians bring to the recognition of these threats? Are our ways of naming evil usable in helping us to understand this destructive capacity, or have they actually been an element in promoting this destructiveness and allowing us to turn a blind eye to it?

Fundamental to human experience is a basic sense that things are not as they should be. Self-consciousness allows humans to stand out from their environment and imagine better alternatives, in relation to which both the natural world and human society are judged as lacking. It would be better not to be cold, hungry, in danger of injury and death from surrounding tribes or carnivorous animals, or subjected to strife within one's own community. The categories of good and evil are absolutized extrapolations from these more concrete experiences of negativity and preferred alternatives.

This capacity to imagine better alternatives is essential to the human capacity to invent artifacts and ways of behaving that incrementally improve daily life. But the danger of translating this capacity into absolutes is that we imagine that these absolutes actually exist, that there is an absolute good that can be set against an absolute evil, and that humans can strive to realize one side of this duality by repudiating the other.

This problem is compounded when the evil side of this polarity is identified with other people and things: with other groups of people over against our group, with women over against men, and with our bodies and the physical world over against our minds. This false naming of evil as physical and social otherness, and the efforts of dominant males to secure themselves against evil by separating themselves from this otherness, creates ideologies that justify the doing of evil to others as a means of overcoming evil!

In this chapter I will examine three traditions of naming evil that have shaped the Western cultural tradition: the Hebrew view, the Platonic-Gnostic view, and the Pauline-Augustinian view. Although these views are not without recoverable elements, they have been constructed from the vantage point of dominant males in a way that has functioned to justify their violent power over women, other subjugated people, and the earth.

HEBREW VIEWS OF EVIL

Jewish thought, in the Hebrew scriptures and the Talmud, did not accept the concept of a fall from original goodness that rendered humans incapable of doing good or pleasing God and therefore needing a savior to render them acceptable to God. For the Jewish tradition, humans retain their freedom to choose good or evil, and to be pleasing or unpleasing to God accordingly. Early rabbinic ethics would speak of the "two impulses," the impulse to good and the impulse to evil, both a part of human nature.[1]

Some apocalyptic thinkers imagined a cosmic fall, in which human history had fallen under the sway of evil powers that biased human nature and society toward the evil impulse. But humans were still thought of as capable of choosing good, even in the midst of this sway of cosmic evil. God was in charge of history and would finally intervene to put an end to evil and to vindicate the righteous who had walked in the right path, and had suffered for doing so, during the time of the reign of evil.[2]

What exactly is being named as "evil" in these Jewish writings? It is here that we find a problematic mixture of ethical and ethnocentric-cultic judgments. Cultic concepts of evil are deeply entwined with the dualism of purity and pollution. God is all Holy, and the places where God can be approached must be pure and holy. Defilement not only renders a person unacceptable to approach holy places; but also, if defilement intrudes into the holy places, a violent response is mandated, calling down vengeance against the defiler.[3]

This concept of evil as the unholy is identified with the gentile world, particularly with their cults, but in some sense with their culture and their very being. The intrusion of artifacts from alien cults defiles the holy. But pollution is also closely associated with sexuality and reproduction, especially with the female blood of menstruation and birth. Male bodily wastes, especially semen spilled in "wet dreams," and the bodies of the dead are also defiling. Some rabbis identified the evil impulse with the sexual impulse. As Judith Plaskow has noted, this exhibits a deep anxiety about sexuality. While the sexual impulse is necessary for the good of reproduction, nevertheless there is deep concern to control and channel it.[4]

This concept of purity and pollution creates a pattern in Jewish religion of carefully delineated separations, the sabbath from ordinary days, the sanctuary of the temple from the outer courts, Jew from gentile, male from female. While these separations also strive to balance and provide a place for each, nevertheless there is a definite hierarchy of more and less pure, with the total purity of God at the center and total impurity as the outer darkness.

In some sense, as Plaskow notes, women become the "gentile within," the necessary impurity within the holy people.[5] In order

for men to approach God, they have to separate from contact
with women and abstain from sexuality. For example, when the
Torah is given to the men of Israel, they prepare themselves for
this hierophany by "not going near a woman for three days."[6]
This means that women must be distanced from holy places. Only
Israelite men stand in assembly to receive God's Law. Women are
banished to the outer court in the temple (along with gentiles),
and banned even from that space when they are "in their impurity." In the synagogue they are segregated in a balcony covered
by a curtain, so their presence cannot be seen by men who might,
by catching sight of them, fall prey to the "evil impulse."[7]

Israel's election places upon it a mandate to be a holy people.
Through this holiness, or greater proximity to God's holiness,
they also are situated in a central relation to God's work of creation and redemption. It was on their behalf that God created the
world. Election and the mandate to holiness provide Israel with a
land claim. The land of Canaan has been designated by God as
their promised land. They have a superior right to this land because they alone can make it holy, while the polluted people who
live there deserve, precisely because of their unholiness, to be
driven out of this land.

The book of Joshua manifests the most extreme version of the
ethnocentric-cultic concept of Israel's relationship to its God.
Through this relation to its God, it is empowered to enter a land
whose soil it had not tilled, to seize cities it has not built,[8] and to
put all the inhabitants of these cities to the sword, one after another, sparing neither women nor children or even domesticated
animals. The book, however, admits that this slaughter was not
actually total. Survivors of the other peoples remained, and this
posed a danger of cultural amalgamation:

> The Lord your God will push them back before you and drive
> them out of your sight, and you shall possess their land, as the
> Lord your God promised you. Therefore be steadfast to observe
> and do all that is written in the book of the law of Moses . . . so

that you may not be mixed with these nations left here among you, or make mention of the names of their gods . . . For if you turn back and join the survivors of these nations left here among you, and intermarry with them, so that you marry their women and they yours, know assuredly that the Lord your God will not continue to drive out these nations before you, but they shall be a snare and a trap for you . . . until you perish from this good land that the Lord your God has given you. (Joshua 23:5–7, 12–13)

Modern archaeology has thrown into doubt the historical accuracy of this account of the Joshua conquest of Canaan. The cities mentioned in the book as having been destroyed by Joshua show no signs of having been destroyed in the twelfth century B.C.E. Most fell into ruins at a much earlier date.[9] But the problem of the book lies not with its historical accuracy, but rather with the terrible mandate it provides for later people, who take this book to be part of Holy Writ, to act out similar patterns of ruthless colonization of conquered lands and extermination or enslavement of their former inhabitants.

In the seventeenth century, English Puritans read their struggle with Native Americans in the mirror of Joshua and claimed a parallel divinely given right to exterminate these indigenous people and take their land.[10] In the nineteenth century, Dutch Puritans in South Africa read a similar mandate to slaughter the Zulus and appropriate their land.[11] In the twentieth century, Jewish Zionists have seen the Palestinians as having no right to the lands they have tilled or the houses and towns they have built. They should be driven out and replaced by the elect people, whose God has never ceased to give them the right to this land.[12]

In contrast to the book of Joshua, other texts of Hebrew scripture show a very different ethical sensitivity to just human relations as central to divine commandment. Unjust treatment of the neighbor, particularly those who are poor, becomes the sin that excites divine wrath. In the book of Amos, written in the

mid-eighth century, we have a sharp change from the amoral eth-
nocentricity of Joshua. Here the God of Israel is preeminently the
God who demands justice for the poor and the oppressed.

In Amos the special relation of Israel to God becomes a liability rather than a privilege. Precisely because of this special relationship, Israel's unethical behavior will be judged with special
severity:

> You only have I known of all the families of the earth; there-
> fore I will punish you for all your iniquities. (Amos 3:2)

Central to these iniquities are crimes against the needy neighbor,
although sexual depravity and violations of the cult are also
judged:

> ... they sell the righteous for silver and the needy for a pair
> of sandals—they who trample the head of the poor in the dust of
> the earth and push the afflicted out of the way; father and son go
> into the same girl, so that my holy name is profaned; they lay
> themselves down beside every altar on garments taken in pledge;
> and in the house of their God they drink wine with fines they im-
> posed. (2:6–8)

Amos particularly attacks those who think that favor can be won
from God by purely cultic activity. Observance of festivals and
sacrificial offerings earn only divine wrath if they ignore God's
major demand, which is justice:

> I hate, I despise your festivals and I take no delight in your
> solemn assemblies. Even though you offer me your burnt offer-
> ings and grain offerings, I will not accept them. . . . But let justice
> roll down like waters and righteousness like an everflowing
> stream. (Amos 5:21–22, 24)

Those who think that Israel's special relation to God guarantees
them victory over their neighbors are in for a shock, according to
Amos. Indeed Israel's crimes against justice will result in the

reversal of the winning of the land. Israel will be driven out of the land into exile:

> . . . your land shall be parceled out by line; you yourself shall die in an unclean land, and Israel shall surely go into exile away from its land. (Amos 7:17)

The fierce ethical judgmentalism of Amos moves, in one line of Hebrew scripture, toward increasing universalism, while other lines shore up religious ethnocentrism with the assurance that divine judgment is only temporary. Israel remains God's elect, and when it repents will be restored to its land and vindicated against its enemies. The small Book of Jonah represents perhaps the fullest development of Hebrew universalism, affirming the equal concern of God for Israel and for the surrounding peoples, whom Israel regarded as its enemies.

The fourth-century writer of the Book of Jonah satirizes Jewish exclusivist nationalism by imagining God demanding that a prophet in the time of the flourishing empire of Assyria go to Nineveh to preach repentance to its inhabitants. The prophet turns and runs the other way, knowing that God is impartial in mercy and will forgive the Ninevites if they repent. But the prophet encounters a series of mishaps in transit, is tossed overboard, and is swallowed by a fish, which belches him up on the shore from which he embarked, and he is forced to carry out his mission.

Reluctantly preaching divine judgment to Israel's enemies, Jonah is disgusted when they repent. God immediately forgives them and withholds the destruction that was in store for them. The climax of the book has God explaining to his reluctant chauvinist prophet his equal concern for all the beings of his creation. In Jonah evil is described only in a general way as "evil ways" and the "violence that is in their hands." The main point is that God is a universal creator, who, like a tender gardener, loves his "plants" equally, labors on their behalf, and desires the welfare of all of them.

PLATONIC AND GNOSTIC VIEWS OF EVIL

It was from the Platonic tradition of Greek philosophy, and its exaggeration in Gnosticism, that Western culture derived the view that evil resides in the physical body and the material world, over against the conscious mind. As we have seen in the account of Plato's creation story, the *Timaeus,* Platonic thought assumes a foundational dualism of mind and matter, or more ultimately, eternal disembodied intellectual "essence" and "mutability." Mutability characterizes the unformed substratum of matter, which is then shaped into the cosmos by the Demiurgos (Creator), by fashioning it according to the eternal essences.

The soul, or the life principle, is also fashioned by the Demiurgos, who then infuses it into the body of the cosmos as its governing power. The soul has the capacity for knowledge; that is, contemplative union with the divine essences. When it is thus united with the essences, it is capable of subduing the body to which it is joined, and governing it. But the soul also contains the lower forces of unruly passions. When the soul loses its contemplative union with the intellectual essences and capitulates to the lower passions, it fails to govern the body but rather becomes governed by the body.

For Plato this is the root of evil. The soul that has fallen under the power of the passions becomes "forgetful" or ignorant of unchangeable truth, and falls prey to variable opinion. It also falls prey to vice, which Plato sees as the manifestations of intemperate, unruly passions, both excesses of food, drink, and sex, and also the vehement, unruly opinion of the demagogue and the crowd. The soul thereby also loses its capacity to return to its heavenly home at death, and is condemned to a cycle of reincarnation.

Plato's *Phaedrus* supplements the *Timaeus* with a mythic presentation of this mixed nature of the soul and its fall from the heavenly world of the gods, where it once dwelt in contemplative union with the eternal essences, into embodiment.[13] When the soul loses sight of the eternal realm of ideas, its "wings" shrivel, and it falls to the earth and takes on a mortal body. Depending on how far it has lost sight of truth, it takes on various levels of social status, ranging from the philosopher, at the highest level, to lower-class people who are involved with external, physical things, such as farmers and artisans, to the extreme traders in vehement untruth, the demagogue and the tyrant.[14]

If the soul continues in its unruly ways, it may then be incarnated into an animal, in which case escape from the cycle of reincarnation is precluded. There is no mention of women at all in this discussion! Judging from the *Timaeus,* one assumes that Plato would think of reincarnation into a woman as an even lower state than the lowest male state, but above the animal, and still capable of rising to male forms and hence eventual escape into disembodied spiritual existence.

In this Platonic view, vice is expressed in excesses of emotion and desire, imbalance and intemperance, while virtue is control that maintains balance and harmony, the body and the emotions working as the docile vehicles of the governing mind. Virtue is possible only if the mind, as the governing principle of the soul and body, remains united with the vision of the eternal, unchangeable truths, while vice is the result of losing that vision and capitulating to the opposite principle of mutability.

Thus mutability, the substratum of matter, is the basis of both vice and mortality. Everything that is not unchangeable and rational, everything that changes, decays, falls into decline and death, expresses this negative drag of material mutability. The dissolution side of the life cycle was, for the Platonist, the manifestation of evil, expressed in everything that was "out of control" in body, mind, and emotions. Ultimate good is escape from the life cycle, the flight of the rational mind to its true home in the disembodied world of immutable, eternal ideas.

For Platonism (including its Greco-Roman descendants in Middle and Neoplatonism) the heavenly home of the soul, freed from the body, lies within the cosmos, in its astral upper level, where it could contemplate the truths that lie "beyond the heavens." Thus Platonism could also see the cosmos as a whole as a "secondary god," a beautiful manifestation of harmonious movement in imitation of the eternal. But it also assumed that this cosmos was hierarchically ordered. The "upper levels" of the planetary spheres above the lunar region were immortal. The planets and stars themselves were made out of a "spiritual matter," like light, that did not decay. The lower sublunar region, between the moon and the earth, was the region of evil spirits, while earthly bodies were those bodies subjected to decay and death.

In Gnosticism (syncretistic philosophical movements of the first to third centuries C.E.) this hierarchical cosmos of Platonism has fallen into more total dualism. In Gnostic thought the entire cosmos, including its planetary upper regions, have been demonized. The divine world of spiritual goodness now lies beyond even the upper regions of the cosmos, in the "heaven beyond the heavens."

Valentinian Gnosticism constructed an etiology of this fallen cosmos. Originally divine being existed in "depth and silence." Gradually this original oneness began to unfold into manifoldness of divine being, through the male-female duality of generation.[15] This process of generation within the heavenly community continues until the divine pleroma of thirty aeons is completed. Each level of the pleroma is united with the one above it through contemplative knowledge, keeping the whole in unity.

But this unity of the divine pleroma (divine community of beings) becomes threatened when an aeon (divine being) at the bottom level, Sophia, fails to accept her mediated relation to the Father and attempts direct, unmediated knowledge of Him. This results in a fissure in the pleroma, an eruption of unruly ignorance.

This unruly ignorance, expelled from the pleroma, becomes the root and substratum of the visible cosmos.

Fallen, demonic power arises in this lower world and shapes a cosmos in a fashion that reflects Plato's description of the Demiurgos shaping the cosmos in the *Timaeus*. But this Demiurgos is now defined as a fallen, demonic power. The cosmos he shapes is a multilayered realm of ignorance and alienation from the true divine being that lies outside and beyond this cosmos. The earth and its embodied beings lie at the dark center of this cosmic prison, at the furthest distance from divine truth and being.

Within some human beings are sparks of divine being, particles of divine light that escaped from the pleroma in the cosmic fall. These sparks of divine being make these elect humans restless in their cosmic and earthly prison house. The divine world also seeks that which is lost to it, sending down messages from above to break through the walls of ignorance and awaken in the entrapped spirits the memory of their former heavenly home. Once awakened, the spirits recognize that not only the earth, but even the planetary spheres and their gods are expressions of ignorance and falsehood. Through withdrawing its life force from the body and the tumultuous passions of the psyche, the spirit begins its journey out of the body, up through the planetary spheres, and finally beyond it to reunite with its true divine community.

The Hermetic text, the *Poimandres,* describes this salvific ascent of the soul:

> The soul's ascent at death. First at the dissolution of the material body you yield up to the demon your sensuous nature now ineffective, and the bodily senses return each to its source among the elements. And thereafter man thrusts upward through the Harmony, and to the first zone he surrenders the power to grow and to decrease, and to the second the machinations of evil cunning, now rendered powerless, and to the third the deceit of concupiscence, now rendered powerless, and to the fourth the

arrogance of dominion, shorn of its ambition, and to the fifth the
impious audacity and the rashness of impulsive deed, and to the
sixth the evil appetites of wealth, now rendered powerless, and
to the seventh zone the lying that ensnares. And then denuded of
the effects of the Harmony, he enters the nature of the Ogdoas,
now in possession of his own power, and with those already
there exalts the Father, and those present rejoice with him at his
presence, and having become like his companions he hears also
certain powers above the eighth sphere exalting God with a
sweet voice. And then in procession they rise up toward the
Father and give themselves up to the Powers, and having become
Powers themselves, enter the Godhead. This is the good end of
those who have attained gnosis: to become God.[16]

In this striking account of the stripping of the soul of the effects
of transitoriness that lie within the sphere of earth and the planetary spheres below the immortal realm of the eighth sphere, evil is
essentially seen as variants of mutability in the soul. Evil impulses,
such as "evil cunning," "deceit of concupiscence," the "arrogance
of dominion," the "evil appetites of wealth," and the "lying that
ensnares" are all located as impulses in the soul, without reference
to any other persons against whom such impulses might be exer-
cised. In other words, evil is not seen relationally as evil done to
others, but as self-contained "motions" in the soul itself, parallel
to the capacity to grow and decrease. The ascent through the
planetary spheres purifies the soul of these "motions" and thus
renders it immutable and eternal, united with the godhead.

THE CHRISTIAN CONCEPT OF THE FALL:
FROM PAUL TO AUGUSTINE

In Christianity we find a fusion of the Jewish ethical and the
Greek metaphysical views of evil. Evil is located both in the freedom of the human will and its choice of disobedience against
God, and in the flawed ontology of mortal being. The fusion of
these two views compounded the dilemma of human entrapment

in sin and evil in Christian teaching, an entrapment for which humans are both culpably guilty and yet incapable of escaping through their own "natural" capacities.

It was St. Paul who laid the foundations of this concept of sin and evil, although its full development awaited the work of the fourth-century Latin theologian, Augustine. Paul's theology draws on a blend of apocalyptic and Gnostic modes of thought. Basic to his theology is a profound dualism between two modes of existence: existence according to the "flesh," which he characterizes as a state of slavery to sin and death, and existence in the Spirit, which he sees as freeing the Christian, through their rebirth in Christ, both to virtuous and loving life and also to the promise of immortality.

The problem in Paul's thought lies in the extent to which he identifies this evil condition with natural or created life, and thus sees redeemed life as something fundamentally transcendent to our original, created potential. In the first chapters of Romans, Paul declares that the nature and will of God are clearly known through the visible creation, and all peoples have the capacity, through their created nature, to do good. But they have all chosen to do evil, so God has "given them up" to an evil and deluded state of life.

Paul's main concern in these chapters is to reject any special privileges of the Jewish people in relation to God and the doing of God's will because they have received the Law. Both Jews and Greeks have sufficient knowledge of what God demands, either through the revealed Law, or through these same commandments known through nature, to do God's will, so both have no excuse for their sinful ways of life that both have chosen voluntarily.

But this concept of our freedom to chose good or evil then changes to a different emphasis on the present inability of people, Jew or Greek, to do good. The choice of sin becomes a state of sin from which people are unable to extricate themselves. This is attributed to Adam, the first human who sinned, and who then

became the corporate source of the present state of human perversity. The Jewish Law in no way helps this state of perversity,
for it only reveals what God wants, but doesn't give the power to
overcome this state of sin that renders us unable to do what God
wants. Thus knowledge of God's commands through the Law
only increases our awareness of sin and makes us guilty, because
it makes us aware that what we do is sin.

In chapters 5 through 7 of Romans, Paul expounds a profound theological anthropology of the divided self, one that
knows what is good, but is unable to unite one's will and being
to that good that one knows and desires to do. It is Christ who
delivers us from the the power of the fleshly and sinful self and
provides us with the power of goodness. Here Paul thinks in
terms of two opposite types of existence, the one derived from
the fallen Adam, which is sin and death, and the other from
Christ, which is goodness and spiritual life. The death and resurrection of Christ breaks the power of the fallen mode of life and
establishes the redeemed mode of life. Through baptism we die
to our Adamic mode of life and rise in the Christic mode of life.

Yet baptism doesn't complete the transformation. It provides
us with the new power of spiritual life, but the old Adamic power
of sin is still present "in our flesh." The baptized live between the
fallen and the redeemed "age," between the Adamic and the
Christic mode of being. They must struggle to unite themselves
fully with the new mode of life and cease to walk in the old ways
"of the flesh." Paul looks forward to a second stage in this transformative process, in which the fleshly and mortal mode of life finally will be destroyed, and the self will be transformed into a
sinless and immortal state of being.

The confusion of creation and sin in Paul lies in his concept of
the relation of sin and death. We have been created with the capacity to do good, and yet have chosen evil. From evil comes mortality. Does this mean that prior to some historical choice of sin by
the first human, humans were not subject to mortality? Paul never

says this, but this would be the conclusion that the church fathers would draw. On the redemptive side of the dualism, baptism not only roots us in the principle of goodness, but also of immortal life. We thus look forward to the shedding of the mortal body, subject to decay, and being transformed into an immortal and celestial body, similar to that of the stars (1 Corinthians 15:35–50).

It is in this identification of sin with death, and goodness with immortal life, in a celestial body purged of its capacity to decay, that we recognize Paul's quasi-Gnostic cosmology. Paul takes for granted the two-storied cosmology of contemporary philosophy. On the upper level, the celestial bodies are made of a type of matter that is spiritual or "lightlike" and immortal. In the sublunar realm of air and earth, there are the bodies that are subject to decay. This lower realm of earth and air is seen as governed by demonic powers that trap us in sin and death.

Paul uses cosmological terms, such as principalities and powers and elementary spirits (*stoicheia*), to express this concept of demonic powers that enslave us and rule over us. The Jewish Law stands on the boundaries of these demonic powers, for its commandments are spiritual; but lacking the spiritual power to do what it commands, those who attempt to obey it without the Spirit only reveal thereby their enslavement to the *stoicheia* (Galatians 4:3, 9).

Baptism in Christ frees us from the power of the demonic spirits that enslave us, and that correspond to the Adamic mode of life that is "from the earth, earthly." It puts us into communion with the spiritual power, which is from "heaven." Paul also thinks that this demonic control over the cosmos has a fixed epoch in world history, beginning with Adam and lasting until Christ completes the subjugation of the fallen powers to God. Thus he speaks of enslavement to sin as the power of this "age" (*aeon*), as well as of this present "world" (*cosmos*).

The redemptive work of Christ is seen not only as giving the baptized the power of virtue and uniting them with the power of

immortal life, which can transform their fleshly bodies into spiritual, immortal bodies at the resurrection, but also as overcoming the subjugation of the cosmos itself to its "bondage to
decay." When Christ completes the reconciliation of creation to
God, the fallen powers that presently reign over it will be re-
united to God, and the cosmos as a whole liberated into the immortal life of celestial bodies.

> For the creation waits with eager longing for the revealing of
> the sons of God, for the creation was subjected to futility, not of
> its own will but by the will of him who subjected it in hope; be-
> cause the creation itself will be set free from its bondage to decay
> and obtain the glorious liberty of the children of God. We know
> that the whole creation has been groaning in travail together
> until now; and not only the creation, but we ourselves who have
> the first fruits of the Spirit, groan inwardly, as we wait for adop-
> tion as sons, the redemption of our bodies. (Romans 8:19–23)

When Paul speaks of "sin" whose "wages" are death, what
kind of thing does he have in mind? When we look at Paul's lists
of "sins" in Romans 2: 29–31 and Galatians 5:19, the over-
whelming emphasis is on violations of relationships to other people, such as covetousness, malice, envy, murder, strife, deceit,
slander, insolence, boastfulness, faithlessness, heartlessness, ruth-
lessness, jealousy, anger, selfishness, and "party spirit." Some sins
relate to abuse of one's body, such as drunkenness; others to sexual excess and "unnaturalness," such as licentiousness and ho-
mosexuality; others to violations of the true understanding of
God, such as idolatry and sorcery.

But Paul is also notable for what he does not think is sinful:
namely, the whole body of the Jewish laws about kosher food,
sabbath, and holy day observances. He is aware of "weak" members of his congregation, who have been taught to feel guilty
about violations of such laws, and he seeks an ethic of mutual

tolerance and forbearance between those with different opinions of such matters (Romans 14; 1 Corinthians 8). But for him, central to redemption in Christ is liberation from belief that such observances made a salvific difference. Christ frees the Christian from these laws, as well as teaches them that salvation itself is a gift from God that is given by faith, and not as a result of keeping commandments.

Yet Paul is no antinomian. Once we have been united to the life power of God, we must indeed struggle to walk in a path of conduct that is characterized by love, joy, peace, patience, kindness, faithfulness, and self-control, and to avoid their negative counterparts. Paul's strong emphasis on the morality of loving relation is rooted in his understanding of the Church as the Body of Christ. The prime indicator of being in Christ is to be in the Church as a community of loving relationship. Yet, despite his strong communitarian ethic, Paul, like the author of the Poimandres, finally thinks that the solution to evil is to free the self from the "fleshly" body subject to "decay."

Paul's dualistic cosmo-anthropology was so difficult for many early Christians to grasp that it seems to have been put aside for a generation for the more commonsensical Jewish ethic of free will and the "two tendencies." In the mid-second century, the problematic of the Pauline view was accentuated by a radicalized expression of it in the teaching of Marcion and his followers. Marcion was a Christian teacher from Pontus who attempted to systematize the Pauline teachings.

Marcion read the Pauline "antitheses" of slavery and freedom, sin and grace, law and spirit, death and immortal life, as the expressions of two divine Powers: one, lower divine Power, was the Creator of the cosmos, the God of the Hebrew scriptures. This was the jealous and angry God of the Law. Christ was the son, not of this lower Creator God, but of an unknown God from a transcendent heavenly world whose nature was that of

love and forgiveness apart from the Law. Baptism frees us from
the power of the Creator God of "this world" (*cosmos*), and
unites us to the power of the transcendent God of love.

The Christianity that became dominant by 200 C.E. was one
that rejected such radical dualisms of creation and redemption in
favor of a reaffirmation of the Jewish view of the essential goodness of creation. The God who created the world, and the God
revealed in the Redeemer, Christ, are one and the same. This
means that Christ does not cancel creation, but indeed remani-
fests the divine power that underlies and sustains creation. Evil
arises because humans, gifted with free will, "turn away" from
and lose touch with that sustaining power of God that is our true
nature, our *imago dei*, given in creation.

Redemption is an evolutionary process, begun in the Law and
the prophets, fulfilled in Christ and completed through the
Church, whereby creation is reconciled and enters into the fullness of unity with that same "Logos" and "Spirit" that created
the world in the beginning. This is the "cosmic Christology" of
the anti-Gnostic church fathers, such as Justin Martyr and
Irenaeus, both of whom retained a strong element of the Jewish
belief in a millennial age of a redeemed physical cosmos.

Yet these Christian teachers also presupposed the Pauline
identification of sin with death and redemption with the risen,
immortal body. How is this concept of redemption from sin as
liberation from mortality reconciled with redemption as renewal
and fulfillment of the creation? Irenaeus's solution is to suppose
that the original creation in the "image of God" was an immature state. Although sustained by the Word and Spirit of God as
their ground of being, humans are also given free will to turn
away from God. Free will is the root of sin, but also of the final
perfection of creation, for we are finally united with God only
when we choose this relation voluntarily.[17]

Origen, a brilliant Christian teacher in Alexandria (185–254
C.E.) attempted a more Gnostic solution to the relation of sin and

death. For him the original creation was a spiritual community
of intelligent spirits (*logikai*) attached to the Logos of God. But
these spirits, having free will, turned from their source of being
and "fell away" into outer darkness. God then organized a visible cosmos around the various levels of their fall. The angelic
spirits of the planetary spheres, human spirits in carnal bodies
and demonic spirits in the infernal region, each express the various "levels" of fallenness (fallenness here is seen as ontic and
moral, but expressed, in some sense, spatially).

Origen regards "matter" as changeable, taking on different
appearances of density and mortality depending on its degree of
fallenness from its divine source.

> The material substance of this world, possessing a nature ad-
> mitting of all possible transformations, is, when dragged down
> to beings of a lower nature, moulded into the crasser and more
> solid condition of a body, so as to distinguish those visible and
> varying forms of the world, but when it becomes the servant of
> the more perfect and more blessed beings, it shines in the splen-
> dor of celestial bodies, and adorns either the angels of God or the
> sons of the resurrection with clothing of a spiritual body.[18]

Redemption is a gradual process of pedagogy of the fallen,
materialized souls, by which they learn to willingly reunite their
wills with the will of God. Through successive reincarnations,
the souls ascend back through the planetary spheres to union
with God. Eventually the whole material, visible world will disappear, as even the demonic spirits are gathered back into their
original union in the spiritual community of heaven.

Origen's bold effort to connect original and final creation was
too radical for dominant Christianity. His theories of the preexistent spirits, reincarnation, and universal salvation, including
even the demons, were rejected. Yet Eastern Christianity remained
deeply imbued with many of his basic premises. Although the
Cappadocian church fathers of the fourth century, Gregory

Nyssa, Gregory Nazianzus, and Basil the Great, describe the original creation in terms drawn from Genesis 1–3, they too assume that the original Adam and Eve possessed an immortal body.[19]

The choice of sin by the primal parents loosened their union with God and made their bodies mortal and subject to decay and death. The idea in Genesis 3:7 that Adam and Eve made themselves clothes after the fall (which was translated in the Septuagint used by the Greek Fathers as "coats of skin") was understood by them as referring to this mortalization of the body due to sin. Sin and death also brought about the sexual impulse, both in order to compensate for mortality through propagation, but also as the manifestation of the sinful nature of the fallen body.

For the Eastern fathers, redemption is a transformation through the power of Christ that allows us to gradually withdraw the powers of the soul from the sinful body. Abstinence from sex, fasting, even curtailment of sleep in night prayer, express this strengthening of the soul by its withdrawal from the death powers of the fleshly body. The final expression of redemption in the resurrected body will complete this restoration of the original immortal body, casting off the "coats of skin" of the fallen body. The "spiritual body," like the ascended soul in the *Poimandres,* will lose all those qualities of changeability that mark it as finite and corruptible.[20]

These Christian perspectives on nature, sin, mortality, and redemption from sin and death were refined in the teachings of St. Augustine in the late fourth and early fifth centuries. Augustine also became the great interpreter of Pauline theological anthropology for the Western church. In his youth Augustine had been attracted to Manichaeanism, a Gnostic dualistic religion, and was an adherent of this sect for nine years. But Manichaeanism eventually failed to satisfy Augustine's quest for understanding of the nature of good and evil, and he repudiated it.

Christian Neoplatonism enabled Augustine to overcome the Manichaean concept of two competing spiritual powers, the luminous "light" power of God and the "dark" power of matter, which is the source of evil. The soul was seen as a particle of the "light" substance of God, while evil in humans came from the contrary power of evil derived from the body. The body and the material world derive not from God, but from the powers of darkness.

Augustine rejected this dualism through a Neoplatonic ontological monism in which there is only one source of being, God. Both the soul and the body of humans are essentially good, but non-divine, created entities. Humans, created good, are endowed with freedom of will. This freedom of will makes possible their choice of good or evil. The choice of evil is not impelled by an contrary power, but is an irrational choice of nonbeing, against being. Evil is thus defined as a defect, a negation of good. In Augustine's language, in his *Confessions*:

> I inquired what iniquity was, and ascertained it not to be a substance, but a perversion of the will, bent aside from thee, O God, the Supreme Substance, toward these lower things.[21]

Despite Augustine's affirmation that all that is, is from God and is thereby good, there remains in his thought the Platonic version of the anti-body, anti-material hierarchy. God as Supreme Being is immaterial, and one is in communion with God by turning "upward" to the immaterial, against those bodily "lower things," which have lesser being and goodness. The mind, although created, has a "natural" affinity for God, as immaterial Mind. The intellectual journey to truth and the moral journey to goodness is one with the journey from bodily beings to disembodied Being.

Augustine refined his teachings on anthropology in his conflict with Pelagianism in the early fifth century. Pelagius was a Christian teacher who was primarily concerned with strengthening his students in their capacity to "do good and avoid evil." He grounded his anthropology in a firm affirmation of the essential goodness of human nature as "image of God." Creation itself was, for Pelagius, the foundational "grace" or gift of God. God also gave humans complete freedom of will, and therefore the capacity to choose good or evil. Pelagius also rejected the concept that humans were undying prior to sin. For him sin brought negative consequences to the soul, but the body is naturally mortal.[22]

By the exercise of free will, humans have sinned and chosen evil. This choice weakens human understanding of good and also creates a social climate that disposes one to evil. But it doesn't change the essential capacity to choose good, which remains our basic human nature created by God. Divine grace thus is a pedagogical process in which God, through the Law and the prophets and then through Christ, shows us again the right path, but we remain capable of making the choice for good. As we choose good, we also strengthen our capacity (habits) of doing good, and we can, through exercise of free will, become closer and closer to achieving perfection.

Pelagius's teachings seemed quite unexceptional to most of the Eastern teachers of Christianity, according as it did with their own concepts of free will and of Christ as the renewer of creation. It was the North African church, and especially Augustine, who were enraged by this confident moralism and who set out to refute it as heresy. Pelagius's view of nature and free will was, for Augustine, an insulting negation of his whole experience of his conversion, as a transformation through redeeming grace that was given him by God from beyond and over against his own perverted nature. Augustine's experience resonated deeply with the Pauline sense of the divided self, unable to do what it wills, that "law in the members that wars against the law of the mind."[23]

In a series of letters and treatises, Augustine hammered out the anthropology of transcendent grace, and of the fallen self that has lost the freedom to do what it wills, which would shape Western Christianity. This fallen state of humanity is contrasted with what Augustine believes to be the original created state of Adam. The original human was given both a good nature and freedom of will. Adam truly had the capacity to do the good that he willed, and thus to earn merit with God. This capacity to align his will with God's also held the original Adam in an undying condition. Thus the original Adam was able both not to sin and not to die, not because he was incapable of sin or death, but because he could will to unite himself with God (I use generic male pronouns here intentionally).

However, this capacity was lost when Adam chose sin and self-will over God's will. This choice lost him (and all humans thereafter) his original undying existence, and also his original capacity to choose good. It also means that now no man can exercise his will unselfishly. All of his acts are corrupted by self-will, including the apparent choice of virtue and knowledge. This state of bondage of the will cannot be remedied by acts of the will, but only by a transforming grace that comes from God through the redemptive work of Jesus Christ. This grace transforms his corrupted will, and empowers the will to do the good that it wills, but that it cannot do in its present, corrupted state.[24]

Since this redeeming grace is given by God without regard to any prior meritorious acts, for Augustine this can only be God's arbitrary sovereign choice of some humans, while allowing the rest of them their deserved perdition. This leads Augustine to his distinctive teachings on predestination and on the perseverance of the saints.[25] For all eternity God has chosen and predestined some to receive this transforming grace of redemption, and also to receive additional infusions of grace that allow the self to persevere in goodness. The redeemed self will experience its ultimate transformation in the resurrected body. The redeemed state is not simply a return to, but an improvement on, the original state of man. The original Adam was able not to sin and not to die, while the man redeemed in Christ is so transformed by divine grace that he is no longer able to sin, and finally, no longer able to die.

Augustine's concept of the original, fallen and redeemed "man" was closely related to his views of sexuality, and by implication relations of men with women. He believed that although women are equally redeemable, they are "by nature" under male subjugation. The male alone possesses the image of God, and woman is related to the divine "image" only under the "male as her head." Unlike some of the Eastern church fathers, Augustine thinks that sex and reproduction would have taken place in paradise, but it would have taken place without sexual feeling (concupiscence), and as a purely rational act.[26]

An essential result of the fall is the loss of the ability to perform the sexual act for procreation (its only legitimate purpose) sinlessly, that is, without lust. It is this sinful nature of the sexual act, even in marriage, although allowed there for the sake of procreation, that is the mechanism for the transmission of the fallen state of the original Adam to all his descendents. All humans are born with the same tainted nature into which Adam fell, through the sinful nature of the sexual act by which every human is generated.[27]

It follows, then, that the basic struggle to do the good that he willed, but felt himself unable to do in his unregenerate state, was for Augustine paradigmatically a sexual struggle, a struggle against his continuing desire for sexual activity, even though he clearly saw it as shameful and a degradation of his "integrity." Only through the gift of divine grace beyond his fallen nature, transforming his will, was Augustine finally able to give up sexual activity and desires and to lead a celibate life.[28]

Such views led not only to a concept of marriage as a lower status of virtue for Christians, but also imply an instrumental view of women in the sexual act, as receptacles of male sinful concupiscence and as rightly "used" only for procreation. Strikingly absent here is any idea of sex as an expression of loving relationship. Women, naturally subordinate, were to be redeemed by subordinating themselves all the more to the will of their husbands, or to other men in authority over them. Redeemed males express their redemption by eschewing sexual relations with women.

CONCLUSIONS

This classical Christian understanding of sin as both ethical and metaphysical, as both disobedience and finitude, has imparted a mixed heritage to the Western world. It is a powerful and compelling analysis that cannot be lightly dismissed by optimistic claims of easily recoverable innocence and virtue. Yet it is a heritage that is also deeply problematic, one that has contributed as much to the justification of evil as to the repentant overcoming of evil. These problematic aspects of the Christian view must be rooted out before its positive elements can be reclaimed in a new form.

The notion that humanity is culpable for its own finitude has laid upon Christians an untenable burden of guilt. Although we may evaluate our mortality as tragic, or seek to embrace it as natural, what mortality is not is sin, or the fruit of sin. The (preapocalyptic) Hebrew view that mortality is our natural condition, which we share with all other earth beings, and that redemption is the fullness of life within these finite limits, is a more authentic ethic for ecological living.

The evaluation of mortal life as evil and the fruit of sin has lent itself to an earth-fleeing ethic and spirituality, which has undoubtedly contributed very centrally to the neglect of the earth, to the denial of our commonality with plants and animals, and to the despising of the work of sustaining the day-to-day processes of finite but renewable life. By evaluating such finite but renewable life as sin and death, by comparison with "immortal" life, we have re-versed the realities of life and death. Death as deliverance from mortality is preferred to the only real life available to us.

The separations of the holy from the unholy, the spiritual from the carnal, and immortal from mortal life have also man-dated phobic relations to the death side of the life cycle, to decay, dead bodies, and the life fluids of sex and reproduction. These phobic patterns have been used to structure social apartheid along gender and ethnic lines. Such phobic patterns also express the inability to integrate the death and decomposition side of the life cycle constructively, turning wastes into toxic poisons rather than matter for new organisms. Thus the very effort to separate oneself in a sphere of purity against "pollution" creates pollu-tion.

Such despising of finite but renewable life is closely related to the despising of women as birth givers. Both the Jewish and the Greek traditions contributed to the compounded Christian scape-goating of women for both sin and death, the source of both im-purity and finitude. Tentative beginnings of an egalitarian view of male-female relations in early Christianity were quickly over-whelmed by this woman-blaming tradition. Not only is woman's "natural" subordination justified anew, but limitless victimization of women is justified by attributing the origins of sin and death to female insubordination. Through woman, "man" lost his "origi-nal, natural" immortality.

The negation of woman as the "mortal other," which the male must negate in order to grasp his lost "immortality," is also extended to other victimized groups. Religious, social, sexual, and racial-ethnic "aliens" have been viewed through the same dualistic lens that separates the godly from the ungodly and the spiritual from the carnal. Either conquest and subjugation or genocidal destruction has been justified as a way of dealing with such aliens who threaten the purity and power of the "men of God."

The reconstruction of the ethical tradition must begin by a clear separation of the questions of finitude from those of sin. Finitude is not our fault, nor is escape from it within our capacities. Mature spirituality frees us from ego-clinging for acceptance of the life processes of which we are inescapably a part. Within the bounds of finitude and mortality, there is certainly much missed plenitude that is outside our control or decision-making; that is tragic, but is not "sin."

What is appropriately called sin belongs to a more specific sphere of human freedom where we have the possibility of enhancing life or stifling it. It is the realm where competitive hate abounds, and also passive acquiescence to needless victimization. It is not easy to delineate exactly this region of culpable evil, for the boundaries between freedom and fate are fluid, and humans have greatly extended their power over things once thought unchangeable.

The central issue of "sin" as distinct from finitude is the misuse of freedom to exploit other humans and the earth and thus to violate the basic relations that sustain life. Life is sustained by biotic relationality, in which the whole attains a plenitude through mutual limits in interdependency. When one part of the life community exalts itself at the expense of the other parts, life is diminished for the exploited. Ultimately exploiters subvert the bases of their own lives as well. An expanding cycle of poisonous hostility and violence is generated.

The question mark over the Christian ethic is the extent to which it has contributed to this very effect of exploitative violence through the misnaming of death as sin. I suggest that in its quest to escape from mortal life, and its projection of the blame for sin and death onto the victims of exploitative violence, the Christian definition of sin has served to promote, more than to avoid, this cycle of violence.

There are certainly also recoverable elements for an ethic of eco-justice from our Christian heritage. One of these is the

Hebraic understanding of evil as unjust relations between peoples, and the destructive effect this has on the earth (to be explored more fully in chapter 8). Repentance means special advocacy of those who have been victimized by systems of oppressive power. This is the source of the call of liberation theologies for a "preferential option for the poor."

From the Pauline-Augustinian tradition, we derive a profound existentialist recognition of the divided self, acting against its own interests and desires. In the concept of inherited sin, we also recognize that evil is not simply the sum of individual decisions. We do not start with a clean slate, but we inherit historical systems of culture and social organization that bias our minds and wills negatively. Our freedom to chose good is not only limited by the fluid boundaries of finitude, but also distorted by a heritage of deception and injustice masquerading as good.

We are called to exercise our real but finite freedom within these limits and in struggle against these distortions. This means that, while we should not hold ourselves culpable for the entire system of sin, much less for biological mortality, we also should not imagine ourselves purely innocent either. We are an integral part of this whole reality. We need not only compassionate solidarity with those who are most victimized, but also realistic acknowledgment of how we have benefited from such injustices. Only by eschewing paranoid projection of all evil onto malignant "aliens" can we begin to reconstruct the tissues of relationship in a way that produces more biotic plenitude and less toxic violence.

Sin, then, as that sort of evil for which we must hold ourselves accountable, lies in distortion of relationship, the absolutizing of the rights to life and power of one side of a relation against the other parts with which it is, in fact, interdependent. It lies further in the insistent perseverance in the resultant cycle of violence, the refusal to empathize with the victimized underside of such power, and the erection of systems of control and cultures of deceit to maintain and justify such unjust power.

6

Paradise Lost and the Fall into Patriarchy

In this chapter I will examine a new "fall story," which is emerging from the ecofeminist movement: the story of the fall into patriarchy. In this story it is presumed that both nonhuman nature and also humans have an inherent capacity for biophilic mutuality, although there is often the suggestion that human females are relatively or absolutely better at mutuality than human males. It is further suggested that there was an original social order in which women and female modes of relationality dominated, and all was benign between the genders and in the human-nature relationship. But this state was lost about the time of the emergence of early urban civilizations, with the development of patriarchy.

There are elements in the underlying values of this story with which I would agree. But there are also dangers of reversed forms of scapegoating and untenable assumptions about "nature" as "originally" paradisaical. In this chapter I will summarize briefly the roots and some of the major forms of this hypothesis of the "lost paradise" in contemporary ecological and feminist theory. I will then examine in some detail the work of some contemporary paleoanthropologists, and ask whether this hypothesis can be

verified historically. In a concluding section, I will seek to sort out
the psychic and the social aspects of this "story," what is useful
and what may be misleading about it.

THE LOST PARADISE AND RADICAL ECOLOGY

Stories of a lost paradise have two major roots in Western
thought, the biblical story of Eden and the Greek story of the
Golden Age. The Eden story envisions an idyllic time when the
first man and his wife dwelt in a garden, "with every tree that is
pleasant to the sight and good for food." Forbidden the fruit of
one tree, the tree of the knowledge of good and evil, humans sin
by taking this fruit. They are expelled from the garden, and made
to dwell in a harsh land of "cursed ground," which brings forth
thorns and thistles, where the man must toil to till the ground by
the sweat of his brow and the woman is subjugated to the man
(Genesis 2–3).

In the Golden Age myth, as told by the Greek poet Hesiod,
there was once a happy race of mortals who were free from trou-
ble and wearisome labor and safe from disease. After Prometheus
stole fire from the gods to allow humans to develop technology,
Zeus punished humanity by sending the woman Pandora, who
makes the mistake of opening the box given to her as a gift by
Zeus. As a result all the diseases and troubles that afflict humanity were let loose.[1]

Both of these stories are shaped by males to blame women, especially as wives, for all the troubles of hard labor and physical
illness. Both of them imagine the idyllic time as one prior to hunting, agriculture, and technology, a gatherer paradise when humans could simply stretch forth their hand to pluck the fruits of
an abundant earth. The stories seem to be compounded of two
elements, an idealized memory of preagricultural societies and
idealized (male) childhood.[2] The adult male resents the wife,
whom he must support by his labor, and idealizes his lost nurture

by an all-giving mother. Woman-blaming for the lost paradise
may have psycho-familial roots, roots that go back to primal
human social patterns.

Ecofeminist theories of the lost paradise often include the idea
of original matriarchy. This story envisions a time prior to patriarchy, in which women ruled over men. It is a story found in
many cultures, often associated with male puberty rites.[3] In the
late nineteenth century, some anthropologists popularized a theory of human development in which society progressed from an
initial stage of promiscuity to a period of matriarchal rule, followed by patriarchy.[4] The theory was claimed by Friedrich
Engels and became a part of Marxist thought.[5] It also had great
influence on classical archaeology and became a standard element in the interpretation of the development of Greek culture
from its ancient Minoan roots.[6]

The nineteenth-century version of this theory of primitive matriarchy did not see it as a better world to which we should return.
Rather, in German classical anthropology, it is seen as a period of
"immanence," in which the human spirit is controlled by "dark
forces." Patriarchy represents a higher stage of development in
which the "transcendent Spirit" triumphs over "nature."[7] In
Marxist thought, however, it is seen as original communism, a
time of primitive egalitarianism that was undone by unjust male
and class rule. Final communism will supersede these unjust social
systems, bringing back original communist equality, but on a
higher level of technological development.[8]

Some feminist thinkers, such as Matilda Joslyn Gage, picked
up on the theme of original matriarchy, seeing it not as a primitive time, but a time of high culture in early Egyptian and Near
Eastern civilization, when women were in the ascendancy in family, religion, and society. The worship of the Mother Goddess
was the divine principle of this benevolent female rule. This
Golden Age of human society was overthrown by the regressive
influence of patriarchal religion and social organization, which

Gage identified particularly with the Jewish and Christian traditions. In order for women to be liberated today, they must throw
off this patriarchal Jewish and Christian heritage.[9]

In the 1920s mainstream anthropology generally rejected the
theory of original matriarchy, together with global efforts to
trace "stages of human development."[10] But the literature en-
shrining these ideas of original matriarchy, idealized as a lost paradise, was revived and repopularized in the 1960s and forms a
major source of contemporary ecofeminist concepts of female-
centered lost past.[11] This idea has been popularized in radical
ecological, feminist, and ecofeminist writings in various forms.

One such expression is found in creation spirituality, represented by Dominican theologian Matthew Fox. For Fox, "original blessing" is the foundational truth. This truth is primarily
theological; that is, it is intended to assert an understanding of
creation as originally and essentially good.[12] Fallenness or evil is
secondary and recent in earth history. While evil is a reality that
alienates us from our creational goodness, original blessing remains the true nature of all things.

Fox stresses the primacy of original blessing by citing the
great age of the cosmos, 18 billion years, in contrast to the recent
appearance of humans, 4 million years ago. Thus original blessing is 17,996,000,000 years older than sin. But Fox often suggests a more recent beginning of sin. Sin began with the rise of
patriarchy some four thousand to six thousand years ago.[13]

Fox believes that human alienation has not been cured, but
rather has been deepened by what he sees as a false Christian theology of fall and redemption. This false and alienated mode of
thought has been imposed on indigenous peoples of the rest of
the world who retained, until Western Christian colonization,
cultures of harmony with "nature."[14] Fox's creation spirituality
stresses forms of meditation, liturgy, and therapy designed to free
us from cultures of alienation and restore our harmony with the
original blessing that remains the true "nature" of things.

Another version of lost paradise is found in deep ecology and the Earth First! movement. For Earth First! radical environmental activists, it is human technological control over "nature," beginning with agriculture, that is the root of the destruction of "nature" and human relations to "nature." The ideal relation of humans to "nature" is represented by hunter-gatherer societies, groups that not only existed in the past, as the form of human society that sustained humans on the earth for millions of years, but which exist in dwindling wilderness areas. Their wisdom must be rediscovered and emulated today.[15]

Earth First!ers focus on wilderness areas and seek to disrupt further destruction of remaining uncut forests. In contrast to ecofeminism, they stress anthropocentrism, rather than patriarchy, as the false thinking that underlies human destruction of "nature." Their preference for wilderness and an idealized hunting society as the "image" of the original harmony of humans and "nature" seems to reflect a masculine imagination quite different from the idea of the "good life" that appears in ecofeminism, where settled agricultural villages, domestic life, and the arts find a place. This movement has been criticized by animal rights ecofeminists for its idealization of hunting and its obliviousness to issues of male domination of women and of animal rights.[16]

The hypothesis of a lost paradise also is found in the thought of feminist philosopher Mary Daly. Daly, like Fox, comes from the Roman Catholic tradition, and like Fox was trained in Thomistic scholastic theology in France in the 1960s. Unlike Fox, however, Daly has repudiated not only Roman Catholicism, but Christianity as a whole, as a religion of unredeemable evil. As Daly has moved from a Christian reformist to a post-Christian and increasingly separatist feminism in her later work, she has rejected all male-dominated culture throughout "recorded" history as evil and seems to regard females as having a radically different "nature" from males.[17]

Daly accepts the theory of original matriarchy found in writers such as Elizabeth Gould Davis, *The First Sex*.[18] For Davis, patriarchy as a global system of evil is recent, about six thousand years old. Before that a gynocentric world flourished, in which women were in control of their own lives, bonded with each other and with the nonhuman world of animals and the cosmos. Daly sees her project of feminist theory as putting women back in touch with that original "wild" and "lusty" world of women and nature and freeing them from patriarchal systems of evil.

Daly's major message is a basic and powerfully stated dualism between good and evil, life and death. Women have the capacity for true life that is vigorous, and in dynamic communion with animals, earth, and stars. Males lack such capacity. They are by "nature" parasitic, feeding off the true life-bearers and creators, setting up necrophilic mummeries of real life and insight. This spurious, parasitic maleness is the source of evil, the basis for generating a fallacious world of delusion that reverses all true principles and life and spreads a network of death over the fabric of life.

For Daly, most females have been seduced into cooperation with this "phallocratic" system of "necrophilia." They have become "fembots," robotized tools of male power, whose true life energy has been drained out of them and used to feed the vampirelike system of patriarchy.[19] Liberation comes for women by breaking the chains of false consciousness that hold them in bondage. For Daly the question is not so much the past history of the unfallen world, but rather of resurrecting it from underneath its smothered existence behind patriarchal false consciousness. The world of gynocentric life exists now, behind or as the Background of the patriarchal system of lies and death. Patriarchal false consciousness is the fallacious Foreground that women must deconstruct, reject, and leave. As they leave behind the patriarchal Foreground, they can leap into authentic life and reconnect with each other and with the real world of biotic interconnections.

Carol Christ is also a feminist of Christian background whose spiritual journey had led her to reject Christianity as essentially a culture of patriarchal oppression and war. She also believes that there was a gynocentric world of peace, gender equality, and harmony with "nature" behind the rise of patriarchy. However, she is more interested than Fox or Daly in locating that cultural shift historically.

Christ would agree with Fox that Christian fall/redemption spirituality is the problem, but would reject his belief that there is an alternative "true Christianity" that is ecofeminist. Christianity and other religions of patriarchal transcendence have taught us to look away from the mutable world of nature with its cycles of birth, death and decay, and regeneration, and its tragic costs of eating and being eaten. These religious cultures have taught us to identify our true selves with our capacity for abstract consciousness and to ally this abstracted self with an intellectual God outside of this process of mutability.[20]

In recent years Christ has put much emphasis on archaeological evidence from early urban agricultural towns in southeastern Europe, Turkey, and the Aegean islands, as interpreted particularly by Marija Gimbutas. Christ sees Gimbutas's work as proving that such a gynocentric, peaceful, egalitarian, and ecologically harmonious world once existed, prior to the rise of patriarchal warrior cultures in the bronze age (that is, 4500–2800 B.C.E.).[21] She has also joined the feminist Wicca movement and believes that, through its rituals that enshrine the natural energies and rhythms of nature and its immanent Goddess, we are put back in touch with that same Goddess who was worshiped by these ancient prepatriarchal cultures.[22]

Marija Gimbutas is an archaeologist who has worked to interpret the cult images and decorative symbolism found in Neolithic towns, such as Catal Hüyük in Anatolia. The excavation of these towns by archaeologists in the last thirty years has pushed the history of town life in the eastern Mediterranean back several millennia, showing that complex towns with extensive trade, agriculture, and livestock existed as far back as the eighth millennium B.C.E.

Catal Hüyük, a seventh-millennium town excavated by British archaeologist James Mellaart in the 1960s,[23] is particularly cited as proof of this benign matricentric society. Its lack of centralized public buildings, its female-identified cult objects in its many small shrines, and the fact that women had larger work and sleeping platforms than men in the houses are seen as evidence of high female status, lack of social hierarchy, and shared leadership between men and women. Its lack of a fortified city wall, military images, or evidence that it was ever conquered in its nine-hundred-year history are seen as indications of a nonviolent culture that existed prior to the advent of warfare.

Gimbutas has also studied a number of other sites of towns in "Old Europe" in the region of northern Greece and the Balkans. She has concluded that a relatively uniform culture existed in this region from upper Paleolithic times, being carried over from hunting-gathering societies into early agricultural towns. She sees these towns as having a social and political order of independent theocratic city-states ruled by queen/priestesses. They were socially unstratified, without hierarchies of wealthy rulers over against serf or slave laborers, but rather consisted of relatively equal households of rich "middle-class" farmers, traders, and artisans.[24]

Gimbutas believes that these societies also lacked any gender ranking. Males and females, although having different work roles, were seen as of equal value. They were matrilineal, tracing descent through the mother, who then associated herself with either a brother or husband who "supervised trade and agriculture." The central focus of worship was the Goddess, who incarnated the life energies of humans, animals, and plants in the cyclical process of birth, death, and regeneration.

The symbols on pottery, dress, sculptures, and mural art all reflect different aspects of this worship of this Goddess in her threefold aspect as giver of life, taker of life, and renewer of life. Females were the primary cult leaders, as the biological representatives of this work of generation and regeneration, while males and male symbols are appended to the Goddess and her priestesses in an auxiliary relationship. The female represents the "creative and eternal" aspect of nature, the male the "spontaneous and ephemeral" aspect of nature. Represented by male animals (bulls especially), phalluses, and ithyphallic animal-masked men, the male appears as "adjunct of the Goddess."[25]

Gimbutas sees this prosperous, egalitarian (in terms of both gender and class), peaceful, and ecologically harmonious world as having been violently overthrown by a series of invasions from patriarchal pastoralists, who came from the Pontic steppes in successive waves between 4500 B.C.E. and 2800 B.C.E. This was a militaristic, horse-riding society, ruled solely by males. Unlike agriculture, where, Gimbutas says, women predominated as food producers, pastoral control of animals is entirely in the hands of males and gives women little role or power. These "Kurgan" invaders lacked the high artistic culture of the Old European settlements. Their primary divine image was the sun, identified with the male. They subdued the early peaceful agricultural settlements, either destroying them or overlaying the earlier gynocentric culture with their patriarchal militarist one.[26]

This storyline of a once peaceful, gynocentric, agrarian world violently overthrown by militarist patriarchal invaders from the north has been popularized by Riane Eisler, in *The Chalice and the Blade,* who uses this view of prehistory to inspire contemporary Americans to reclaim such a peaceful and egalitarian "partnership" society today.[27] Unquestionably this story has powerful mythic appeal for people in the late twentieth century, deeply concerned by ecological and militarist threats to the earth; but is it really history?

One major problem with it is its post-Christian Romantic construction of the "feminine" as essentially and unchangingly

nurturant, benign, and peaceful, promoting mutuality and partnership. However good such values may seem for us today, to
project them on an ancient Neolithic people and to presume that
these must have been their values and their understanding of
both "woman" and "nature," on the grounds that they had a
"goddess-dominated" culture and society, is very questionable.
The stereotypic linking of these qualities with "women" and
"nature" together is also problematic.

James Mellaart, who is frequently cited by Christ, Eisler, and
others as corroborating Gimbutas's interpretation through his
excavations of Catal Hüyük and other early Anatolia towns, em-
phatically states that the scanty archaeological evidence can afford no basis for knowing how these towns were ordered socially
and politically. Mellaart sees evidence of a priestly class and of
social stratification, although not an extreme one, in Catal
Hüyük. He does not see Catal Hüyük and its surrounding as a
pacific culture. Rather, its builders created a city architecture in
which the blank outside walls of the densely packed houses provided an excellent defensive barrier against invaders. This defensive strategy worked to ward off such invaders as there may have
been during the nine hundred years (6500 B.C.E. to 5600 B.C.E.)
of its existence on its original site.

Mellaart also notes that Catal Hüyük society was well supplied with weapons: clubs, spears, daggers, bows and arrows,
and slingshots. There is a clear male-female distinction in associ-
ations with material culture; men were buried with weapons as
well as other artifacts, such as belt fasteners, and women with
mirrors, jewelry, and cosmetics. It is misleading to speak of Catal
Hüyük religion as focused solely on a goddess, for the actual
shrines show us two major complementary symbols, the Goddess
as representative of both birth and death and the bull as the sym-
bol of male virility. Male use of weapons was associated with
hunting, although they were available for defense against human
attackers as well.[28]

The Goddess is seen as the source of life, for humans, plants, and animals. She is typically depicted with arms raised and legs spread in the birthing position. Often the bull's head with curved horns appears beneath her outstretched legs, indicating that male virility saw itself as finding its source in her fecundity, but also as being the favored offspring of her generative power. The female breast also frequently appears, but symbolically mingled with the power of death. The breasts are often molded over the skulls of scavengers, such as vultures, with jaws or beaks protruding through the open nipples.

Catal Hüyük was concerned as much with death as with life. It practiced the exposure of corpses to vultures and insects that picked the bones clean, which were then buried under the platforms in the houses. Human skulls and images of vultures picking at the flesh of corpses appear frequently in the shrines. The association of the female breast with this work of vultures must have promoted an awesome, but not necessarily benign, view of women.

Both women and men were in the priestly class in different roles. This and the fact that female platforms in houses were larger than those associated with men, and that children were always buried with women and never with men, are often cited as indication of female power. But the relation between female sacral roles and political power is not automatic. The larger female platforms suggest that women did the child care and most of the indoor handicraft work, and thus needed larger work benches.

The fact that no centralized palace or other public buildings have been found is partly the result of the limited excavation, which concentrated on what Mellaart saw as the "priestly quarter." If this pattern actually continued throughout, we would have evidence for a dispersed form of political leadership, but this does not automatically translate into shared power between men and women. Catal Hüyük might have been organized around clan groups, in which several households each had their clan shrine. But how this translated into political power across gender or across the whole society is unknown.

Mellaart notes that the number of head wounds on the skeletons suggests that there was much quarreling and fighting among the inhabitants of the town, reflecting the "rabbit-warren" nature of the closely packed quarters of the town. Houses in Catal Hüyük were entered through the roof by ladders, something like the Pueblo Indian apartment towns in the American Southwest. There were no streets or alleys separating the rooms, but small courtyards were used to deposit trash and human wastes. In Mellaart one finds no dramatic story of "Kurgan" patriarchal warriors overthrowing peaceful agriculturalists in a several-millennia sweep from the steppes. Trade contacts from Mesopotamia are seen as the primary source of cultural changes that have been noted between Early and Middle Bronze age towns in Anatolia (c. 1900 B.C.E.).[29]

None of this disproves the possibility of some aspects of these Old European cultures that might have been more egalitarian and also more female-identified, at least culturally, than the cultures that succeeded them in the eastern Mediterranean. But it does suggest that feminists should not quickly build such evidence into a comprehensive story of an Eden-like world that was present not only in this limited region, but also, according to Christ, in "Africa, China, Indus Valley, and the Americas," prior to the rise of patriarchy.[30]

Why is it that Christ and others find this story of an idyllic prepatriarchal, gynocentric society so important? I suggest that this story plays an important mythical role in their thought. By uncovering a world before patriarchy, one also provides warrant for faith that such a society can happen again. The story affirms a faith in the nonessentiality of relations of domination. But this faith claim needs to be sorted out from what we can prove or not prove about prehistory, where we need to be more tentative and open to new evidence.

PALEOANTHROPOLOGY AND GENDER

Was there a world of ecofeminist harmony that was lost sometime between the Neolithic agricultural revolution and the emergence of classical civilizations? If we could recover that world, would it provide a model of egalitarian gender relations and harmony with nature for today? In the last several decades, there have been major advances in paleoanthropology through the study of the remains of ancient hominids. Comparison with the behavior of primates, particularly chimpanzees, also has been used to reconstruct the patterns of early hominid development. Such reconstructions are still hypothetical. But they provide important dialogue partners with the ecofeminist quest for understanding of prepatriarchal societies and the origins of patriarchy.

Many paleoanthropologists, such as Richard Leakey, believe that chimpanzees and humans shared a common ancestor; the line leading to humans split from that of chimpanzees about 4 million years ago.[31] After considerable evolutionary experimentation, and the extinction of hominid lines that proved unsuccessful, *Homo habilis,* using stone tools, emerged about 2 million years ago.

Further advances in the ability to refine tools, create carrying containers, and communicate in complex language emerged gradually, enabling humans to hunt larger animals, replacing earlier patterns of scavenging dead animals or hunting small or immature animals. This development of hunting larger animals with weapons took place about 500,000 years ago, while the development of pastoralism and gardening took place between 12,000 and 10,000 years ago, providing the basis for more complex villages and then early urban communities.

Leakey claims that human evolutionary development took place originally in the savanna regions of Africa. Only after the development of the hunting-gathering pattern of life did the ancestors of *Homo sapiens, Homo erectus,* move out of Africa and spread into south Asia and Europe (about 350,000 years ago), eventually finding their way across the Pacific and into the Americas. The migration was driven by gradual population expansion and the need to colonize new regions for hunting and gathering, a mode of life that can only sustain a limited population in any region. By about 10,000 B.C.E., humans had expanded into the temperate and even lower arctic regions of Europe and Asia, and were widely dispersed in the Pacific and the Americas.

Probably the development of large-scale hunting and of fire allowed humans to survive in colder climates, cooking and preserving food and living in caves during the winter. Meat-eating may have greatly increased its share of the human diet in this period, particularly during the upper Paleolithic Ice Age. In colder areas, where vegetation was absent in winter, meat perhaps became the primary staple of the human diet. Mark Cohen, in *The Food Crisis in Prehistory,*[32] suggests that this era of concentration on hunting as the main component of the human diet led to a destruction of many large mammals. Expanding human population thus struck its first ecological crisis.

The response to this crisis of expanding population and dwindling herds was to turn to a more intensive gathering of foods that had hitherto been ignored: smaller animals, including rodents, fish, and shellfish, and also tubers, grains, and other vegetable foods. This increasing dependence on vegetable foods precipitated the development of agriculture. Tribal groups began to mark off fields with wild grains as "theirs" for managed harvesting, and then began to scatter the seeds to renew the next harvest. Fixed cultivation and grain storage made permanent villages necessary.

Nancy Tanner draws from studies of the social organization observed in chimpanzees today for clues of early hominid society during the gathering stage. The core social organization of chimpanzees she sees as matricentric. The basic social tie is that of mother and child. From the biological tie of birth-giver and suckler of the child, the mother also assumes the basic roles of food-gatherer for herself and for her young offspring. A primary social group of mother, immature offspring, and sometimes older daughters and their offspring is formed. This may continue as a tie between sisters after the death of the mother.[33]

Adolescent males, however, tend to split off and scavenge for themselves individually or in male sibling pairs. They seek sexual satisfaction from females of other matricentric groups, sometimes winning such favors in exchange for the food they have gathered. Some females are drawn into pairing relationships with males. But the relation is unstable and reverts to the matricentric pattern as the female bears more offspring with other males. Tanner sees early hominids as following a similar pattern.[34]

Paleoanthropologist Margaret Ehrenberg also sees early hominid society as matricentric. Moreover, she sees the female, particularly as mother, as taking the leading role in key human evolution, contrary to male anthropologists, who have regarded males as hunters playing the leading roles in evolution. It is females as mothers who are the primary food-sharers, and thus create the core of human social organization. Males generally gather for themselves, eating on the spot, rather than carrying food back to a site to share with others. It is the female who socializes males to share.[35]

As both mother and food-sharer, it was women who pioneered bipedalism in order to pick and carry food as they gathered, while also carrying children. They also were the inventors of containers, to carry both babies and food, to free their hands for gathering. Weaving grasses into carrying containers and then storage baskets is an essential invention by women related to women's combined roles. Most early human tools were probably created first by women, such as digging sticks to uncover insects, and stone tools for cracking, pounding, and grinding food. Such tool use began with chimpanzees, and thus preceded by millions of years the development of weapons by men to hunt larger animals.

Women probably also developed fire to cook food, as well as the arts of treating skins of animals and weaving animal hair for clothing. As plant-gatherers they were the ones who first began to scatter some grain they gathered to assure new growth, and thus became the first agriculturalists. Women's roles thus are key to human biological, social, and technological evolution.

More complex human social organizations can take several forms from this foundation. They can be superstructures erected over this matricentric core of human society, as in matrilineal, matrilocal societies. They can also seek to make the pairing relation more permanent and exclusive, honoring both bloodlines. From the pairing relation they can move to exclusively patrilineal societies, which negate this matricentric core altogether by the fiction that the female has been "transferred" to the control of the male, who then forms the sole true line of progeny.

How the matricentric core of mother-child relations is linked to the family of the father(s) of her children is crucial for understanding female status in society. For example, in a matrilineal society like the Iroquois, the long house and gardens were female-owned and run, while leadership in the warrior confederacy was male. But the male intertribal leaders acknowledged the maternal source of their power. Women named the male league leaders and could veto their decisions.[36]

Do male-dominant societies develop when grown men, split off from the matricentric core, bond together and capture women as wives from other groups? These women as wives might then be seen as possessions and slaves of the men for sex, reproduction, and work. A refinement of bride-capture is bride-purchase. The female in either case is taken out of her matrifocal kinship group and attached to the male and his kin, being defined as a subordinate possession of her husband.[37] The spontaneously altruistic maternal ethic of sharing food with children is thus turned into forced labor as service to a ruling husband.

According to paleoanthropologist Richard Leakey, matricentric scavenging/hunting-gathering societies were quite stable. They sustained hominid and early human society for millions of years, until the beginnings of pastoral and agricultural life some 12,000 to 10,000 years ago. Some examples have lasted into the twentieth century, although almost all such societies are being extinguished today by the encroachment of westernized patterns.[38]

The !Kung-San of the Kalahari desert is one group that has been studied as an example of a matrifocal hunting-gathering society that has lasted into the twentieth century, although it is rapidly being forced by the government into sedentary male-dominated households. The most stable hunting-gathering societies have been maintained in climates where animal and plant food is available year round and human population is widely scattered. The core food-gathering band of about thirty people roam together in a territory where their rights are accepted by other groups. Plant food provides the majority of the diet (70 percent to 80 percent). Women are the gatherers and processors of plant food, and they also gather insects and capture small rodents and lizards.

Males hunt alone or in pairs with an adolescent male. The food they capture is much more occasional than that provided by the women. Hunting is granted a high prestige, and the capture of a large animal becomes the occasion of a feast for the community. But the !Kung-San also have developed a strong ethic of egalitarianism that prevents any male from becoming dominant on the basis of hunting prowess. The successful hunter is to be modest and play down his success. He does not gain status over others by such success, but rather is acknowledged through his willingness to share his kill. Nothing is saved long term, but the fruits of gathering are shared within a few days.[39]

The seemingly arid climate of the desert provided the !Kung-San an abundant living, based on skillful use of all the resources of their environment, including insect food. Traditionally women and children in their groups and men in theirs could gather enough to sustain the whole community in a few hours each day, although the men were much more likely to return empty-handed from hunting. This meant that there was considerable leisure time, in which the community gathered for intense social life: trance-dancing, story telling, exchange of gifts, and rites of passage.

Each core group understands itself as linked to several others in complex kin relations, and these gather in larger groups periodically through the year. Although women are in charge of child-care, their work is balanced by the hours spent by men in hunting, so the work hours of men and women are approximately equal. Men spend about twenty-one hours a week hunting, and women twelve hours a week gathering food. Women carry small children with them and do most of the food processing.

In virtually all the hunting-gathering societies that have been studied, a basic gender division of labor seems to have developed, in which women and smaller children gather plant food, and men are in charge of hunting larger animals. Studies of these societies have shown that vegetable foods are the major part of the diet (around 70 percent), and have suggested that the role of hunting has been greatly exaggerated in anthropological studies. Many tools have been automatically classified as hunting tools, used by men, when they may have been grinding tools used by women. Also the digging sticks, carrying baskets, and vegetable foods disappear from the archaeological record, while arrowheads and animal bones remain. This, combined with the imposition of modern male-dominant prejudices, has skewed the picture of pre-historical human societies.

Female power and prestige in hunter-gatherer societies is rooted in organized control by women of the food that they supply to the group. When the females of a kin group are split from each other, and women are incorporated under the control of husbands, women lose this power and prestige. Women do not necessarily do less work in male-dominated societies. Indeed, in many male-dominated tribal groups today, women work longer than men. Women do the child care, gathering or planting, harvesting, food processing, make most of the clothing and containers, seek and carry wood and water, and do the cleaning. Long hours of female labor are the basis for more leisure for men, leisure to be spent in rituals of male-bonding.

The key issue of female power and prestige seems to be the extent of women's control of their own products as a female group. How does this square with Cohen's suggestions of a food crisis in the late Paleolithic period leading to an increased diversification of foods and then to the Neolithic agricultural revolution? Cohen believes that we should see in modern hunter-gatherers not a picture of ancient ones of 500,000 to 10,000 years ago, but rather a new adaptation that began as the large animals became scarcer. If this is the case, high male prestige in hunting is archaic, having actually become a minor part of the survival of the group. The predominant plant-gathering of women represents a more recent adaptation to disappearing wildlife.

If, as I have suggested, the loss of a major contribution to the food supply, and collective control over that contribution, undermine the female power base in hunter-gatherer societies, then we might suppose that female power would have declined in the period of migrations and intensified hunting. However, female power would have been renewed and expanded as wildlife declined and human communities turned to alternative sources of food, animal and vegetable, most of it supplied by women. The transition to more sedentary patterns, focused on harvesting wild plants and then on gardening, very likely was led by women. Women were thus closely linked with plant cultivation in early Neolithic villages.

In gardening societies women often are seen as owning the household, which was also the setting for childcare and for female collective labor in preparing food and making baskets, clothes, and other artifacts of daily life. The fields, which women cultivated, also are seen as belonging to women. Men thus became auxiliary to a female-led Neolithic revolution. Their contribution through hunting continued to carry status, but it declined as the actual contribution to the diet. Small domesticated animals generally are seen as belonging to women, herds of larger animals to men.[40]

If hunter-gatherer groups passed through a considerable period where hunting was the major part of the diet, and only later became more reliant on the female gathering and then gardening roles, this might suggest various adaptations of social patterns. In some regions, especially very cold or hot, dry ones, where edible plants were sparse, the male hunting role allowed men to predominate in prestige and power. Patrilocal and patrilineal social patterns might develop. Women were captured or traded into clans of the men who were to be their husbands and were seen as subservient to them.

As wildlife became scarcer, these groups adapted to the food crisis by becoming pastoralists. From following herds and culling limited numbers each season, tribal groups began to define these herds as "belonging" to them. As herds of larger animals were domesticated, they were defined as the property of the leading men of the clan. Thus pastoralism strengthened and confirmed nascent patriarchal social patterns. Women were traded from one clan to another in exchange for cattle or other animals, equating both women and animals as property of dominant males.

Other groups adapted to the crisis of declining wildlife by much more intensive exploitation of the diverse food options in their region. Women's role as gatherer expanded and was consolidated, allowing matrilineal hunter-gathers, such as the !Kung-San, to continue in marginal areas up to the twentieth century.

A third group, which became the main line of human development, moved from intensified plant-gathering to agriculture. During a considerable period of transition into Neolithic farming villages, women's prestige and power may have expanded. There is good evidence that in the proto-Neolithic and Neolithic periods in the ancient Near East, female fecundity was seen as the primal expression of the life force, and male virility, while also celebrated, was seen as dependent on it. This may also have been the pattern in the Indus Valley region.[41]

What happened to undermine this female-centered culture of Neolithic farming villages and early civilizations? Did militant patriarchal pastoralists from the North invade and subjugate groups with a totally opposite culture? I would suggest a more complex pattern. The bull cult and hunting rituals of male bonding were not so docilely "adjunct to the Goddess" as Gimbutas and others claim. Moreover, the view of woman as death-bringer, as well as source of life, carried ambivalent feelings toward female power and male dependency on it. (We don't have to decide here whether males or females shaped these symbols. Both may have shaped them, but also read them from different perspectives.)

Although actual hunting receded as a food source, the weapons of hunting remained identified with males. As humans became sedentary, population expanded and differences of accumulated wealth appeared. Social stratification within settlements, conflicts with rival settlements, and challenges from migrating nomads increased. The weapons of hunting were at hand to become the weapons of war, owned and controlled by males.[42]

Another key element lay in the male ownership of herds of larger animals. When plow agriculture was invented, by yoking cattle and using them to pull large digging tools, men were able to redefine both land and its products as belonging to them. Thus as Ehrenberg shows, between 6000 B.C.E. and 2000 B.C.E. we see several shifts that allow for the emergence of patriarchy. Before plow agriculture, plants and gardening are a female sphere. Once the plow pulled by cattle is invented, it is men only who are shown doing the plowing, as well as the milking of these animals.[43]

Whether or not it was invading males who first seized the tools of animal hunting as the tools of war, the males defending their settlements against such invasions would have quickly learned to reciprocate. The plow was the tool of male dominance over animals and land. Together with the sword, these tools become the means for male conquest of other men and finally of their own women. These tools and weapons were not simply imposed on the ancient Near Eastern cities by outside "aliens." They also reflected internal developments related to sedentary life, population expansion, and accumulation.

Competition for resources—not just from outside immigrants, but also from within—led to early urbanization. Priestly elites arose who monopolized new knowledge and symbolic power, that is, literacy and astronomical calculations. A warrior class also developed among males who adapted male hunting skills into organized defense against competing human groups. Thus we have the foundations of priestly, scribal, and warrior aristocracies of the classical cultures of the ancient Near East. These aristocracies created fortified urban areas and defined the surrounding peasant villages as serf labor under their control.

Increased warfare led to the defeat of attacking groups and then to offensive war. The adult males of conquered populations were killed, and females and children enslaved. As aristocracies defined new legal social systems of control over land, and over peasant and slave labor, male-female relations within the ruling group was redefined. Women of the ruling group, who may have shared in earlier stages of aristocratic power, become redefined in law codes of the period from 3000 B.C.E. to 500 B.C.E. This is reflected in the Babylonian code of Hammurabi, the Hebraic Law codes, and the sixth-century Athenian codes of Solon.[44]

These codes defined women as strictly subordinate to the males of their own family and to those of their husband's family. In this way the classical patriarchal legal and social patterns of the classical world were constructed, based on the hierarchy of aristocracies over serf and slave labor, their control of land and of knowledge, and the subordination of women to men within these ruling aristocracies.

One should not assume that subordination of women is always the first subordination, only then followed by slavery and class hierarchy. Some aristocracies of early cities may have evolved from gardening patterns that enshrined female agricultural power, and first allowed for some male-female parity as priestesses and queens. As systems of slavery and class hierarchy were erected, eventually women of the aristocracy became redefined as subordinate. This seems to have happened as a later stage of the patriarchal revolution of some early urban civilizations.[45]

CONTEMPORARY ANTHROPOLOGY AND GENDER

This sketch of human evolution into early urban civilization is very general and hypothetical, and by no means can be assumed to be final. Contemporary indigenous, non-Western cultures can offer a complementary perspective for evaluating the factors that may have undermined matricentric societies and led to patriarchy.

Peggy Reeves Sanday, in her book *Female Power and Male Dominance: On the Origins of Sexual Inequality,* studied 150 tribal societies in an effort to discern basic patterns that make for gender parity or male dominance in early human development.[46] She defined gender equality not as sameness of male-female roles, but rather as a balance of power between the genders, based in most cases on men and women having different spheres of activity. In her study she was able to discern a number of correlations characterizing societies of relative gender parity versus those that are male-dominated.

Societies with gender parity virtually always have creation myths that attribute the creation either to a female or a male and female together. By contrast male-dominant societies typically have male-only creation stories. Male-dominant societies also have rigid gender segregation and little male parenting of smaller children. More egalitarian societies have less gender segregation. Gender lines are more fluid, and women and men do a lot of work together. There is not a rigid concept of some work as only for men or only for women. Typically males are more integrated into early childcare in such societies as well.

Of the societies that she studied, Sanday found that 32 percent were characterized by gender equality, where women had economic and political power in balance with that of men and there was no male aggressive violence against women. Twenty-eight percent of the societies she studied were markedly male-dominated. In these societies women, while doing much of the labor, were excluded from economic and political decision making and were subject to a high level of male aggression in the form of beating and rape.

However, Sanday also found an intermediate group of some 40 percent of the societies, which she characterized as conflictual. Here women had considerable economic power, based on organized control of their productive labor, but they were excluded from areas of political decisions monopolized by males. Males, although lacking full actual dominance, had developed ritualized dominance based on male-bonding clubs and rites, in which they acted out myths of the overthrow of female (maternal) power by men.[47] It is this conflictual group that I think helps us to understand the internal psychosocial vulnerability of matricentric social organization that leads to its subversion by male domination.

The psychosocial weakness of matricentric society lies in its difficulty in drawing in the contribution of the grown male without either conceding to this male a dominating role over women, or else producing a demoralized male deeply resentful of women. The root problem lies in the extension of the female childbearing and suckling functions into making the mother the dominant parent, together with primary food-gathering and food-sharing roles. Males are then somewhat auxiliary to the life-sustaining processes, both in food production and in reproduction, and can experience this as uncertainty about the male role.[48]

While the female role is built into the process of life-reproduction and food-gathering, the male role has to be constructed socially. Societies that fail to develop an adequately affirmative role for men, one that gives men prestige parallel to that of women but prevents their assuming aggressive dominance over women, risk developing the resentful male, who defines his masculinity in hostile negation of women. The symbolic negation of women in conflictual societies provides the myths through which actual dominance over women is promoted and justified.

The societies that have achieved gender parity in Sanday's study were societies that either had elaborately structured mutual acknowledgment of male and female prestige and power, where women conceded power roles to men and men acknowledged that they received these from women, or else societies of considerable gender-role fluidity. The Mbuti (pygmys) are an example of the first type. In the *Molimo* ceremony, undertaken periodically to awaken the powers of life in the forest, the all-giver of life, an old woman scatters the fire and men gather the embers together again. Later an old woman ties the men together. When men acknowledge their defeat and give gifts to the woman, they are untied by the old woman and blessed. Thus the ceremony serves as a continual righting of the balance of male-female power.[49]

The (traditional) Balinese are an example of role fluidity. Every child was seen as male-female unity. Gender differentiation develops in adolescence, but considerable cross-dressing and role fluidity based on individual interests were allowed. After marriage people again became androgynous.[50] Pacific, gender-egalitarian societies generally have lived in mild climates with abundant resources and stabilized populations that prevent intense competition with other human groups. Such societies thus did not face an adversarial struggle for survival with their human or nonhuman surroundings.

But the stability of such gender-balanced societies can be upset by a number of factors. New methods of agriculture and food storage may lead to rapid expansion of population, creating more crowded housing patterns. Competition for resources arises both within the society and over against nearby rivals. The male tools of organized hunting are converted into those of warfare with other human groups, while within the society class hierarchies and male domination develop.

When there is a conflict over resources, with harsh climatic conditions and competing groups, such conflicts often seem to be acted out, not only externally, in an adversarial view of other people and of nature, but also internally, in male definitions of women. The female body becomes the symbolic terrain on which the struggle for resources is acted out. The female body, particularly in menstruation and sexual relations, is seen as dangerous to male potency. Men strengthen themselves, particularly for hunting and war, by avoidance of women in these conditions.[51]

In these male definitions of female sexuality and blood as dangerous to male potency, there is a symbolic reversal of life and death in which women, the life-givers, are defined as threats of death, and male acts of killing are defined as sources of life. The male warrior God as transcendent source of all life, demoting the Goddess of birth and growth as the bearer of sin and death, is the ultimate expression of this reversal.

Why does the conflict of men against nature and other social groups get expressed in hostility toward women in their own societies as well? One aspect of the scapegoating of women by males under stress can be explained by the basic insecurity of the mother-parented male who makes his way to adult male status through mother-negation. Sanday suggests that, under environmental stress, scapegoating of women is accentuated in those societies that already have conflictual patterns; that is, where male resentment of female maternity has not been successfully balanced by adult male cultural roles.[52]

CONCLUSIONS

One has to ask whether elements of male resentment are not built into the matricentric pattern. The matricentric core of human society remains, even under male hierarchies, and continually reproduces the insecure, resentful male, who emancipates himself from his mother by negation of women. Unlike his sister, becoming an adult does not give the boy a ready way into becoming a nurturer himself. Rather, the male ego seems to oscillate between domination of inferiors and subjugation to superiors.

Modern societies that have long been officially patriarchal retain this matricentric core of the family. When the patriarchal superstructure fails to function, the matricentric core of the female-headed household, sometimes a three-generational female-headed household, emerges as the survival unit. This is as true of the slums of industrial America as it is of the *bantustans* of South Africa.[53] This mother-children-siblings core family, to which males from other families loosely attach themselves, might be a stable, successful unit in a gathering economy; but in an industrial or colonial economy, such families command the poorest resources and form the impoverished bottom rung of society.

In such female-headed households, the mother or adult female group becomes the main provider, working long hours at low pay, while also trying to play the nurturing role in the family. The husbands and fathers are marginal visitors, and all too often the sons grow up to repeat the same patterns. Adult male prestige, denied as economic prowess, is acted out through sexual and physical domination of women. The unemployed son or husband, demoralized by the dominant patriarchal and hierarchical society, disdains to help with housework and childcare lest he compromise his "masculinity" thereby.

But the males of the ruling class, while seemingly afforded an overabundance of proofs of power and prestige, exhibit a limitless appetite for more such validations to fill the bottomless void of male insecurity. The endless quest for absolute power and control, now fueled by modern technology of industry and war, thus brings human society to the brink of annihilation. A recent paradigm of this was seen in the 1991 Persian Gulf War in which a patriarchal Anglo-American faced a patriarchal Arab across a desert filled with modern death machinery, each refusing to concede to the other lest he "lose face."

In gatherer and early gardening societies, built on the matricentric core of the human family, women often had real power and prestige, when food-gathering and agriculture also meant female control of resources. Such societies achieved real gender parity of power when they constructed ways of drawing in the adult male contribution to work and parenting, conceding to him real and symbolic spheres of prestige and power, while limiting male aggression. But the conditions of such societies began to break down as the agricultural revolution moved toward more crowded urban societies about five thousand years ago, and only remnants still exist today.

There can be no literal return to a Neolithic matricentric village as a basis of gender parity today. Reclaiming the memory of these earlier cultures, and valuing the cultures and spiritualities that still subsist today among indigenous peoples who preserve remnants of earlier patterns, can be immensely valuable to the wholeness we seek. But we also need to learn the lessons of the weaknesses of the matricentric core of human society that made it vulnerable to patriarchy. This critique is absent in female-identified visions, such as those of Daly or Christ.

The separatist vision of Mary Daly takes the feminist critique of patriarchy into a denouement where the male is negated as a fellow human. This undermines the humanist promise of feminism and offers no real hope of resolving the male-female conflict in society. Carol Christ, along with Marija Gimbutas and Riane Eisler, seek an egalitarian society. They assume that a matricentric society was and would be one where such equality of men and women, as well as harmony with "nature," would be promoted. But they have failed to recognize the problems for male adult identity when the male remains only the "son of the Great Mother," and a responsible adult male is absent.

If, as I have suggested, this matricentric pattern is itself the breeding ground of male resentment and violence, rooted in male strategies of exploitative subversion of women's power, then a new pattern of mutual parenting must balance maternal primacy in reproduction. We need to structure new forms of gender parity. This must begin by changing a pattern that goes back to the beginnings of hominid development and even earlier; that is, the social construction of the primacy of maternal gestation into the primacy of early childhood nurture and domestic labor by women. Men and women must share fully the parenting of children from birth and the domestic work associated with daily life.

A genuine change in the pattern of parenting must be understood, not as a slight adjustment toward males "helping" females with childcare, but a fundamental reconstruction of the primary roots of culture, transforming the gender imaging of child-parent relations and the movement into adulthood for both males and females. This implies a reconstruction of the relation of the domestic core of society to the larger society. One must look at all the hierarchies of exploitation and control that emanate out of the family pattern of female mothering and domestic labor.

Can such a shift from gender asymmetry to shared homemaking and nurture of new life make any significant difference in the huge systems of violence and destruction of the earth that presently threaten the earth? Simply seen in isolation, such changes can do little and may be used to psychologize and privatize complex structural problems. We must work on new understandings of culture and power relations in all dimensions of society.

Yet we must also see their interconnections, and their deepest roots in male socialization into violence through mother negation. To create a new society, we will need men (and women) with new psyches. Patriarchal family patterns are basic to shaping the old psyches. New egalitarian family patterns will be essential to shaping new psyches in which women can be affirmed as partners, and men commit themselves to sustaining ongoing life on earth.

7

Constructing the Systems
of Domination

This chapter will survey major elements in social structure and culture that both shaped and reflected the systems of patriarchal domination that the West inherits from its past. I will look at the patterns of domination and its justification in the Mesopotamian, Hebrew, and Greek worlds during the primary era of the emergence and consolidation of patriarchal, classist, and militarist societies and cultures. I will then look at the way these social and cultural patterns of domination were reshaped by the synthesis of asceticism, apocalypticism, and Christianity in the Middle Ages and then reshaped again by Calvinism, the scientific revolution, colonialism, and industrialization in the sixteenth to nineteenth centuries, giving us the world of poverty, war, and ecological crisis that we now face.

There is no suggestion here that either the West or Christian tradition is uniquely responsible for these evils. Indeed, the second millennium B.C.E. to mid-first millennium C.E. also saw somewhat similar patriarchal, hierarchical, and militarist societies emerge in other regions of classical culture, such as the Indus Valley, China, and Mesoamerica. Western Europe was able to take a new kind of global power role primarily during the modern era of colonialism, during which time its new scientific and industrial patterns were imperialistically imposed on the rest of the world.

THE ANCIENT MEDITERRANEAN EMPIRES: MESOPOTAMIA

The stages that shaped the patriarchal world of emerging empires of the late fourth millennium B.C.E., when writing and hence "history" began, are difficult to trace, as we have seen in the previous chapter. We can imaginatively reconstruct these steps from the resulting system. But the earlier patterns remain unknown, tantalizingly suggested by artistic and archaeological artifacts and traces of suppressed female power in later myth.[1]

The Sumerian cities of Ur, Uruk, Nippur, Kish, and Lagash were planted between 4000 B.C.E and 3000 B.C.E., and the system of cuneiform writing was perfected by the end of that period. The earliest tablets that give account records, laws, and legends of the Sumerians are a thousand years later, from the third millennium.[2] In these records the patrilineal family, slavery, an aristocratic priesthood, and a warrior nobility, who control most of the land and rule over a peasantry as well as a slave labor force, are all firmly established.

One historian of ancient Babylonia dates the beginnings of slavery to 4000 B.C.E., thus making it coincide with the origins of these cities.[3] If this is so, then the patriarchal reordering of the family, its definition of land as patrilineal property, the scribal religious elites who controlled written records, the development of war, and the warrior nobility probably all emerged as part of an interconnected process. Slaves came from groups conquered in war, where the custom was to kill the adult males and enslave the women and children. But slaves also originated from the poor, those who fell into debt and sold their children, wives, and even themselves to pay their debts. Abandoned surplus children also supplied slaves. In all these categories, women predominated. Even male household slaves were female-identified, lacking legal paternity and known by their mother's name, since their mother's sexual and reproductive potency, as well as their labor, was owned by the master of the household.[4]

The importance of the institution of slavery in Sumeria is suggested by the fact that it provides the dominant metaphor for all hierarchy, including the divine-human relationship. An early Sumerian story of the creation of humans imagines a time before there were humans, when the gods had to do their own work. At one point the gods go "on strike," throwing down their picks and shovels and refusing to work. The solution is to create human beings as slaves of the gods to free the gods from physical labor.[5] The same idea appears in the *Enuma Elish,* the Babylonian creation epic (which was discussed in chapter 1). Here Marduk creates "man" by mixing the blood of Tiamat's slain consort, Kingu, with clay. "He shall be charged with the service of the gods that they might be at ease."[6]

Although class hierarchy of royal and priestly families was strongly established, women within these families played roles of real power, but they did so as extensions of male power. Queens, as wives of kings, were delegated large palace and temple complexes, where they governed their human and material assets. It was also customary to place princesses, as daughters of kings, as priestesses and rulers of temple complexes. These female governors of temple and palace property were appointed because of their relation to their husbands and fathers. They were dependent on them for their power, although third-millennium Sumerian tradition does record one reigning queen, Ku-Baba, the ruler of Kish.[7]

Babylonian society clearly saw women as competent economic administrators, and leading families made use of both male and female family members to govern their extended lands and work force. Yet the patrilineal and patrilocal family system created problems of alienation of family property through the dowries of daughters who are attached by marriage to other male lineages. One strategy to prevent this was to focus dowries on "movables," jewelry and household goods, bestowing lands and slaves on daughters very sparingly in comparison to sons.[8] But Babylonian society also worked out several ways in which daughters could remain attached to their father's household.

One such method was the legal fiction of a daughter who inherited from her father "as a son," in the case of a man who lacked a son. Here the daughter could be appointed to be her father's "son," her husband would then move into her family's household, and her children would be attached to her father's lineage rather than to that of her husband.[9] Another strategy was to keep royal daughters unmarried. The institution of the *naditu,* or community of priestesses, who remain unmarried and administer temple property was such a method. Although the *naditu* could not marry, they could adopt a child from their own lineage, who could then inherit their property.[10] In this way the patrilineal family could keep the property it gave to its daughters under its extended power.

The analysis of women's history through the three-millennia history of Mesopotamian city-states and empires (to the end of the Persian period in 331 B.C.E.) is still rudimentary, but there seems to be a pattern of decline of women's status over this period. Women become more firmly subordinate to fathers and husbands, the status of institutions like *naditus* decline, and women are no longer given wide spheres of government, as seemed to have been the practice in some third- and second-millennia societies.[11]

When we turn to the mythological realm, the idea of goddesses remains very powerful, but they are increasingly subordinate to male deities in the pantheon. In the *Enuma Elish,* as we have already noted in chapter 1, the central Babylonian creation story focuses on the defeat of the ancient Mother Goddess,

Tiamat, and the construction of the cosmos out of her dead body by the reigning god, Marduk.

A second myth of renewal of nature played a key role in Ancient Near Eastern and also Egyptian society. In this myth the god-king is defeated by the powers of drought and death and resurrected by his goddess sister-wife. In the Sumerian version of this story, however, Inanna appears as an imperious queen, challenging her sister Ereshkigal, Queen of the Underworld. Inanna makes her own descent into the underworld and provides means for her own eventual release. She punishes her male consort, Dumuzi, Shepherd-King of Uruk, for failing to be sufficiently attentive to her needs by consigning him to the underworld for half of the year.

In the parallel Canaanite story of Anath and Ba'al, from the second millennium B.C.E., Anath also is imperious, storming into the presence of her divine Father, El, and pulling his gray hair, to protest the dishonor of her husband, Ba'al. Anath goes into action when Ba'al is defeated by his brother Mot, god of drought and death. She kills Mot in battle and resurrects Ba'al, seating him again on the royal throne.

In the two versions of this story of seasonal regeneration, the goddess represents the abiding cosmic powers of life, and the king-consort the seasonal powers of dying and rising vegetation and cycles of drought and rain. Both Inanna and Anath are imagined as highly domineering, capable of great anger and power, in the manner of queens, not nurturing mothers. But Inanna fights for her own honor and power. It is her drama of descent and resurrection that is central, while Anath's power is put entirely on behalf of the honor and power of her consort, Ba'al.

Although ancient Near Eastern cultural consciousness never lost a sense of female power as foundational to the cosmos and society, we seem to see here a process in which this female-identified cosmic power is increasingly domesticated. It is seen either as conquered by force, and turned into "matter" for male cosmic technology, or else it is put totally at the disposal of the god-kings, who are reestablished on their thrones through the power of the goddess.

WOMEN IN ANCIENT ISRAEL

Women's status in ancient Israel varies, for the records span a thousand years and quite diverse political and economic systems. But Israel exhibits from the beginning the marks of a strongly patriarchal society of peasant pastoralists. Unlike Mesopotamian society, where class hierarchy was central, and gender hierarchy was modified by spheres of female power within family systems, Israel exhibits resistance to the class hierarchy of the urban agricultural world into which it entered as settlers of Canaan.[12]

In Hebrew thought the ideal remained one of equality of men as householders who come together as the assembly of Israel. Although slavery is accepted, this is to be modified in the case of Hebrew slaves. The God who liberated his people from slavery does not allow Hebrews to be held as slaves in perpetuity. Periodic redistribution of land and cancellation of debts is imagined as the means to overcome accumulated property distinctions and restore the ideal of equality between male householders.[13]

However, in this system of male community, females are rigorously marginalized. Women do not receive the Torah from God on Sinai. They are banished so that men can be pure to receive God's covenant.[14] The covenant is given to the male assembly of Israel, and women are defined by it but are not members of it in their own right. The ceremonies of initiation into membership in the covenant, circumcision and *bar mitzvah*, are exclusively male. Women are excluded from studying the Law and have only limited areas of observance of it. They also cannot inherit property, except as placeholders for male heirs, nor can they testify or make contracts.[15] In relation to both God and society, woman lacks autonomous personhood and is represented by the male head of family.

Hebrew myth expresses not only the subordination of female power, but even the suppression of the memory of it. This is revealed in many key stories. One is the creation of Eve from Adam's rib to be his helpmeet. This story banishes entirely the birthing mother as the source of human life. Instead the male is defined as the original and normative person, created from clay and breath by a Father God acting without female consort. The female is fashioned out of the "side" of the male to be auxiliary to him by the Father God. This story reflects the final stage of the male puberty drama, where woman as mother is not only overthrown but disappears, and woman as wife is "created" as a secondary being, adjunct to her husband.[16]

A second key biblical story is the attempted sacrifice of Isaac by Abraham. Central to the Abraham story is his paramount need for a male heir from his legitimate wife, Sarah, a male heir who will be the source of the paternal lineage of the people of Israel. When this child is finally born, miraculously, in his and Sarah's old age, nevertheless Abraham must prove his total loyalty to the patriarchal God by showing his willingness to sacrifice this son. In so doing the right of the mother to her own children is so totally negated as to be absent as even a factor in the drama.[17]

The institution of kingship and city life with the Davidic monarchy conflicted with earlier male egalitarian ideals. It also brought Israel into closer proximity to the Canaanite patterns of renewal of kingship through annual rituals of death and rebirth and marriage with the Goddess. There is evidence that elements of Goddess worship were present for much of the history of the Solomonic temple, but these were rigorously banished from legitimacy by Yahwist reformers who shaped the existing biblical documents.[18]

One way to handle this threat of the Goddess was to assimilate the symbols of the sacred marriage, but to reverse its gender pattern. In the Babylonian myths, the Goddess is primary and the god-king represents the human community elevated to divine status through her. In the Hebrew use of sacred marriage symbolism, however, God is elevated above the cosmic process altogether, preexisting the world and creating it by his Word. A female deity is banished from the heavens, although remnants of a female personification of the divine remain in the Wisdom and Shekhinah figures. In these figures the divine feminine represents God's immanence within creation, subordinate to a male transcendence.[19]

In Hebrew scripture the covenant of God and Israel comes to be imaged as a marriage. But in this marriage the male is the divine "Lord," while the human community is identified as subordinate wife. This transcendent Lord, who espouses Israel as his wife, also claims to be the authentic source of earth's fecundity, thereby negating the rival claims of Ba'al and Anath. Israel as "whore" is defined as the counterpart to Israel as wife, the image of the woman punished by her Lord for infidelity.[20]

> She did not know that it was I [God] who gave her the grain, the wine and the oil . . . Therefore I will take back my grain in its time and my wine in its season and I will take away my wool and my flax . . . I will punish her for the festival days of the Ba'als . . . when she went after her lovers, and forgot me, says the Lord. (Hosea 2:8, 9, 13)

In Hebrew thought the line between divine and human is more rigidly drawn, and gender hierarchy is used to demarcate the realm of the divine and the holy from the realm of the human and the unclean, with the female representing both the creaturely and the unclean. Procreational potency is denied to the female and to the earth and appropriated by a male divine power that stands above and outside the earth. This divine Lord also appropriates the power of drought and infertility, using these to punish those who seek after Ba'al (the name of Anath is never mentioned in the Bible) as the source of renewal of agricultural fecundity.

WOMEN IN CLASSICAL ATHENS

When we turn to classical Athens, we find a culture that, like the Mesopotamian cultures, had strong goddess cults and told myths that testify to archaic female power. But it also exhibits a vehement struggle to subdue matricentric power, a struggle that remains overt rather than banished from memory, as in the Hebrew stories. Hellenic culture stood on the heritage of ancient Mycenae, a patriarchal and warrior society of the late Bronze Age (1400 B.C.E–1000 B.C.E.), which in turn drew on the memory of Minoan culture of the second millennium. Although efforts to portray Minoan society as totally egalitarian, without class or gender hierarchy, is probably exaggerated, it is likely that—even more than in the early Mesopotamian world—women stood as peers with men in palace elites. Goddesses predominate as symbols of the source of all life.[21]

In the sixth century, Athens was reorganized into a male-citizen society by the lawgiver Solon. In these laws, parallel to Mosaic law, but with more vehement misogyny, women are forbidden all citizen roles and made permanent minors, unable to act as autonomous parties to any civic transaction, economic or political. Women were banished to the back of the house in a strict division of public and private. There they are to toil and spin and raise small children, but are not to appear in the spacious public forums of male political and cultural life.[22] Yet all the public monuments of Greek culture testified to a continuing male consciousness of women's defeated yet still dangerous potency.[23]

The Pandora story, told by the eighth-century farmer-poet Hesiod, makes Zeus's gift of woman as wife a punishment for Prometheus's sin. She brings evil into the world, banishing the

carefree life of male autarchy.[24] In the dramas of the great trage-
dian, Aeschylus, the subordination of motherright to fatherright
is worked out through the trilogy of the *Oresteia,* which culminates in a final contest between the Erinyes, the frightful earth
deities that avenge matricide, and the father-identified Olympian
Goddess Athena. Athena casts the deciding vote for the priority
of the father over the mother with these words:

> Mine is the right to add the final vote,
> And I award it to Orestes' cause.
> For me no mother bore within her womb,
> And, save for Wedlock evermore eschewed,
> I vouch myself the champion of the man,
> Not of the woman, yea, with all my soul,
> In heart, as birth, a father's child alone.
> Thus I will not too heinously regard
> A woman's death who did her husband slay,
> The guardian of her home; and if the votes
> Equal do fall, Orestes shall prevail.[25]

The Earth Mother powers are tamed and become the Eumenides
(Kindly Ones), henceforth to dwell under the Aeropagus as
peaceful collaborators with patriarchal power.

In her study of fifth-century Athenian culture, Page DuBois
has shown how both classical drama and monumental art testify
to the importance of this conflict between Greek male citizen
identity and its excluded opposites. These excluded opposites are
identified as the female, the barbarian, and the animal. The free
Greek male citizen seeks to establish his identity by subduing and
banishing the non-Greek, the nonmale, and the nonhuman from
the citizen circle. One expression of this struggle is the depiction
of Centaurs and Amazons on the public buildings, locked in battle with Greek soldier-citizens.

The Centaur and the Amazon represent the liminal region
where human male and virile animal mingle, and where females
act like warring males. By depicting these figures as defeated, the

Athenians also depicted their triumph over the Persians, the representatives of the "slavish, effeminate" Oriental society, over against which the Athenians contrasted their society of free and equal male citizens. DuBois shows that this distinction broke down in the Peloponnesian War, in which Greek battled Greek. In the Euripidean plays of this period, women represent the patriarchal dilemma of the conquered "alien" within the household, not only as the subjugated female, but also as the representative of other households and alien cultures.[26]

In the society that emerged from the fraternal strife, the Greek city-states would lose their autarchy, as well as their segregation from Near Eastern cultures. Alexander the Great would not only incorporate Greece under his Macedonian rule, but also the whole Persian empire, in a merger of Hellenic and Asian. DuBois sees Plato and then Aristotle working out the new relationship of the Greek male to the female, the barbarian and the animal, through a new metaphor of hierarchy. Rather than powerful but excluded others, over against the Greek male, the new metaphor incorporates the female, the alien, and the animal as "natural" inferiors in a hierarchical "chain of being" that stretches from immaterial divine Logos at the upper end of the hierarchy, to unformed matter at the lower end.[27]

Slavery becomes central to this new metaphor of hierarchy. Although there had been slaves in Athenian society, the free male citizen did not identify himself in relation to them, but rather ignored them, seeing slavery as characteristic of barbaric society. The numbers of slaves greatly increased after the Peloponnesian War, but slavery also invaded Greek consciousness as the model of all relationships between dominant Greek males and "others."

As we have seen, the ontology of this chain of being was developed in Plato's philosophy. But it was in Aristotle, tutor of Alexander the Great, that this social hierarchy of being was explicitly correlated with slavery. The basic relation of domination and subjugation is seen as one in which the ruling "mind" instrumentally appropriates the bodies of others as "tools." Ruling-class Greek males are those in whom reason and thus the capacity to rule predominates. In descending order women, barbarians (as slaves), and animals are seen as beings without this rational capacity, and hence fitted only to be slaves or servile instruments of Greek masculine sovereignty.

Aristotle also developed the view of female impotency suggested in Athena's speech in the *Eumenides*. Procreative power is appropriated as solely the capacity of the male. The female is defined as merely the passive recipient and "incubator" of the male seed, which alone contains the generative power. The female herself comes about through a maternal failure of this process of formation, in which the female matter is not fully formed by the male potency. The result is a defective being, lacking in full rationality, moral will, and physical strength, and thus unsuited to autonomy.[28] Thus, as do the Hebrew myths, Aristotle deprives earth and femaleness of generative power and demotes them to being passive receivers and/or subverters of a transcendent male potency.

This metaphor of ontological hierarchy as a social hierarchy, with its descending levels of rationality and hence of fitness for servility, would be appropriated into Christianity in the early centuries of the Common Era and henceforth shape Western culture well into the modern period. Yet, even as Plato and Aristotle were shaping the Greek male claims to preeminent sovereignty over all that was "naturally" inferior, we also see the beginning of the "failure of nerve" of classical culture, the flight from the woman, the body, and the earth into ascetic negation.

THE ASCETIC FLIGHT FROM EARTH

Although asceticism was to dominate Christianity almost from its beginnings until the Renaissance and Reformation, and remain influential to the present, asceticism did not originate in Christianity. Rather its roots lie in movements in both Judaism and Hellenism that express an increasing pessimism with the capacity of male cultural and political elites to create a "good earth" and their desire to escape from the mortal bounds of the body and the earth altogether.

Already in Plato the "fall" of the soul into the body is seen either as punishment or a temporary period of "testing." The ideal state of the soul is as a disembodied spirit dwelling in its "native star." Life in the body is defined as a process of "mortification," in preparation for release from the cycle of reincarnation. In the era of Roman imperial conquest of the Greek and Near Eastern worlds (late first century B.C.E to first century C.E.), this mood of pessimism and world alienation, expressed in apocalypticism and Gnosticism, deepened among thinkers in these regions.

Both Gnostic and apocalyptic thought contained elements of social protest against patriarchal and imperial domination. Apocalyptic writers protested on behalf of the oppressed nations and the poor who were the victims of imperialism. Gnosticism contained nascent elements of gender emancipation. The transcendent divine world was imagined as androgynous, and both women and men were seen as released from gender roles into a new, spiritually androgynous wholeness.[29]

Christianity was shaped by both of these anticosmic systems of thought, but it also struggled to curb their more radical elements. It affirmed a modified view of the goodness of the body and the earth as God's good (but temporary) creation, but it did so in a way that continued the Hebrew and Greek identifications of the cosmos and the body with patriarchal hierarchy. The patriarchal social order was reaffirmed as the "order of creation," and the victims of it were enjoined to patiently submit to it until they were released from its rule at death.

The Christian system of thought that emerged by the end of the fourth century, in thinkers such as St. Augustine, can be characterized as a conservative fusion of patriarchy, asceticism, and apocalyptic. For Augustine, patriarchy is the natural order of society, reflecting the innate inferiority of women, their lack of a capacity for headship, and their subjugation to the male as the representative of the "image of God." Both slavery and imperial rule, although not God's ideal mandate for society, are the necessary instruments to curb the unruly passions of "fallen men." The church is justified in using the military power of the state to keep order, and also to enforce orthodoxy against heresy.[30] Celibacy is the optimal state of life by which Christians prepare themselves for the end of this world and the immortal world to come.

This Augustinian synthesis of Gnosticism, apocalypticism, and Christianity shaped the dominant perspective of the Latin medieval world. Its otherworldly pessimism was reinforced by the collapse of the Western Roman empire as a political entity. Augustine's own life coincided with critical stages in this collapse. He wrote his monumental work on world history, *The City of God,* shortly after the city of Rome had been sacked by the Goths (and in response to pagan charges that Christianity itself contributed to the collapse of Rome). As he lay dying in 430 C.E., his own North African city of Hippo was under siege by the Vandals.

For the next thousand years, western Europe would live in the shadow of the collapse of the Roman empire, seeing its own world as one of decline in preparation for the end of the world.[31] The Roman empire (which had organized into one vast political system a region from England and Spain in the west across North Africa and Egypt to Syria and Asian Minor) was the culminating form of a three-thousand-year history of Mediterranean empire-building that began in the kingdoms of Assyria, Persia, and Egypt. For this world system to collapse and fall apart into chaos (as far as the West was concerned; the Eastern half of the empire experienced a different history) was indeed "apocalyptic," and confirmed the worldview that believed that earth's history itself had run its course.

The primary causes of this collapse of the Western half of the empire was economic, a top-heavy imperial bureaucracy that drained the cities of their wealth, and the inability of the Roman armies to fend off the movements of Celtic and Germanic peoples to the north, indeed the increasing takeover of the Roman army by these "barbarian" chiefs. Three millennia of exploitation of the lands surrounding the Mediterranean Sea also took its ecological toll. The irrigation methods of farming in the Tigris-Euphrates Valley caused, even in the second millennium B.C.E., a process of salinization that gradually turned this fertile crescent into a desert.[32]

Phoenician, Greek, and Roman use of wood as the primary fuel, as well as material for all types of construction, denuded the forests of Lebanon, Greece, and Italy. Strip-mining and quarrying also ripped the ground cover and soil from hills. These hills, stripped of their cover, then became subject to vast soil erosion as torrential rains washed away the unprotected earth. Grazing sheep and goats completed the destruction of forest life. Deforestation dried up mountain springs, and soil erosion created malaria-filled swamps. This, together with inadequate disposal of sewage, often caused epidemics in crowded cities such as Rome.

Almost all wild herds of larger mammals also were destroyed in Greece during the Classical period, and the Roman obsession with circus games wiped out vast herds of wild animals in Africa and Asia as far east as India. Elephants, rhinoceros, and zebras became extinct in North Africa, lions disappeared from Greece and Eastern Asia, and tigers from Iran. Ecological destruction was certainly one contributing factor to the collapse of the empire, and one that has generally been ignored by historians.[33]

Although much of this ecological damage has remained, the collapse of the empire, the fading of cities, and the return to subsistence farming helped restore the land. Here Christian asceticism played a positive role in its very hostility to accumulation of wealth. Monastic communities in western Europe not only were centers for the preservation of literary culture, but they also created a new union of subsistence agriculture with egalitarian spiritual community. St. Benedict united intellect and labor by decreeing that monks do their own domestic and agricultural work.[34] All too soon, however, monasteries succumbed to the temptation to accrue wealth and to farm through exploited serf labor.

For those seeking an ecological ethic for a new era of collapse of empire, the heritage of Christian asceticism is Janus-faced. One side of this tradition, with its hostility to women, sexuality, and the body, and its contempt for the material world in favor of life after death, reinforces the patterns of neglect of and flight from the earth. But asceticism can also be understood, not as rejection of the body and the earth, but rather as a rejection of exploitation and excess, and thus as a return to egalitarian simple living in harmony with other humans and with nature. Even fasting, in moderation, and the adoption of a vegetarian diet can restore a healthy body, rather than express a sick negation of the body.

Asceticism in this sense can be seen as a "restoration of paradise." The monk restores communal property, overcoming the exploitative division of God's creation into private property that came about through the fall.[35] The monk befriends animals who minister to him, overcoming the enmity between humans and animals that came about after the Flood (Genesis 9:2–3).[36] If St. Francis can be seen as the patron saint of conservation and the animal-rights movement, with his reverence for all nature as our sisters and brothers, St. Benedict, according to philosopher René Dubos, should be the patron saint of stewardship, restoration, and sustainable use of nature.[37]

Christian asceticism was deeply ambivalent toward woman. One side of ascetic thought (and one that particularly appealed to ascetic women) imagined freedom from marriage and childbearing as liberating women from subordination in the patriarchal family. By adopting celibacy women overcame the "curse of Eve," were restored in Christ to equality with man, and enabled to act as active agents in Christian preaching and ministry.[38] But this liberation was predicated on a rejection of women's sexual and reproductive roles as inherently debasing. Male ascetics spoke of the virginal woman as having become "spiritually male," since for them femaleness was inherently inferior.[39]

But this egalitarian asceticism was quickly overshadowed by a misogynist perspective that saw female sexuality and childbearing as the essence of both sin and death. Through sexual reproduction comes the transmission of sin and mortal, corruptible life. The disembodied male soul was the bastion of "eternal life" that must be fortified against woman as the embodiment of mortal life.[40] In order to secure himself against a fall into corruptible life, the male ascetic should flee even the most distant presence of women.[41] Even ascetic women, for these male ascetics, were too dangerously sexual. Ascetic women were increasingly deprived of their minor roles in public ministry, such as deaconess, and cloistered in convents, where obedience to God was to be expressed in total obedience to male ecclesiastical authority.[42]

This ambivalence toward women was closely related to Christian ambivalence toward physical nature. As Carolyn Merchant has shown in her study of the rise of science, the medieval paradigm of nature was organic.[43] The earth and the whole cosmos was seen as one vast body in which all parts are interconnected. But, as she also shows, the dominant version of this organic metaphor was hierarchical. It is as a hierarchically ordered body that the cosmos becomes the analogy for the hierarchical society. The rulers are the head, the warriors the heart, and the workers the stomach, hands, and feet.[44]

St. Paul inaugurated the ecclesiastical version of this hierarchical body when he made the church the "body," under Christ as its head, analogous to the relation of husband as head and woman as "his body" in (patriarchal) marriage (Ephesians 5:21–33). Medieval thinkers continued to elaborate this concept of the hierarchically ordered body as a metaphor for ecclesiastical, feudal, and domestic hierarchies. This hierarchically ordered body slips over into dualism between mind and body, since the "head" is seen as the seat of "reason," the nonbodily power that must rule over the body but not succumb to it.

For medieval spirituality this hierarchically ordered cosmos could also be seen as a "ladder" for ascent to God. Thus, in the thirteenth-century classic by St. Bonaventure, *The Mind's Road to God,* the contemplative starts out by contemplating physical nature. There he sees the traces of God's presence in "sensible" nature. But this contemplation of God through physical nature is the lowest stage of a contemplative ascent that must be soon superseded by "higher" stages. The contemplative withdraws into the soul and sees the traces of God within his own intellectual powers. He then moves from these images in the mind to the archetypes of the eternal essence, and from there begins to glimpse the Mind of God as the source of these essences. This ascent leads finally to a contemplative encounter with Godself.[45]

But this same view of earth and sense experience, as the first rung of an iconic, sacramental cosmos, also carried its negative message. Nature lay under a curse. The fall of humanity precipitated the cosmos into a state of bondage. It is under the sway of the Devil, who is the Prince of this World.[46] The earth, and the sublunar sphere of air around it, particularly was believed to be filled with demonic spirits. All that is not redeemed and brought under the rule of Christ (and the church), that is, non-Christian lands and peoples, but also the "wild" animals and forests not yet domesticated, are the Devil's realm. To venture out into "nature" outside of "Christian" society is to risk encounter with demons. Those who sought knowledge of nature outside of the church's control did so by making a pact with the Devil.

This view of the demonic, unredeemed realm could also be directed toward women and sexuality as the "enemy within." In the witch-hunts that gripped European society in the fifteenth to seventeenth centuries, this geography of demonic, fallen nature over against the redeemed sphere, under "Christian" ecclesiastical and social control, was played out primarily on the bodies of women, particularly elderly village women. According to the fifteenth-century Dominican Inquisitors Heinrich Kraemer and Jacob Sprenger, women, by their very nature, are hostile to Christian faith; and woman's creation from the bent rib of Adam meant, not only woman's secondary and inferior nature, but a nature ever resistant to accepting its proper subordination.[47]

From this perverse nature comes woman's proneness to witchcraft, an evil from which the male has been preserved by incarnation of Christ (as a male). Women, even in old age, are imagined as sexually insatiable. It is this lustfulness that not only drags males into sin, but also draws women to accept a pact with the Devil, sealed with icy sexual intercourse. Witches are seen as using their powers particularly to "impede the venereal act," both by rendering men impotent and also by causing infertility and miscarriage in women, as well as various other disasters in nature (bad weather, miscarriages of cows).

Witches also were seen as consorting with untamed nature through animal familiars and flying off into the forest to celebrate their nocturnal "sabbaths." Thus the persecution of witches made women the focus for the war against the demonic as nonhuman, non-Christian, nonmale and nonrational. Wild forests, untamed animals, heretics and pagans, sexuality and sensual feeling met as woman. This obsession with woman as witch was by no means confined to the Middle Ages or to Catholicism, but would be continued in Protestantism and provide major metaphors, both for early scientific investigation of nature and also European colonization of "pagan" lands.

THE REFORMATION AND THE SCIENTIFIC REVOLUTION

The Calvinist Reformation and the scientific revolution are two expressions of a crucial turning point in the Western concept of nature. In these two movements the medieval Christian struggle between the sacramental and the demonic was recast. Calvinism made major contributions to the dismemberment of the medieval sacramental sense of nature (in contrast to both Lutheranism and Anglicanism, which retained much more of the sacramental liturgical culture). Calvinism radicalized the split between nature and grace in Christian thought. It saw nature as totally depraved. No residue of a divine presence remained in nature that could sustain any "natural" knowledge of God or relation to God.

Although, according to Calvin, the "book of nature" and human conscience once revealed God, since the fall this ability to know God through creation has been broken. Saving knowledge of God now can only descend from God's revealed Word in scripture, telling of God's redemptive work in Christ.[48] The interconnections between creation and redemption, cosmic Logos and Christ, woven by classical Christianity were broken into duality. This also meant that one could not expect to encounter any experience of God in art, mysticism, or experiences of nature, nor could there be any traces of authentic knowledge of God in non-Christian people.

Calvinist reformers were notable in their iconoclastic hostility toward visual art in churches. Stained glass, statues, and carvings in the church buildings that fell into their hands were smashed,[49] and Calvinist worship was barren of all visual symbolism. The preacher, dressed in the somber black of the academic robe, and the pulpit became the central features of the church, with the altar reduced to a plain "communion table." The ear alone was the aperture of experience of God. The word, proclaimed in scripture and sermon, and music were the primary means of mediation of the divine presence. All the other senses were suspect;

nothing one could see, touch, smell, or taste could be trustworthy bearers of the divine.

Even the bread and "juice" of the Eucharist were seen, not so much as a physical embodiment Christ, as an intellectual reminder of a message about Christ's salvific act for us completed in the past.[50] Thus Calvinism promoted the victory of word culture over visual culture. Because of the excitement with the discovery of the printed and vernacular word, Calvinist worship carried great power in its classical era. But today, in a culture saturated with the manipulated "word," the Calvinist legacy in Western Christianity contributes to a pervasive feeling of boredom with worship and life in general. Endless technological hypes cannot fill the vacuum left by the death of sensible experiences of wonder and mystery.

Although Calvinism dismantled the sacramental cosmos of medieval Christianity, it maintained and reinforced its demonic universe. The fallen world, especially untamed nature and also other human groups outside the Calvinist church, were under the sway of the Devil. Everything "pagan," including Roman Catholics as well as unconverted Indians and Africans, was the playground of demonic powers. But it was women who were the gateway of the Devil within the community of the saints itself. If women were strictly obedient to their fathers, husbands, ministers, and magistrates, they were redeemed as "goodwives." But in any independence of women lurked heresy and witchcraft.

Among Protestants, Calvinists became the primary witchhunters, both in England and Scotland and in New England. They also became the major formulators of the new understanding of the patriarchal family as the key institution for both church and state. It is not accidental that William Perkins, the same divine who was a leading formulator of the Puritan vision of the patriarchal family in his *Christian Oeconomie* (1590), also wrote one of the major treatises promoting witch persecution: *A Discourse on the Damned Art of Witchcraft* (1596). Like his

Dominican counterparts, Perkins sees women as the gender primarily prone to witchcraft, both because of their natural "weakness of mind" and also because of their resistance to accepting their rightful place under male authority.[51]

The Reformation era of the sixteenth and seventeenth centuries saw major changes in social hierarchy and the relation of the domestic sphere of the family to public life. Males of the middle and upper classes came closer together as one educated mercantile and landed elite. At the same time, peasants were being deprived of rights of communal land and reduced to landless laborers. Thus a new class hierarchy of capital and labor was being constructed out of the dissolution of the feudal system.

Women of the upper classes were losing access to public power through possession of land, and the universities remained closed to them. Women of the peasant and artisan classes were losing access to skilled work in areas such as medicine and midwifery, brewing, and printing. All women *qua* women were marginalized in the private sphere of the family, under the headship of their husbands.[52] Modification of class hierarchy between upper and middle classes of men was compensated for by a more rigid gender hierarchy between men and women. Puritanism was in the mainstream of this development of the middle-class patriarchal family.

The relationship of the scientific revolution to Puritanism, not to mention to witchcraft persecution and to the strengthening of the patriarchal family, remain largely unexplored. It has usually been assumed in Western intellectual history that the rise of science in the seventeenth century was a major factor in dispelling the kind of "superstitious" views of nature that promoted the persecution of witches. But recent studies suggest a closer and more complex relation between these phenomena of the period than has been generally recognized.[53]

Francis Bacon (1561–1626), Lord Chancellor of England under James I, is seen as the "father" of the scientific method. In his treatise, *Novum Organum* (1620), he details the inductive method of empirical knowledge that proceeds from observation of natural phenomenon to increasing generalization, always returning to experimental observation to check these generalizations. Yet Bacon's rhetoric of the "new knowledge" is replete with images drawn from witch-hunting. (James I was himself a great promoter of witch persecution.)[54] The scientific laboratory is described in language taken from the Inquisitor's chamber, in which nature is "vexed" and put to the test and thereby "forced to yield her secrets."

This inquisitional imagery should not simply be seen as a "cultural accident," but has several effects that still shape scientific thought. One of these is the assumption that the laboratory situation, where entities in nature are taken out of their normal environment and put under special stress conditions, yields the "purest" truth about nature. A second assumption is the belief in the objectivity of the "inquisitor," whose motivations and presence in constructing the experiment need not be taken into account in the results.

Bacon's thought is pervaded by images of nature as a female to be coerced, "penetrated," conquered, and forced to "yield," the language of rape and subjugation of women, while the scientist is imaged as the epitome of masculine power over such "feminine" nature.[55] Bacon ties the scientific revolution to the Christian myth of fall and redemption. Through the sin of Eve, "nature" fell out of "man's" control, but through scientific knowledge this fall will be reversed and "nature" restored to man's dominion, as representative of God's dominion over the earth.[56] For Bacon, scientific knowledge is fundamentally a tool of power, the capacity to subjugate and rule over "nature."

René Descartes (1595–1650) is a second foundational figure for modern scientific thought. Yet Descartes's famous method of inquiry is antiempirical. In line with the Platonic and scholastic tradition, sense impressions are seen as unreliable. Truth is

obtained by moving inward to abstract reasoning and there discovering the "first principles," by which all other knowledge can
be deduced. These first principles Descartes finds in the thinking
mind itself, which cannot doubt its own existence, and in God,
the perfect correlate of this thinking mind, whose perfection
assures the human mind that its rational logic cannot be de-
ceived.[57]

Descartes's method yields a radical version of the dualism between mind and matter. The thinking mind is transcendent and
stands over against matter, which by its nature is mindless and
soulless, divisible into smaller and smaller elements, moving me-
chanically according to laws of causality. In Descartes we see the
pervasive metaphor of the "machine" for all physical nature, even
the human body. The result is a radical denial that material reality
itself is capable of producing reason or any innate animation.

Descartes reduced animals to "automata," which appear to
be lifelike but are actually moved by mechanical power, like
clocks. This view also was used to justify vivisectional experimentation on animals, by assuring the experimenters that the
cries and writhings of animals were mere mechanical reflexes.
Since animals lack "soul," they cannot possibly "feel." [58] In effect, Descartes severed the continuum between organic body, life,
sensibility, and thought. This continuum was split into thought,
found in God and the human mind, and dead matter in motion.

Descartes's dualism of mind and matter also reflected a dualism between two truths: the truths of religion, revealed in Catholic doctrine, and the truths of science, found through scientific
method. This dualism also permits a split between fact and value,
allowing scientific truth to be regarded as "objective" and
"value-free," while the questions of ethics and values can retreat
to a segregated realm of the soul. Descartes and other scientists
who also wanted to be orthodox Christians (Catholic or Protestant), promoted this split because it allowed them to live in two

worlds, without having these two worlds impinge upon one another.[59] The "university" of discourse, in which all branches of knowledge cohere, which was the quest of medieval Europe, was fragmented, with fateful effects that have only begun to be recognized.

Isaac Newton (1642–1727), a generation after Descartes, integrated the experimental and mathematical methods of knowledge. Newton's *Mathematical Principles of Natural Philosophy* (1687) laid the foundations for modern physics until Einstein. For Newton matter is reducible to atomic particles moving in a spatial void, through the laws of force and gravity. Newton also saw himself as a "natural" theologian. The mechanical universe demanded a "clock-maker," and that clock-maker was God, who not only constructed the machine of the universe and embedded the laws of motion into it, but intervened from time to time to correct its irregularities.[60]

Newtonian physics was the paradigm of the new mechanical universe, which could be reduced to "resources" and appropriated as power and wealth by the new ruling elites of Europe. Nature was "exorcized" of both benign and evil "spirits." Animist traditions of science, exemplified by the "natural magicians," such as Giordano Bruno, Tommaso Campanella, and Paracelsus (with their dangerous sympathies toward the protests of subjugated peasantry),[61] were defeated. This left the mechanical model of the universe in firm control of science up the present time.

All innate spiritual elements having been eliminated from nature, human spirit need no longer interact with nature as a fellow being, but could see itself, like the clock-maker God, as transcendent to it, knowing it and ruling it from outside. Soon this presupposition of God could itself be discarded, leaving the scientists, together with the rulers of state and industry, in charge of passive matter, infinitely reconstructible to serve their interests.

COLONIALISM AND INDUSTRIALISM

In Western European society, the application of science to technological control over nature marched side by side with colonialism. Not accidentally, the science of bodies in motion pioneered by Galileo was closely related to ballistics, the technology of military projectiles.[62] Thus the new science was married early to the technology of war. From the sixteenth century until the dissolution of colonial empires (beginning with the American Revolution and mostly completed after World War II), western European expansionist states would appropriate the vast territories of North and South America, much of Asia and Africa, and the Pacific, vying in the early twentieth century for the partition of the Middle East and North Africa from the Ottoman empire.

The Spanish and the Portuguese were first on the scene of colonial expansion, using new naval technology to circumnavigate the globe and then carving out vast regions of control, exploitation, and settlement. The Spanish seized Central and South America in the sixteenth century, coming as gold hunters, but soon settling down as sugar producers. The international trade routes carried slaves from Africa to the Americas, gold, sugar, furs, and spices to Europe, and returned with the manufactured goods of the "Mother country."

This era of colonization decisively reshaped the human, plant, and animal ecologies of colonized regions. War and disease exterminated millions of "native peoples," and reduced those who were left to slaves and serfs in the mines and plantations of the new international trade economy. New plants and animals were introduced, reshaping ecosystems. Forests were stripped for the agro-plantations, devastating fragile rain forest ecologies in a tragedy that still continues today in regions such as Guatemala and Brazil.[63]

This vast process of stripping the Americas of their gold and silver, together with the slave and agro-export trades, laid the foundations for western European capitalism. The capital accumulation that made the industrial revolution in England and western Europe possible was derived in large part from colonialism. The regions thus depleted of their wealth were rendered impoverished and dependent on the economies of the colonizing nations whose "development" they had financed through the exploitation of their lands and labor. The wealth accrued by this vast process of exploitation of land and labor would fuel new levels of technological revolution, transforming material resources into new forms of energy and mechanical work, control of disease, and increasing speed of communication and travel.

This experience of increasing power for technological transformation of daily life was expressed in the optimistic vision of endless "progress," translated into "revolution" among European workers and colonized people, who were the "underside" of this Western capitalist "progress." Western elites imagined that this technological way of life would gradually conquer all problems of material scarcity and even push back the limits of human mortality. And they sought to sell this vision to colonized people as "development."[64]

However, in the last quarter of the twentieth century, this dream of infinite progress began to turn into a nightmare. We have already detailed the dimensions of that nightmare in chapter 4, the colliding trajectories of population explosion, dwindling food supply, climate change, soil erosion and drought, declining supplies of fossil fuels, toxic waste, the growing gap between concentrated wealth and increasing poverty, and the militarism that seeks to keep the system of exploitation in place for those who profit from it.

CONCLUSIONS

Is civilization salvageable for sustainable life on earth, or is the very process of shaping urban and agricultural entities, departing from the hunter-gatherer mode of human life, the root of unfolding evil, as the Earth First! radicals believe? In the story of civilization I have sketched here, there are elements of tragedy and of sin, in the sense defined in chapter 5, intertwined. There is tragedy in the finitude of the human perspective, which pursues limited good for its community and is little able to visualize the interrelated train of destruction that may be set in motion thereby, such as the salinization of soils through irrigation.

But there are also elements of sin in the sense of culpable evil in this story. The roots of this evil lie, as we have suggested, in patterns of domination, whereby male elites in power deny their interdependency with women, exploiting human labor and the biotic community around them. They seek to exalt their own power infinitely, by draining the lives of these other humans and nonhuman sources of life on which they depend. They create cultures of deceit, which justify this exploitation by negating the value of those they use, while denying their own dependence on them.

Symbolically this culture of deceit has passed through three mythic patterns. In the first mythic pattern, the male acknowledges his dependency on the mother (as woman and as earth), but he also co-opts her as the means to his power and the lap upon which he is enthroned as king of the universe. This ancient myth of the Goddess with enthroned male king on her lap continues in the Catholic iconography of Mary and the infant Christ.

The second mythic phase negates this dependency by seeking to separate the immortal soul or spirit from the mortal body. The positive dependency on mother and nature is denied, but their potency is recognized negatively as demonic power. In the third mythic phase, there is an effort to sterilize the power of nature altogether, imagining it as dead stuff totally malleable in the hands of men in power. Although this is the myth of dominance that has triumphed in modern science, it was already suggested in the Babylonian myth of the universe constructed out of the dead body of Tiamat.

What modern science and industrialism have added is not so much new forms of domination, as the enormous increase in productive and destructive power and the lengthening of the lines of hierarchical exploitation. The system of domination has grown increasingly global; at the same time, the links of interdependency between the human and biotic parts in the chain have grown increasingly remote from each other. It becomes increasingly difficult for elites in modern cities even to recognize these links or to imagine the ripple effects of destruction unleashed by the operations of their daily lives.

Thus the search for an ecological culture and society seems to demand three elements: (1) the rebuilding of primary and regional communities, in which people can understand and take responsibility for the ecosystem of which they are a part; (2) just relations between humans that accept the right of all members of the community to an equitable share in the means of subsistence; and (3) an overcoming of the culture of competitive alienation and domination for compassionate solidarity. Are there elements in Christian culture that are reclaimable for this task? In Part Four of this volume, I will explore two lines of Christian tradition as a beginning effort to answer this question.

Healing

8

Healing the World:
The Covenantal Tradition

In this and the following chapters, I will explore two lines of the biblical thought and Christian traditions that have reclaimable resources for an ecological spirituality and practice: the covenantal tradition and the sacramental tradition. I want to make clear at the outset what I am *not* doing in this exploration. I am *not* assuming that these are the only or the best religious traditions for ecological ethics and spirituality; and I am *not* assuming that these traditions can be reclaimed and made usable without change.

Both these traditions are marked by a legacy of patriarchalism and must be reinterpreted, if they are to be genuinely affirming of dominated women, men, and nature. Even then the question of whether they can be adequately liberated and made liberating will remain. Nor do I in any way discount that there are resources for ecological spirituality and practice in other traditions, Native American, African, and Pacific indigenous traditions, and also Asian spiritualities, such as Taoism and Buddhism. All of these many ways should be honored and their resources for ecological spirituality and practice developed.

In focusing on these two Christian traditions, I make several presuppositions. First, I assume that there is no ready-made ecological spirituality and ethic in past traditions. The ecological crisis is new to human experience. This does not mean that humans have not devastated their environment before. But as long as populations remained small and human technology weak, these devastations were remediable by migration, retreat from top-heavy urban centers, or adaptation of new techniques. Nature appeared a huge, inexhaustible source of life, and humans small. Only after the bombs of Hiroshima and Nagasaki did humans begin to recognize the possibility that they could destroy the planet by their own expropriated power. The radical nature of this new face of ecological devastation means that all past human traditions are inadequate in the face of it. Whatever useful elements may exist in, for example, Native American or Taoist thought, must be reinterpreted to make them usable in the face of both new scientific knowledge and the destructive power of the technology it has made possible.

My second assumption is that each tradition is best explored by those who claim community in that tradition. This does not preclude conversions into other traditions or communication between them. Indeed I believe that we must ultimately draw upon all our spiritual resources in a global community of interrelated spiritual traditions. But the plumbing of each tradition, and its reinterpretation for today's crises, is a profound task that needs to begin in the context of communities of accountability. Those people for whom Taoism or Pueblo Indian spirituality are their native traditions are those best suited to dig these roots and offer their fruits to the rest of us. Those without these roots should be cautious in claiming plants not our own, respectful of those who speak from within.

The Christian tradition is one of those communities of accountability that has profoundly valuable themes for ecological spirituality and practice. It also has problematic defects and bears significant responsibility for the legacy of domination of women and nature. But, for that reason, its liberating potential should not be disregarded. Those too alienated from this tradition to allow it to speak to them have every right to seek other spiritual traditions that can nurture them. But the vast majority of the more than 1 billion Christians of the world can be lured into an ecological consciousness only if they see that it grows in some ways from the soil in which they are planted.

THE COVENANTAL TRADITION: HEBRAIC ROOTS

The Bible has been made to appear to Western Christians to be much more antinature than it is by a particular line of biblical interpretation, shaped in nineteenth-century western European Protestantism, that thought in terms of a sharp dualism between history and nature. History was seen as the true realm of the human, ascendant over "nature," and, for that reason, the authentic sphere of the presence of the true "God" of the Bible. "Nature" was understood as subhuman, as the sphere of necessity, and the realm to be negated in order to ascend into humanness and freedom. Divinities revealed in and though nature were, by definition, false gods.[1]

More recent explorations of the Bible, undertaken out of ecological concern, have shown that this modern European dualism of history and nature distorts the biblical perspective. The Hebraic understanding of the God of Israel did not set history against nature, but rather experienced God as Lord of heaven and earth, whose power filled all aspects of their lives.[2] The same steadfast love of God is present when God "spread out the earth on the waters, . . . made the great lights," made "the sun to rule over the day, . . . the moon and stars to rule over the night," and when God "brought Israel out from among them. . . . with a strong hand and an outstretched arm, . . . divided the Red Sea in two . . . and made Israel pass through the midst of it . . . but overthrew Pharaoh and his army in the Red Sea" (Psalm 136:6–15).

This is one lived reality in time and place that is not differentiated into separate spheres of "creation" and "redemption." The God made present in historical acts of deliverance is at the same time the God who "made heaven and earth." Nor is it appropriate to say that the affirmation of redemption from Egypt precedes and is more foundational than the affirmation of God as Creator,[3] or vice versa. Israel experienced both divine judgment and divine blessing in relation to threatening neighbors, and also in relation to storms and droughts. They praised God for deliverance from enemies and for the miracles of fertile fields and starry night skies. In contrast to Greek thought, which saw reality as moving in geometric space, Hebraic thought saw reality as "event."

The Hebraic view of relationship to God is undoubtedly highly androcentric, anthropocentric, and ethnocentric. God is seen as relating to this particular people through the male leadership of this people. But this does not preclude more inclusive perspectives, a God who also relates lovingly to other people, a God who related directly to women without intermediaries, and a God who relates to nature apart from human mediation. In chapter 5 we discussed ethnocentrism and universalism in the Hebrew Bible. One can also point to stories, such as Hagar's encounter with God in the wilderness, that break both the ethnocentric and the patriarchal mediations of God.[4]

However, for the purposes of this chapter, I will focus particularly on the testimony to a God who relates directly to nature, whether or not it is a nature of benefit to humans. Although the metaphor of God as "maker" is modeled after the artisan shaping artifacts, God is seen as creating a living world, not "dead things." God is seen as taking profound pleasure in this work of creation, and the creation, in turn, responds to God with praise. God "rejoices" in the world "he" creates, and the planets, mountains, brooks, animals, and plants return this rejoicing in their relation to God. The relation of God and "nature" is often animistically interpersonal.[5]

Psalm 29 speaks of God present in the storm, whose "voice . . . thunders over many waters," whose thunder "breaks the cedars of Lebanon, . . . makes Lebanon skip like a calf and Siron like a young wild ox." In Psalm 65 God visits the earth in the rain showers, watering its furrows abundantly, blessing its growth. The earth responds with overflowing abundance: "The hills gird themselves with joy, the meadows clothe themselves with flocks, the valleys deck themselves with grain, they shout and sing together for joy" (9–13).

The blessing of God's presence is found not only in those spheres of nature under human cultivation, where humans seek benefit from nature. In an extended rebuke to human arrogance, the God who speaks to Job from the whirlwind makes clear that God is equally present in places and times in nature to which humans have no access. "Where were you when I laid the foundation of the earth, when the morning stars sang together, and all the heavenly beings shouted for joy? . . . Have you entered into the springs of the sea, or walked in the recesses of the deep?"

God also provides for the wild animals not under human control:

> Can you hunt the prey for the lion or satisfy the appetite of the young lions . . . ? Who provides for the raven its prey, when its young ones cry to God . . . ? Do you know when the mountain goats give birth? Do you observe the calving of the deer? . . . Who has let the wild ass go free . . . which I have given the steppe for its home . . . ? It scorns the tumult of the city; it does not hear the shouts of the driver. It ranges the mountains as its pasture. . . . Is it by your wisdom that the hawk soars . . . Is it at your command that the eagle mounts up and makes its nest on high? (Job 38–39)

God is present not only in blessings in society and nature, but also in social and natural disasters. Indeed, even to differentiate "social" from "natural" reflects too much the modern dualism. In the Hebraic texts these are knit together in one holistic experience, in which defeats at the hands of conquering enemies and the storms and droughts that bring human works to naught are seen as aspects of one picture that testifies to divine judgment upon human sin. In both blessing and curse, success and disaster, God is sovereign, hence all events have moral meaning and purpose.

In a description that reflects the ecological disasters of ancient irrigated agriculture, the Psalmist declares, "He turns rivers into a desert, springs of water into thirsty ground, a fruitful land into a salty waste, because of the wickedness of its inhabitants." At the same time, God can reverse this disaster for the needy: "He turns a desert into pools of water, a parched land into springs of water. And there he lets the hungry live . . . they sow fields and plant vineyards and get a fruitful yield" (Psalm 107:33–36).

Much of the ecological critique of the Bible has focused on the concept of "dominion" over nature granted to "man" by God.[6] However, despite some hyperbolic claims to have given "man" power over "all" of nature, the biblical picture is one of keen awareness of the limits of human power. One such limit is human transience. In the words of Ecclesiasticus (17:1–2): "The Lord created man out of the earth and turned him back to it again. He gave to men few days, a limited time, but granted them authority over the things upon the earth."

Moreover, as biblical scholars have been quick to reply, human authority over nature remains always delegated authority. Nature is not private property to be done with as one wishes, but stewardship over an earth that remains ultimately God's.[7] To abuse this trust in destructive relations to nature is to bring divine wrath upon one's head. God, not "men," is in control of nature. Neither nature's blessings nor nature's destructive power is handed over into autonomous human hands.

Humans can hope for blessings if they are faithful to God and just toward one another, and can expect devastating wreckage when they are not. But even "good works" are not assurance of blessing, for sometimes God makes the righteous suffer, while the wicked thrive. When disaster strikes the righteous man, nature itself teaches him that in this too lies the work of God:

> But ask the animals, and they will teach you; the birds of the air, and they will tell you; ask the plants of the earth, and they will teach you; and the fish of the sea will declare to you. Who among all these does not know that the hand of the Lord has done this? In his hand is the life of every living thing and the breath of every human being. (Job 12: 7–10)

Hebrew thought knit the covenantal relation of God to Israel in a close relation to the gift of the "land." In chapter 5 we have shown how this concept of the "promised land" can be acted out in ethnocentric violence against other people whose ancient tenure in that same land is discredited because of their lack of relation to (this) God. But the other side of this same perspective is the understanding that Israel's own tenure in the land is contingent on its righteousness. The gift of the land is not a possession that can be held apart from relation to God. If Israel "pollutes" the land with iniquity, "the land will vomit you out for defiling it, as it vomited out the nation that was before you" (Leviticus 18:28).[8]

One of the major fruits of this Hebraic understanding of the covenantal relationship between justice and prosperity in the land is found in sabbatical legislation. This legislation describes a series of concentric cycles, the seven-day cycle, the seven-year cycle, and the seven-times-seven-year cycle or Jubilee. In each successive cycle, land, animals, and humans are to rest and be restored, in deeper and more thoroughgoing ways, culminating in a periodic "permanent revolution" in the fiftieth year.[9]

The six-day cycle assures a day of rest every seven days, not only to the farmer, but also to his human and animal work force: "Six days you shall do your work, but on the seventh day you shall rest, so that your ox and your donkey may have relief, and your homeborn slave and resident alien may be refreshed" (Exodus 23:12). In this cycle the community of Israel imitates God's own creative pattern in making the world, laboring for six days and resting on the seventh.

In the seven-year cycle, attention is given to the rights of the poor and to wild animals, as well as to the renewal of the land itself: "For six years you shall sow your land and gather its yield; but the seventh year you shall let it rest and lie fallow, so that the poor of your people may eat; and what they leave the wild animals may eat. You shall do the same with your vineyard and your olive orchard" (Exodus 23:10–11). In addition, male Hebrew slaves are to be set free without debt in the seventh year (Exodus 21:2). Parallel legislation in Leviticus on the seventh-year sabbath mentions slave and hired laborers and animals allowed to rest during the sabbatical year, living off the untilled land like the farmer (Leviticus 25:6–7).

In the fiftieth year, there is to be yet more profound renovation of relationships between humans, animals, and land, restoring just balance between them. The Jubilee year is to be announced by a trumpet sounded throughout the land: "You shall hallow the fiftieth year, and you shall proclaim liberty throughout the land to all its inhabitants" (Leviticus 25:10). In this year everyone who has lost their land through debt will be restored, with each one returning to their former property. The lawgiver accentuates the provisional character of all landholding, since the land remains ultimately God's: "The land shall not be sold in perpetuity, for the land is mine, with me you are but aliens and tenants" (Leviticus 25:23).

During the Jubilee Hebrew men and women who have fallen into debt and sold themselves into slavery are to be released, along with their children. Debt too has its limits, and is to be liquidated at the time of the Jubilee. The Lord-servant relationship between God and Israel, manifest in God's liberation of Israel from slavery, is guarantee against permanent Hebrew slavery. "They and their children with them shall go free in the Jubilee year. For to me the people of Israel are servants; they are my servants whom I brought out from the land of Egypt; I am the Lord your God" (Leviticus 25:54–55).

As in the seven-year cycle, the Jubilee year is also a time when the earth lies fallow, animals and human laborers rest. But, more radically, it is a time of periodic righting of unjust relations, undoing the enslavements of human to humans, the losses and confiscations of land, that have created classes of rich and poor in Israel. The norm of a just community is one of free householders with land equitably apportioned among them.

Scholars have doubted whether the Jubilee laws were ever fully applied, although there is evidence of partial application of these laws at different times. Their importance, however, lies in providing a model of redemptive eco-justice. Unlike apocalyptic models of redemption, the Jubilee vision does not promise a "once-for-all" destruction of evil. Humans will drift into unjust relations between each other, they will overwork animals and exploit land. But this drift is not to be allowed to establish itself as a permanent "order." Rather, it is to be recognized as a disorder that must be corrected periodically, so that human society regains its right eco-social relationships and starts afresh.

This vision of periodic righting of relationships is also projected on a more absolute messianic future, although still a future within history. This future time will bring a final fulfillment of the covenant of creation, restoring peace between people and healing nature's enmity. In Isaiah even the carnivorous conflict between animals will be overcome in the Peaceable Kingdom:

> For I am about to create new heavens and a new earth; the former things shall not be remembered or come to mind. But be glad and rejoice forever in what I am creating, for I am about to create Jerusalem as a joy and its people as a delight . . . No more shall the sound of weeping be heard in it or the cry of distress.

No more shall there be in it an infant that lives but a few days, or an old person who does not live out a lifetime . . . They shall build houses and inhabit them, they shall plant vineyards and eat their fruit. They shall not build and another inhabit; they shall not plant and another eat; for like the days of a tree shall the days of my people be.

Before they call I will answer, while they are yet speaking I will hear. The wolf and the lamb shall feed together, the lion shall eat straw like the ox. But the serpent—its food shall be dust. They shall not hurt or destroy on all my holy mountain, says the Lord. (Isaiah 65:17–22, 24–25)

THE COVENANT IN CHRISTIAN TRADITION

This intimate unity between justice and right relations to nature in the covenantal relation between God and Israel is largely lost in the New Testament. It was probably important in Jesus' own understanding of the coming Kingdom, which he saw himself as commissioned to announce. The reports of Jesus' teachings in the synoptic gospels reflect strong elements of the Jubilee vision of renewal.[10]

The fullest account of the Lord's Prayer in Matthew 6:9–13 shows an understanding of God's Kingdom as the establishment of justice and right relations on earth: "God's will be done on earth." This hope for earthly renewal is spelled out in three terse statements: "Give us this day our daily bread. Forgive us our debts as we also have forgiven our debtors. Do not bring us to the time of trial, but rescue us from evil." The reference to debts probably should be understood in the Jubilee tradition of liquidation of debts, and not simply spiritualized as "sins" (in the Christian sense).[11]

The text from Isaiah, which Luke has Jesus take for the inauguration of his ministry in his hometown synagogue in Nazareth, also reflects the Jubilee tradition. The "Year of the Lord's Favor" is defined in terms of "good news to the poor," "release to the captives," "recovery of sight to the blind," and letting "the oppressed go free" (Luke 4:18–19).[12] However, in both these texts, the sabbatical legislation about restoration of land, letting animals rest, and the soil lie fallow are absent. The concern is for interhuman justice, but no longer from the perspective of farmers and their relation to animals and to land.

As Christianity developed, even these concerns for this-worldly justice would fade, to be replaced by a cosmological and spiritualized understanding of the work of Jesus as Messiah. Even though Christianity claimed to be the people of the "new covenant," the covenantal concepts of relationship to the land would be discarded. Christianity replaced the Jewish ethnic view of peoplehood with a universalist imperial view of God's "new people." It reinterpreted the promised land as the whole cosmos, and particularly as that part of the cosmos transcendent to earth, or "heaven." This meant that the concrete eco-justice perspective of Hebrew law vanished.

Thus the covenant idea lay fallow for most of the Middle Ages. However, the sixteenth century saw major recoveries of this concept among Zwinglian and Calvinist reformers and also the radical, Anabaptist wing of the Reformation. The emergence of European nationalism and the close links of Puritan reformers with some forms of militant nationalism revived the ancient connection between an elect nation and its national homeland. This concept, as we have seen earlier, would be carried by Puritan settlers to America and South Africa.

Anabaptist reformers stressed the conflict between the church as a covenanted community and the state. They saw the church as a redeemed community that stood for countercultural values, such as radical equality of persons, rejection of war and luxury, against the dominant ethos. A few movements, such as Gerrard Winstanley's Digger movement in England in 1649 and 1650, carried this concept into a communistic rejection of private property and the affirmation of the right of landless peasants, displaced by the enclosure movement, to reclaim common lands.[13]

This concept of the covenanted community as a religious state bound together by common principles would play a major role in the shaping of American political identity. In a sermon addressed to the Massachusetts Bay colonists in 1630, while still on shipboard, John Winthrop spelled out the Puritan vision of covenanted commonwealth:

> Thus stands the cause of God betweene God and us. Wee are entered into Covenant with him for this worke, we have taken out a Commission, the Lord hath given us leave to draw our owne Articles, . . . we have hereupon besought him of favour and blessing. How if the Lord shall please to heare us, and bring us in peace to the place wee desire, then hath hee ratified this Covenant and sealed our Commission and will expect a strickt performance of the Articles contained in it . . .[14]

Drawing on the precedent of God's covenant with Israel, Winthrop solemnly warned the new covenanters that if they violated these statutes, they could expect severe punishment from God.

To avoid divine wrath they must "do justly and love mercy and walk humbly with our God" (Micah 6:8), so the community could be "knit together as one man," hold together in brotherly affection and be ready to "abridge ourselves of superfluities" in order to minister to each other in times of necessity. The community must rejoice together, mourn together, labor and suffer together, keeping before their eyes their common life as one Body in the Lord. If they did this, the Lord "will be our God and will delight to dwell amongst us as His own people and will command blessing upon our ways."[15]

Winthrop also links this understanding of the Massachusetts Bay Colony as a covenanted people with that of a promised land that will thrive if the people are righteous, but will eject them if they are not:

> If our hearts turn away so that we will not obey, but shall be seduced and worship other gods, our pleasures and profits and serve them, it is propounded unto us this day, we shall surely perish out of the good Land whither we pass over this vast sea to possess it.[16]

This Puritan use of the covenant theme as the religious basis of a political community would play a major role in the development of the idea of American Constitution as a social contract, voluntarily entered into by all parties (male householders), and hence resting on the consent of the governed. These biblical and Puritan roots of American national identity are a source of much of the best and the worst in American culture; both notions of America as an Elect nation, especially favored by God to impose its will as divine law upon others, and also movements of prophetic self-criticism and national reform of social evils.[17]

The biblical concept of covenanted people was patriarchal; it was androcentric, anthropocentric, and ethnocentric. The Puritan revival of this idea in England and in America continued these exclusivist patterns. The covenant of the Massachusetts Bay Colonists was understood fundamentally as a contract between male householders. This meant that neither women, nor slaves, nor Indians, nor white male servants, nor nonchurch members were party to the contract.

The constitutional government constructed by the males of the merchant and planter classes of the thirteen colonies 150 years later would have the same restrictions, with the exception of church membership. All these other groups of people were understood as dependents without autonomous citizenship status. They were presumed to be represented by the collective headship of the male householder.

In the nineteenth and twentieth centuries, the United States would see a series of reform movements—universal manhood suffrage, abolitionism, women's suffrage, and the civil rights movement—that would seek to redress these limitations. The goal, still not perfectly achieved, has been for equal civil status for all adults, regardless of religion, race, gender, or "previous condition of servitude."

This has also meant widening the "religious-ethnic" limits of the American covenantal community. The Puritans saw the covenant as restricted to members of their faith community. The American social contract has needed to be continually stretched to include those who were not Anglo-Saxon Protestants, to Catholics, Jews, African-Americans, Asians, Hispanics. Attacks on Arab-Americans and Muslims during the 1991 Persian Gulf War is the latest strain in this process of expanding the American identity to genuinely include all who live in this land.[18]

THE COVENANT AND THE RIGHTS OF NATURE

Until the 1970s, however, there was little challenge in American culture to the anthropocentric assumptions of American constitutional life. The idea that "natural rights" might be expanded to include the "rights of nature" still strikes most Americans as somewhat bizarre. Recently several movements have begun to ask whether beings other than human might have "civil rights." Environmentalists have asked "whether trees have standing," seeking legal rights for species and environments. The animal rights movement has sought to extend civil rights to animals as individual persons.[19]

Environmentalists and animal rights activists have operated on different ethical perspectives, and this has caused sectarian conflicts between them. Animal rights ethical philosophy has focused on the rights of animals as individuals. It has focused primarily on domesticated or captive animals, the abusive treatment of animals in factory farms and in scientific laboratories. It draws on the deep emotional bonding of the human relationship with the pet, animals that live in the household with the rights to care and affection of a family member. This relationship to pets should not be trivialized, for it is the main arena where urban humans experience interspecies love and communication and come to recognize the personhood of animals.

The horror that is felt at the abuse of such animals on farms or in laboratories draws on this emotive bonding to the pet. But this is not simply a matter of sentimentality, but of a call for moral consistency. How can humans recognize the personhood of one dog and not of all dogs? How can we care deeply about the well-being of an animal who is a member of our household and let other animals of that same species undergo the cruelest torture and neglect?[20]

The interpersonal model of relation to animals is criticized by environmentalists. It means that the category of "animal rights" is extended primarily to certain "favorite" animals, primarily mammals. Some birds, fish, and reptiles may also be included. Insects, which are the vast majority of animal species, do not draw the same response. The traditional line between humans who possess "soul" and animals that do not is extended downward to include categories of animals. But a line is still drawn between a category of beings to be respected on the basis of "sentience," and those who lack sentience and hence lack "rights."[21]

Tom Regan, in his writings, represents the most throughgoing effort to assimilate nonhuman mammals into the category of moral rights based on consciousness. Going beyond many animal rights activists, who cite animal sentience and hence ability to feel pain as the basis for protection from painful procedures, Regan defines mammals as possessing all the requirements of personhood. Mammals not only experience both joy and pain, but also are purposive. They evidence goal-directed behavior that suggests an element of imagination of future possibilities. Recognition of persons, places, and events experienced before also indicates an element of memory. Like persons, mammals have psychopersonal identity over time.[22]

Such qualities of personhood prove, for Regan, that all the same rights that liberal society extends to the human person should be extended equally to the mammal. This means not only that animals should not be subjected to painful processes on farms or laboratories, but they should not be used for experiments, raised for food, hunted or trapped, or killed before their time, any more than we would treat a human person in any of these ways. Like humans, animals have an unconditional right to life. This is a moral right intrinsic to their nature as persons, which cannot be abridged by legal statutes that define them as property.

Despite Regan's definition of animals as conscious, purposive, and capable of decisions, he does not think animals are able to know right and wrong, and hence are not moral agents. They are moral patients, who are acted upon by moral agents who must be called to account, but they cannot be defined as culpable for their own acts. This does not prevent society from killing the rabid dog that threatens others, in situations of conflicts between rights to life. But animal life is morally innocent, and hence has the claim to the protection of innocent life, like small children.[23]

Regan recognizes that if animals could no longer be raised for food or used for scientific or commercial experiments, the population of animals on the earth would be quickly reduced by perhaps 20 billion to 30 billion. Many subspecies of animals that have been bred for human use would disappear, since humans would not raise pigs or cattle simply so they could enjoy a long, happy life. Like human population control, animal population should be reduced by not breeding, rather than by killing living animals.

A vast reduction of the animal population is itself no problem for Regan, since the value of the animal lies in the value of each individual, not in numbers or species. Human responsibility to animals is to let them be, presumably in wild habitats where they can take care of themselves. Regan has harsh words for environmentalists who are concerned for species and biotic communities, rather than for individual animals, calling them "environmental fascists." In his view the last member of an endangered species is no more valuable than the 2-millionth animal of that species. Each one is equally valuable as an individual.[24]

Environmental ethicists, by contrast, are concerned with the health of biotic communities and the maximization of diversity of species within their habitats. Hence they are more concerned about the life of a few insects of an endangered species than they are about the life of the 2-millionth deer in a park where deer are overrunning the carrying capacity of their habitat. This concern for endangered species is often defended on anthropocentric grounds: that each plant or animal species that disappears removes a potential source of knowledge about the earth that might be valuable for food or medicine.

But the value of species goes beyond these utilitarian criteria. Each species of plant or animal is a distinct evolutionary form of life, and thus, as a species, has unique value in its own right. Environmentalists operate from the principle that maximization of diversity of species promotes the health of the whole biotic community. Although natural evolution results in extinction of species over time, the recent human impact on the earth has accelerated this process of extinction in a very dangerous way, and hence humans must assert a role of explicit guardianship over endangered species.[25]

Environmentalists see animal rights activists as operating out of a misplaced sentimentality for particular favorite animals, which often results in greater hurt to these animals. Thus, for example, in cases where monitored culling of herds of deer or horses in state parks has been stopped on grounds of sentimental feelings for these types of animals, the result has been ecological disaster. Not only have proliferating herds of horses or deer stripped the forests and grasses for food, but finally have died in large numbers from starvation, a form of death more painful that if their numbers had been kept within limits through periodic shooting.[26]

The call to let animals "be" in the wild itself suggests a longing to return to a simpler world, where human power over the rest of life was limited and most animals indeed could "be" in untapped wilderness. But the enormous proliferation of human population and the capacity of humans to invade every environment, even the most inaccessible, does not leave us with this *laissez-faire* option toward animals. Like it or not, if the diverse biota of earth are to be protected and preserved, it will only be by the human community asserting an enlightened guardianship over it.[27]

This means close observation of nature, so that we can learn how a healthy biotic community is sustained through complex interchanges of plants and animals. But it also means that we become conscious promoters and restorers of such habitats; that is, they are no longer "on their own." Thus the biblical concept of humans as the "image of God," into whose hands care of nature is given, assumes a more profoundly ethical meaning. Not only does this role of humans give no mandate to destructive use of nature, but it also places a much more comprehensive responsibility for the preservation of nature in human hands. It is the human species that is accountable to the God of life to care for and protect the vast panoply of life forms produced by millennia of earth's creativity.[28]

But the concerns of animal rights activists should also be heard. There needs to be a place for moral sensitivity to the quality of life of highly sentient animals that most resemble humans in their capacity, not only to feel pain, but also to enjoy life, remember and imagine, and interrelate socially with their own species, as well as with humans. Such animals should not be subjected to painful experiments or caged in small, isolated cells where they are never allowed to romp or interact with others. These rights to quality of life are inherent in these animals themselves, not simply in terms of human relations to them.

The sheer numbers of animals used in laboratories far exceeds scientific necessity, and there is no excuse for the cruelty with which these animals are treated. Factory farming necessitates the use of artificial hormones and antibiotics on animals that are cruel to these animals themselves, not to mention their dubious results for the health of humans who consume the meat.[29] Meateating as the centerpiece of the affluent diet is questionable in the light of the need to feed starving millions. All these considerations suggest a vastly reduced use of animals in laboratories, and many fewer animals raised for food. In both contexts their rights to "humane" and natural conditions of life should be protected.

However, I am not sure that all these considerations add up to a moral mandate to eliminate either of these practices entirely. The demand of the animal rights movement for absolute vegetarianism, as an expression of the unconditional rights of animals to life, does not seem to me morally convincing. Many of these writers, such as Tom Regan, extend this principle primarily to mammal flesh, and are unclear about extending it to fish and fowl, much less "lesser life."[30] In an understanding of nature as continuous, how can such a line be drawn between animals with rights to life and those without such rights?

The attempt to derive this mandate from "nature" runs into the contradictory reality of predation as an unavoidable part of nature. Not only do carnivorous animals depend for their existence on eating other animals, but all life forms exist through an interdependency of consuming and being consumed. Even the bodies of large mammals must eventually decay, providing food for worms and insects. Nor is it sufficient to claim that one does not eat beings with whom one can have an interpersonal relation. As a vegetable gardener, I expend great loving care over each plant for months of every year and feel great pain when I see one that is ill, but I still intend to eat them.

It is likely that some humans, from the beginning of animal hunting, have felt pangs of guilt about eating animals. This is expressed in the biblical tradition that, in the original creation, both humans and animals were vegetarians. Meat-eating, and the predator-prey relation of humans and animals, represent a fall into an inferior moral state. In the covenant of God with Noah after the flood, it is said:

> The fear and dread of you shall rest on every animal on earth, and on every bird of the air, on everything that creeps on the ground, and on all the fish of the sea; into your hand they are delivered. Every moving thing that lives shall be food for you, and just as I gave you the green plants [in the original creation], [now] I give you everything. (Genesis 9:2–3)

Limits to human consumption of animals are imposed: "Only, you shall not eat flesh with its life, that is, its blood" (Genesis 9:4). In this limitation against eating animal blood, or shedding human blood, the biblical text recognizes the fundamental commonality between warm-blooded mammals and humans; both share the same blood of life.

Those who inherit from biblical culture a vision of redemption as return to Paradise have sometimes pointed to these texts to affirm that one expression of redeemed life is vegetarianism. We thereby restore the original peaceful relations between humans and animals, as we saw in the Isaiah text above. But this view stumbles on the fact that at least a major group of animals also eat other animals. Do we regard their predation as an expression of "fallen nature"? The lines between eating "higher" and "lower" animals, and even the eating of plants, seem arbitrary.

The consumer-consumed relation is an inevitable part of the biotic condition. Consequently the effort to escape from the ambiguity of killing other life in order to live is finally impossible.

Nevertheless there are compelling moral reasons for a mostly vegetarian diet, particularly for affluent people. Both justice to animals and concern for a just food ethic for the whole of humanity demands greatly reduced meat-eating, and the boycott of meat produced in factory farming. (Some meat is now available in "health food" stores that claims to be produced by "natural" animal raising.) A second reason to avoid meat is to express our solidarity with the hungry millions of humans who can only be adequately fed if affluent people eat lower on the food chain.

But we can hardly impose a vegetarian ethic on third-world peasants for whom the eating of the occasional chicken or pig that grows up in the barnyard is an indispensable part of an otherwise very limited diet. The possibility of having many forms of alternative protein, and hence a healthy diet without meat, is the luxury of the affluent. So it is we of affluent nations, whose supermarkets are filled with a great variety of foods from all over the world, who can and should adopt a near-vegetarian diet for the sake of the rights of both animals and other humans.

Christopher Stone—the philosopher of law whose famous brief defended the legal standing of trees, in the 1969 case of the Sierra Club versus the Disney Enterprises development of the Mineral King Valley into a huge resort[31]—has recently suggested that environmental ethics has suffered from "moral monism." Whether they adopt a utilitarian or a deontological view of ethics, the various schools of animal rights or environmental ethics have sought a single set of principles that are all-encompassing. The result is that many realities are ignored or fitted into a scheme of ethical thought that is inappropriate. This seems to me the case with Tom Regan's effort to assimilate animals rights into the framework of moral rights of human persons.

Stone suggests that there is a need for moral pluralism in ecological ethics and in the translation of such ethics into legal principles. By moral pluralism Stone is not speaking of moral
relativism, in which universal ethical standards are abandoned in
favor of cultural pluralism. Rather, he suggests that different
rules of ethics need apply in different contexts or "planes" of reality.[32] The ethical principles applicable to the protection of
human life cannot be exactly identified with those appropriate
for highly sentient mammals.

Yet there is a place for elements of such respect for the individual sentient animal that is different from plants or less sentient
animals. In addition, there are ethical principles that need to be
applied to biotic communities and endangered species that operate on a different plane of values than those applicable to individual mammals in captivity. Perhaps the most important issue
here, in Stone's call for "moral pluralism," is a recognition of
both the usefulness but also the inadequacy of defining "nature"
solely through the rubric of "individual rights." American culture needs to be able to think in terms of community relationships. We need to learn to envision humans and nonhumans in
biotic communities, in which a plurality of values needs to be
balanced in relation to each other.[33]

The rights of sentient animals to be free of excessive pain and
to enjoy a modicum of qualitative life, even if their final fate is
the human dinner table; the need for "wilderness" habitats to
have a balance of predator and prey, if some animals are not to
destroy their own carrying capacity; the need to preserve biotic
diversity and prevent rapid extinction of species—all these are
values that need to be defended. The ethical basis for each of
these various values needs to be clarified in a rich tapestry of
rights, values, and duties of humans to the other life forms toward which we must assume the responsibility of guardianship.[34]

A covenantal vision of the relation of humans to other life forms acknowledges the special place of humans in this relationship as caretakers, caretakers who did not create and do not absolutely own the rest of life, but who are ultimately accountable for its welfare to the true source of life, God. This covenantal vision recognizes that humans and other life forms are part of one family, sisters and brothers in one community of interdependence. Although we have limited rights of use of other life forms, and also responsibilities of care and protection toward them, there is an ultimate thouness at the heart of every other living being, whether it be a great mountain lion or swaying bacteria, that declares its otherness from us.[35]

The covenantal relation between humans and all other life forms, as one family united by one source of life, forbids this otherness from being translated into destructive hostility. We have no right to wipe out any other life form because it is different from us. But rather, we encounter each other being simultaneously as "other" and as kin, as indeed we encounter each human person. The plant stretching toward the sun, the animal whose eyes warily encounter ours as it pauses in its tasks, reveal their own being in and for themselves.

This means that the other life forms finally cannot simply pass into our power as property, as "things" without their own life and being. Each has its own distinct relation to God as source of life, and not necessarily for our purposes, a vision eloquently revealed in the voice of God to Job from the whirlwind. Thus, even in order to make use of animals and plants for food and clothing and other needs, there must remain an ultimate *caveat* against reducing animals or plants, soils, or mountains to the status of "things" under our power.

Each life form has its own purpose, its own right to exist, its own independent relation to God and to other beings. Encompassing our relation to nature as usable things there must remain the larger sensibility, rooted in the encounter with nature as "thou," as fellow beings each with its own integrity.[36] It is not idle sentiment to thank the animals and plants that provide the sources of our life before we make use of any material thing. The prayer of thanksgiving before every meal is required if we are to begin to be in right relation to our fellow beings in the covenant of creation.

9

Healing the World: The Sacramental Tradition

In this chapter I trace a line of Christian tradition that regards Christ as the cosmic manifestation of God, appearing both as the immanent divine source and ground of creation and its ultimate redemptive healing. Although this cosmological understanding of Christ as both creator and redeemer of the cosmos, and not just of human beings separated from the cosmos, is central to much of New Testament thought, Western Christianity since the late medieval and Reformation periods has ignored this holistic vision. Thus modern searchers for a cosmological spirituality have assumed that this is lacking in Christianity and can only be found in non-Christian perspectives, such as pagan "nature religions" or Asian religions.

Although the cosmological tradition in Christianity needs reinterpretation to be adequate for ecological spirituality, nevertheless it has not been absent. Its possibilities and limits will be discussed in this chapter. I will then explore what it would mean to restore for today the cosmological center of theology and spirituality. Once the cosmos becomes the mediating context of all theological definition and spiritual experience, how does this change our understanding of both "God" and "humans"?

HELLENISTIC ROOTS OF COSMOLOGICAL CHRISTOLOGY

New Testament and early Christian cosmological Christology built on theologies of cosmogenesis in Oriental Hellenism, particularly as these had already been assimilated into Hellenistic Judaism. The mediation of these ideas through Judaism allowed Christians to assimilate ideas of Hellenistic philosophy, while denying their "pagan" origins. Christian theology took over the Hellenistic Jewish apologetic myth that Plato had learned his philosophy from Moses. Thus the similarity of Christian theology to contemporary Platonic thought could be explained away by making Platonism derivative of biblical revelation.[1]

Christianity also took over from Judaism an ideology of religious "purism," over against paganism as "false religion." This dualism still shapes Christian self-understanding, causing it to obscure and deny its actual syncretistic reality. Today this role of Christianity as synthesizer of major Hebraic, Oriental, and Greco-Roman thought should be recognized as a strength, rather than a "secret" to be denied. Certainly Christianity's success as the "winning" religion of late antiquity can hardly be explained apart from this synthesizing process. Today's eco-spiritual crisis demands a synthesizing creativity of even greater expansiveness.

What is called here Oriental Hellenism encompasses both schools of Greek philosophy that had synthesized the Platonic, Stoic, and Peripatetic cosmologies,[2] and also movements that restated this mystical philosophy as "Oriental wisdom," for example, the *Chaldean Oracles* and the Hermetic literature.[3] Out of this speculative milieu there also emerged the Gnostic literature. But the writings I trace here rejected Gnostic anti-cosmic dualism. Instead they affirmed the cosmos as the expression of immanent divinity, within which humans stood as microcosm to macrocosm.

In Middle Platonism the Platonic concept of the transcendent world of Ideas and the Aristotelian concept of the Divine Mind were combined. Also combined were Plato's concept of the World Soul and the Stoic concept of the Logos, which Stoics saw as the

immanent life-power of all beings. There thus developed a cosmogonic story with either a two-part or a three-part sequence.
Neoplatonism in Plotinus fully develops the three-part sequence.[4]

The cosmos is seen as originating in a transcendent divine
being, who is the source of all things. This divine being brings
forth from "himself" a perfect "image" and self-expression, in
which the intellectual essences of all things are contained. This
second God is then also identified with the Demiurgos, who
shapes the cosmos from the intellectual "blueprint" contained in
"his" own mind. The world soul, in turn, expresses this divine
Logos in immanent form as the sustaining power of the cosmos.
Human souls are seen as partaking in the substance of this world
soul or immanent Logos of the cosmos.[5]

This cosmogonic picture was used in Jewish Wisdom literature to describe divine Wisdom as a secondary manifestation of
the Creator God who is God's agent in creating the universe, and
is also the immanent power that sustains the universe. Wisdom is
understood also as the presence of God speaking in revelation.
Through Wisdom human souls come to know God and grow
into virtuous "sons" of God.[6]

Philo, the major philosopher of Hellenistic Judaism, developed a more elaborate philosophical theology. He saw God
bringing forth a secondary expression, the divine Logos, who is
the manifestation of the divine mind. From this Logos radiate the
"Dynameis" or energies of God that create the world. The cosmos is sustained by the power of this immanent Logos. Each
human soul, in turn, reflects the divine logos. Humans and cosmos thus are seen as "brothers" and parallel "sons of God."[7]

THE CHRISTIAN SYNTHESIS: COSMIC CHRISTOLOGY

The term *Christ* originally referred to the Messiah, a figure in
Jewish apocalyptic thought that was seen as appearing at the end
of world history to destroy the forces of evil and renovate the

universe, installing the saints of God there in a blessed existence.
In Jewish apocalyptic thought, there had been no identification
of this figure of the Messiah with cosmogenesis, even though he
was sometimes seen as "preexistent."[8] The Christianity reflected
in the synoptic Gospels also lacks this identification of Christ
with the cosmogonic Logos. However, when we turn to the more
speculative Christian thought found in Paul, the Gospel of John,
and the book of Hebrews, this identification of Christ as redeemer with the cosmogonic Logos has been put together into a
unified vision of the beginning and the end of "all things." One
of the fullest expressions of this cosmological Christology is
found in Colossians 1:15–20:

> He is the image of the invisible God, the firstborn of all cre-
> ation; for in him all things in heaven and on earth were created,
> things visible and invisible, whether thrones or dominions or
> rulers or powers—all things have been created through him and
> for him. He himself is before all things, and in him all things hold
> together. He is the head of the body, the church; he is the begin-
> ning, the firstborn from the dead, so that he might come to have
> first place in everything. For in him all the fullness of God was
> pleased to dwell and through him God was pleased to reconcile
> to himself all things, whether on earth or in heaven, by making
> peace through the blood of his cross.

It is likely that the original form of this hymn stressed primarily the cosmological logos. It has been edited to add the Christo-
logical references to "the church," "the firstborn from the dead,"
and "the blood of the cross."[9] The resulting synthesis brings together the two dramas of creation and redemption in the figure
of the Logos-Christ. This one divine being is seen as (1) the manifestation of God, (2) the immanent presence of God that creates
and sustains the cosmos, and (3) the divine power remanifest at
the end of time, healing the enmity that has divided the cosmos
and reconciling the cosmos to God.

The divine person encountered in Jesus is thereby identified with this Logos-Christ. His redemptive act "through the blood of the cross" is seen as the paradigmatic manifestation of one and the same divine being of the beginning and the end of "all things." As firstborn from the dead and head of the body, the Church, Christ is seen as the power of the new creation, not severed from the cosmos created in the beginning, but the principle through which this cosmos was originally created and now is renewed and reconciled with God. The Church itself is seen cosmologically. It is not simply a group of human believers in this figure, but is the paradigmatic community of the whole renovated cosmos.

The references to "thrones," "dominions," "rulers," and "powers" reflects a Judaeo-Persian apocalyptic cosmology, in which God is seen as ruling the cosmos through angelic agents. The regions of earth, both the primary elements and the nations, and the planetary spheres, were understood as ruled by angelic governors. These angelic spirits were believed to have revolted against God, creating an alienated universe in which evil triumphs over good.[10]

The manifestation of the cosmogonic Logos in the end time thus can be understood as a reincursion of God's primal creative power, subjugating these dissident angelic powers and thereby bringing about a reunified cosmos, reconciled to God, and filled with God's plenary goodness. The culmination of this process of subjugation of the unruly cosmic powers, and the reconciliation of the cosmos with God, is, as Paul puts it in 1 Corinthians 15:25, "So that God may be all in all."

This bold effort to unify cosmogony and eschatology in early Christianity, however, was jeopardized by the conflicting strands of Hebrew and Greek thought that they sought to synthesize. The Hebrew concept of "creation" demanded a cleavage between the being of God and that of created beings, including humans.

Jewish thought originally saw humans as essentially mortal. Redemption was a fulfilled, blessed existence on earth within mortal limits, that is, one hundred years.[11]

Greek thought, by contrast, saw the relation of God and cosmos as emanational. There is ontological continuity between God, the Logos of God, and the cosmos. Each of these realities expresses being on different levels of existence. Thus the world soul and the human soul partake in the being of the divine Logos, which manifests the ultimate source of being. But Greek thought also sees the cosmos as split between a higher planetary realm of immortal being and a sublunar world of mortal being. The soul belongs to the higher realm and has been cast down "unnaturally" into a body. Its task is to escape from the body through turning the mind "upward" and so return at death to disincarnate, immortal blessedness in the stars.

Classical Christianity presented several efforts to unify these disparate worldviews. With the Hebrew view, Christianity insisted that humans were a psychophysical union. The body was essential for wholeness of existence, and the resurrection of the body was intrinsic to salvation. Christ must have a real body, not merely an "appearance" of body. Both of these ideas were to cause great difficulty to those imbued with Platonic thought. Patristic Christianity fended off various efforts to deny a bodily incarnation to Christ and the bodily resurrection of both Christ and humanity.[12]

At the same time, Christianity accepted the Platonic prejudice against "becoming." The transience and mortality of material existence was evil. The solution, found already in Paul, is the strange concept of the "spiritual body," a created vehicle of the soul, but stripped of its mortality. This concept of the transfigured body in redeemed life was applied, not only to humans, but to the whole cosmos. Christians shared with Hellenism the view that the whole cosmos was alive, pervaded by dynamic energy that Christianity identified with the immanent Logos of God.

Even animals and plants had soul, and the human soul shared with them the animal and vegetative soul.[13] Human psychophysical existence was inseparable from this cosmic whole, within which humans stood as microcosm.

One ambitious effort to create a theology in which creation, incarnation, and consummation are unified in one cosmic whole is found in the second-century anti-Gnostic churchman, Irenaeus, as was mentioned in chapter 5. For Irenaeus, creation is itself an incarnation of the Word and Spirit of God, as the ontological ground of bodily existence. The incarnation of the historical Christ is the renewal of this divine power underlying creation. In the incarnation divine power permeates bodily nature in a yet deeper way, so that the bodily becomes the sacramental bearer of the divine, and the divine deifies the bodily.

The Christian sacraments are paradigmatic of this deeper mingling of body and spirit, renewing the life power of creation. As Irenaeus puts it in his refutation of gnostic negation of the body:

> But indeed vain are they who despise the entire dispensation of God and disallow the salvation of the flesh, and treat with contempt its regeneration, maintaining that it is not capable of incorruption. But if this indeed does not attain salvation, then neither did the Lord redeem us with his blood, nor is the cup of the Eucharist the communion of His blood, nor is the bread which we break the communion of His body. For the blood can only come up from the veins and the flesh, and whatsoever else makes up the substance of man, such as the Word of God was actually made . . . And as we are his members, we are also nourished by means of the creation . . . He has acknowledged the cup, which is part of creation, as His own blood, and the bread, which is also part of creation, he has established as His own body, from which he gives increase to our body.[14]

But since for Irenaeus (as for Paul and for all subsequent Christianity) salvation has to do with transcending mortality, the

only way he can finally think about redemption—not just of the
human being, but of the cosmos as a whole—is by assuming that,
through being infused by the immortal life of the divine, it will
overcome its mortality. This redemption of creation, following
the biblical apocalyptic tradition, takes place in two stages. First,
there is the millennial blessedness of earthly life. Irenaeus describes the millennium in images drawn from Hebrew prophecy:

> Then the whole creation shall, according to God's will, ob-
> tain a vast increase, that it might bring forth and sustain fruits,
> such as Isaiah declares . . . And they shall come and rejoice in
> Mount Zion, and shall come come to what is good, and into a
> land of wheat and wine and fruits, of animals and of sheep; that
> their soul shall be as a tree bearing fruit, and they shall hunger no
> more.[15]

Then the whole cosmos will be transformed into a "new heaven
and earth," immortalized, and fully united with the divine life of
God. This final union with the Being of God fulfills the promise
of the original creation:

> And in all these things and by them, the same God the Father
> is manifested, who fashioned man and gave the promise of the
> inheritance of the earth to the fathers, who brought forth the
> creature from bondage at the resurrection of the just and fulfills
> the promises for the Kingdom of his Son . . . For there is one Son,
> who accomplished his Father's will, and one human race also in
> which the mysteries of God are wrought . . . the wisdom of God,
> by means of which his handiwork, confirmed and incorporated
> with his Son, is brought to perfection; that is His offspring, the
> First-begotten Word, should descend to the creature . . . and that
> it should be contained in Him, and, on the other hand, the crea-
> ture should contain the Word, and ascend to Him, passing be-
> yond the angels, and be made after the image and likeness of
> God.[16]

This effort to incorporate the lush Hebraic view of earthly
blessedness into eternal salvation was dropped by mainline

Christianity after the third century. Christ is seen as establishing his millennial reign through the political power of the church and Christian rulers, but this has no effect on renewal of nature, nor does it bring forth a new era of justice between humans.[17] Millennial visions continue in Christianity, but as the preserve of heretical, counterestablishment groups. Dominant Christianity sees the earth as going downhill toward destruction. Although the cosmos too will participate in the resurrected, immortal "new heaven and earth," the focus is on humans and on planetary spheres, not on other forms of earthly life.[18]

DISINTEGRATION AND RENEWAL OF COSMOLOGICAL THEOLOGY

Although a millennial vision of redeemed earth was discarded by dominant Christianity, the cosmogonic Logos, as the principle of creation, continued in medieval Christianity, both Eastern and Western, as the basis of a view of nature as an ontological "ladder" of ascent to God. This view of nature was transmitted to Western Christianity particularly by the writings of Dionysius the Areopagite.[19]

This understanding of nature as emanational stages of descent (the levels of being from God to angelic hierarchies to humans to animals and plants, rocks, mountains, and rivers) is continuous. The "way down" from God to the humblest creature is also the "way up." Hence, as we have seen in Bonaventure's *The Mind's Road to God*, the contemplative ascent to God begins with the contemplation of visible things, and moves upward to contemplative union with the being of God.

This worldview began to disintegrate in the late Middle Ages. Nominalism rejected the Platonic ontological epistemology, which saw in every plant, animal, or other being a disclosure of an eternal essence in the Mind of God. "Ideas" became mere "names" for collections of individuals. For nominalism, also, the universe no longer disclosed the divine essence, but merely the

"ordained will" of God. God was no longer the top of a continuous ontic and epistemological hierarchy, disclosed in visible
things. Rather, God dwelt in a transcendent otherness radically
inaccessible to the human mind and spirit.[20]

Thus one could no longer begin with the perception of visible
things and move upward through the mind's categories to union
with the mind and being of God. The ladder of ascent had been
broken, both ontologically and epistemologically. The distance
between God and humans could only be bridged by divine revelation, not by any "natural" speculative or mystical capacities of
humans. Nominalism reinforced the renewed Augustinianism of
the Reformation in its emphasis on the unbridgeable gap between "fallen nature" and God, making it hostile to mysticism
and to sacramental views of nature.

However, the Renaissance period also saw a great revival of
cosmological mysticism, reinforced by new access to its ancient
Hellenistic sources. Byzantine scholars, fleeing from the Turkish
conquest of Constantinople, would bring to Italy the corpus of
Hermetic literature and the *Chaldean Oracles,* as well as Platonic
and Neoplatonic works previously unknown in the West. Italian
scholars, like Ficino (1433–99), working under the patronage of
Cosimo De Medici, translated these works, initiating a renewed
Neoplatonic cosmic mysticism, often only lightly disguised as
Christianity.[21]

Renaissance scholars were misled by the belief that the
Hermetic literature represented an ancient Egyptian wisdom con-
temporaneous with Moses. They believed it to be a pristine wisdom parallel with the oldest roots of the Bible. Revelation in
Christ renewed and fulfilled this ancient wisdom. Thus the
Renaissance reduplicated the ancient chronological error that
justified the fusion of biblical and Neoplatonic thought.[22]

In the early sixteenth century, Copernicus would challenge the
ancient geocentric cosmology, making the earth as one planet
among others circling the sun. But, for Renaissance Neoplatonists,

this removed the distance from earth to the planetary spheres. The permeation of the whole universe by the animating world soul, consubstantial with the human soul, allowed Renaissance magicians, such as Paracelsus (1493–1541) and Giordano Bruno (1548–1600), to see themselves as empowered to roam freely throughout the cosmos, communing with the nearest plants and rocks and the farthest planets through the faculties of the soul that had affinities with these earthly and celestial elements.[23]

But Bruno was burned to death in 1600 as a heretic. In the seventeenth century, both orthodox theology and orthodox science would distance themselves from Neoplatonic magic. Yet Neoplatonism, in more chastened form, did not die out, but would be continued among the Anglican school of Cambridge Platonists, such as Ralph Cudworth (1617–88) and Henry More (1614–87). These thinkers sought to bridge the sharp dualism of revelation and reason by reestablishing the ontological relation between the divine mind and the human mind. For More, God also indwells in the universe as Spirit of Nature or World Soul.[24] Renewed by grace, the human spirit could once again ascend from outer to inner things and attain to contemplative experience of the divine through Nature.

The eighteenth and nineteenth centuries saw a continual stream of philosophical idealism, which sought to bridge the division of mind and matter with some concept of the divine as the unifying source of both thought and physical things. For the heterodox Jewish philosopher Spinoza (1632–77), God was *natura naturans,* the underlying substance from which arose the physical world and the human mind (*natura naturata*), as mutual reflections of each other.[25]

German idealists Johann Gottlieb Fichte (1762–1814) and Friedrich Wilhelm Schelling (1775–1854) would also expound philosophies of Nature that saw God as the unitary Being underlying both thought and physical things. G. W. F. Hegel (1770–1831) sought to bridge spirit and matter through a dialectical process of thesis (spirit), antithesis (material expression), and synthesis (matter-spirit union), which in turn became the new thesis.

This European quest for a philosophy of nature that united matter and spirit continued to be haunted by the unresolved syncreticism in Christianity of Greek and Hebrew thought. Those who moved toward a more pantheistic communion with deity immanent in nature, such as the English poets Coleridge and Wordsworth, would toy with modes of thought more "pagan" than Christian.[26] In reaction to these trends, Christian theology would seek to establish its "purely biblical" roots by rejecting any presence of God in nature. Yet other Christians would seek to mediate between this opposition, restating forms of cosmological Christology.[27]

TYPES OF CONTEMPORARY ECOLOGICAL THEOLOGY

Although the ecological crisis interjects a new urgency into this quest for a theology of nature, in many ways the tensions between Christian and anti-Christian proposals represent a restatement of this classic tension between Greek and Hebrew thought. For neo-pagan thealogians such as Carol Christ, the pagan gods and particularly the goddesses are being reborn to save us from antinatural Christianity. For Christian ecological thinkers, however, the biblical God and Gaia are not at odds; rightly understood, they are on terms of amity, if not commingling.

Three somewhat different versions of Christian cosmological theology circulate in the contemporary quest for ecological spirituality. One of these is Creation-centered spirituality, represented particularly by Matthew Fox (see chapter 6). Another has been developed by followers of the French paleontologist-philosopher Pierre Teilhard de Chardin (1881–1955), and a third is based on the process theology of Alfred North Whitehead (1861–1947). I will characterize each of these briefly, and then discuss the key elements in them for an ecofeminist theology of nature.

For Fox, original blessing is the intrinsic nature of things. True Christian spirituality remains rooted in this vivid sense of original goodness. Evil is present in history, but as distortion and alienation from original blessing, not as primary reality. Evil can be evaluated as evil only in its negation of primary goodness, which remains our true "nature." Goodness is fundamentally relational. It is the life-giving and celebratory interconnection of all things. Evil is the denial of that interconnection.[28]

In his *The Coming of the Cosmic Christ*, Fox reclaims the classical cosmological Christology we have discussed in this chapter. Christ is not simply confined to the historical Jesus, nor only related to human souls. Christ is the immanent Wisdom of God present in the whole cosmos as its principle of interconnected and abundant life. The cosmic Christ is not only the foundational basis of original blessing in creation, but is its *telos* or direction of fulfillment. Creation moves toward increasing fulfillment of this abundance of life. The cosmic Christ is thus another name for original and final blessing. It is both immanent divinity present in all things in their interconnection, and the fulfilled being of the cosmos, which it seeks to realize.[29]

For Christians, Jesus is the paradigmatic manifestation of cosmic wisdom and goodness. But he is only one such manifestation. The same wisdom and goodness underlies all other religious quests and has been manifest in many other symbolic expressions, such as the Tao, the Buddha, the Great Spirit, and the Goddess. Thus the truth manifest in Jesus is in no way exclusive, but links Christians in "deep ecumenism" with all other religions, not just the "Great Religions," but also native religions that have been despised as "paganism."[30]

Fox also calls for dialogue with secular wisdom cultures, such as psychotherapy, whose antireligious views have often been based on critique of the distortions of religion. The recovery of an ecological spirituality also means that we have to redevelop the "right brain" or intuitive part of our experience and culture atrophied by masculine dominance. This means attention to the arts and liturgy, dance and bodywork, to reawaken our deadened capacities for holistic experience.

I think that Fox is basically on target in these affirmations and values. His chief defect is a certain superficiality. He has, as it were, mapped the territory that needs exploring, but others have to follow up in greater depth.[31] Particularly problematic is his tendency to distort the Christian past by dividing it into two traditions, creation-based and fall/redemption. Although there is some element of truth in this distinction, he appropriates it in too simplistic a manner, exaggerating the similarities to his own views among medieval mystics, such as Meister Eckhardt or Hildegard of Bingen, with whom he identifies himself.[32]

In Fox's account the ambiguities of all these Christian thinkers, and the elements of social hierarchy and spirit-matter dualism in them, are erased. Fox tends to brush off the significant differences between these expressions of past Christian tradition and his view of creation spirituality, rather than grappling with the meaning of these differences. The deep questions of sin and death, which were central to Christian theology, need new answers for today, and not simply a denial that these are real questions.

The second and third types of ecological theology to be summarized here represent important efforts to incorporate new scientific understanding, the new earth story of evolution and the new subatomic physics or quantum mechanics. Teilhard de Chardin, whose writings only became available in the late 1950s due to church censorship, used the new insights from evolution to restate the sweeping cosmic vision of salvation history found 1,700 years earlier in Irenaeus. Not just humans, but all of nature is part of this salvation drama.

For Teilhard, the universe is a total system that ascends in successive systems of organization, from the atomic to the planetary level. This ascent to increasing organizational complexity is also a moral and spiritual ascent, moving toward the unification of consciousness in what Teilhard calls "the Omega Point." The different stages of the evolution of matter, from atomic energy to molecular organization to cellular life to plants and animals and finally humans, are not merely changes of quantitative complexity, but are qualitative leaps to new levels of existence.[33]

The universe evolves along the axis of the complexification of matter. Increasingly complex organization of matter increases the internal "radial energy." It is this interior aspect of the complexification of matter that Teilhard sees as responsible for "boiling points" that bring breakthroughs to new levels of existence. There arises from molecular organization the living cell, then increasingly complex organic beings that become more and more aware, and then human self-consciousness. Everything that appears in the process of cosmogenesis is latent from its beginning, but this does not change the reality of its historical birth, which can appear only when a critical level of evolution is reached.

Teilhard's thought would mesh well with the Gaia hypothesis, for he sees the planet earth as a living organism.[34] Earth is one living organism, not only spatially, but across time. The planet earth grows through stages of development that are not repeatable, any more than the stages of organic growth from fetus to adult are repeatable. Like an organism, it will also eventually die.

The link between geosphere and biosphere is the organic cell, the highest unit of the molecular structure and the simplest unit in the organic structure. The breakthrough to life expresses a new level of centerness and unification, in which the whole structure becomes an organism participating in a common center and a common life. Unlike nonorganic structures that can be split up and each part survive, when the vital center of an organism is cut, the whole structure disintegrates.

Once organic life appears, its profusion ramifies into ordered types. The phyla become self-perpetuating along the lines laid out by specific types, and they cease to be able to cross-fertilize each other. There is a pattern of experimentation in evolution. First there appears the rudimentary type, then a series of modifications and experimentations with that type, until the most efficient form of that species is reached and its reproduction is stabilized around that form. Less successful experiments die out, and evolutionary changes within that species cease. The suppression of penults gives the impression of greater differences between phyla than originally existed when evolution of that group of related species was in progress.

For Teilhard, the evolutionary tree has a privileged axis or *telos*. This *telos* is toward increasing interiorization and centricity, increasing coordination around the directing center of the organism. With vertebrates we arrive at an animal, not held together by an external shell, but from within by a central nervous system. From vertebrates to reptiles to mammals, the nervous system develops a unifying center in the brain. The increasing size and convolutions of the brain correspond to increasingly intelligent species of mammals, until we arrive at *Homo sapiens,* in which conscious thought appears.

For the last 100,000 years, humans have been the privileged axis of evolution, while the animal and plant kingdoms, from which humans arose, diminish. Now the age of animals is over, and the earth is more and more a human earth. Once the level of thought is reached, evolution takes place socially rather than organically. Humans are more adaptable than animals because they add new evolutionary developments, not as adaptations of their bodies, but as culture and technology. Human evolution through culture and technology is through the complementarity of increasing individuality and increasing collectivity.

Teilhard unabashedly sees Christian Western history as the privileged axis of cultural evolution. From the Neolithic revolution, there arose a limited number of classical civilizations, of which the Greco-Roman world was one. From the Renaissance to the twentieth century, a new stage of modernity began, which is now reaching around the globe, transforming all surviving Neolithic and classical cultures. Teilhard sees this new global stage of consciousness and technology as making possible a "noosphere" or world mind that is increasingly unified and centralized. Human minds together increasingly become one unitary Mind.

Teilhard sees this evolution toward unitary Mind as, in some sense, the evolution of immanent deity or the cosmic Christ. As increasingly collective consciousness develops, finally the organic substratum of the planet will die away, and Unitary Mind will be born from the finite earth into eternal life. The universe will fall away and die after having given birth to God, the ultimate communal consciousness, in which all that has gone before is gathered up and made immortal.[35]

This world picture contains some disturbing elements that need to be rejected. One is the way in which traditional hierarchical order has been "laid on its side," in an evolutionary concept of "progress," together with the confident faith in Western civilization and modernity as the privileged axis of this progress. The anticolonial movements and the ecological crisis have put this confidence in Eurocentric progress in grave question. Second, there is the sanguine acceptance of extinction of species as the acceptable price of progress. Does this not imply an acceptance of ethnocidal destruction of other peoples and cultures as also to be tossed aside by the triumphal march of Eurocentric progress?

Finally we must question the vision of the material underpinnings of consciousness as being tossed aside in the eschatological, culminating stage of evolution, a conclusion that contradicts the foundational insight of life and consciousness as the interiority of complexified matter. Surely this means that mind and body, the inside and the outside, cannot finally be separated. What is compelling about Teilhard's thought for today is precisely this insight that mind is the interiority of matter, and it is continuous from the simplest molecule to the most complex organism.

Process theology, as developed by Christian theologians such as John Cobb and Marjorie Suchocki,[36] from A. N. Whitehead's work,[37] has many affinities with the thought of Teilhard de Chardin. Like Teilhard, process theology sees an element of "mentality" present even in the random movements of subatomic particles. "Mentality" is a capacity for interaction, which becomes increasingly self-determining and conscious as matter organizes itself at successive layers of organizational complexity.

Process theology postulates, as underlying this process, a dipolar God. The Primordial Nature of God contains the whole of potentiality of all existing entities at every moment of actualization. This Primordial Nature of God provides the "initial aim" or best potential option for each entity at each occasion of existence. This "initial aim" relates to the total context of the past of that entity at that moment, and thus is interrelated with all that has been, ultimately, in the whole universe.

Each entity has, however, its own subjectivity. It adapts or actualizes this aim of God through actualizing one possibility that can only partially fulfill that aim, and can even thwart that aim in negative choices that are destructive. Thus the God of Process theology "lures," but does not coerce. It offers continual new possibilities, but the choice belongs to existent entities that can negate their own best options. There is freedom and risk in divine creativity, and with this risk, the possibility of evil. This possibility of evil increases as consciousness and power increase on the part of existent entities.

As entities opt for particular choices, these actualizations are taken into the being of God as God's Consequent Nature. The reality of God is thus shaped through interrelation with self-actualizing entities. God not only lures and offers new life, but also suffers, experiencing the pain of destructive choices as well as the pleasure of good choices.

Process theologians also postulate that this Consequent Nature of God, reflecting the memory of all that has been, is taken up in some way into the Primordial Nature of God, not only preserving immortally all that has been, but also incorporating it into the total vision of what could and should have been, to reconcile the evils and missed opportunities of history. In this way all that has been is not only remembered in the eternal being of God, but is redeemed as well.[38]

TOWARD AN ECOFEMINIST THEOCOSMOLOGY

Ecofeminist theology and spirituality has tended to assume that the "Goddess" we need for ecological well-being is the reverse of the God we have had in the Semitic monotheistic traditions; immanent rather than transcendent, female rather than male identified, relational and interactive rather than dominating, pluriform and multicentered rather than uniform and monocentered. But perhaps we need a more imaginative solution to these traditional oppositions than simply their reversal, something more like Nicholas of Cusa's paradoxical "coincidence of opposites," in which the "absolute maximum" and the "absolute minimum" are the same.[39]

As I suggested in chapter 2, something like this coincidence of opposites has appeared, surprisingly, in subatomic physics. Newtonian physics had seen reality as composed of indestructible atoms, like hard billiard balls, moved by external force in a fixed space. God was seen as constructing this world from outside it, like a clock-maker, and setting it to run by its own internal mechanism, but in no way participating in it as an immanent life-force. Eventually this external God was banished altogether as an unnecessary hypothesis. The universe came to be seen as a mechanistic system arising from random accidents.

But, as physicists continued to probe matter, seeking its ultimate "building blocks" or smallest "simple units," out of which everything else was composed by mechanistic combinations, they discovered smaller and smaller units. The atom was made up of vast space in which tiny particles or electrons moved around an extremely concentrated core or nucleus that contained most of the mass of the atom. The relation of the two can be envisioned if we imagine blowing up an atom to the size of the dome of St. Peter's Basilica in Rome. The nucleus would then be the size of a grain of salt.[40]

The nucleus itself was recognized to be held together by a distinct energy, nuclear energy, the same energy that fires the sun, but found rarely in earth in "loose" form. As the physicists penetrated the nucleus, they discovered that this too was composed of various particles, protons and neutrons. As techniques for detection of yet smaller particles increased, more and more particles were counted, until finally it became apparent that the whole concept of "particles," or elementary "building blocks" of matter, needed to be abandoned. What the physicists were discovering were energy fields in which energy "events" appeared and disappeared. Particles appeared out of energy and dissolved back into energy.

At the subatomic level, the classical distinction between matter and energy disappears. Matter is energy moving in defined patterns of relationality. At the level of the "absolute minimum," the appearance of physical "stuff" disappears into a voidlike web of relationships, relationships in which the whole universe is finally interconnected and in which the observer also stands as part of the process. We cannot observe anything "objectively," for the very act of observation affects what we observe.

As we move below the "absolute minimum" of the tiniest particles into the dancing void of energy patterns that build up the "appearance" of solid objects on the macroscopic level, we also recognize that this is also the "absolute maximum," the matrix of all interconnections of the whole universe. This matrix of dancing energy operates with a "rationality," predictable patterns that result in a fixed number of possibilities. Thus what we have traditionally called "God," the "mind," or rational pattern holding all things together, and what we have called "matter," the "ground" of physical objects, come together. The disintegration of the many into infinitely small "bits," and the One, or unifying whole that connects all things together, coincide.

How do we connect ourselves and the meaning of our lives to these worlds of the very small and the very big, standing in between the dancing void of energy that underlies the atomic structure of our bodies and the universe, whose galaxies, stretching over vast space and time, dwarf our histories? Even our bodies, despite the appearance of continuity over time, are continually dying and being reborn in every second. Over a period of seven years, every molecule of our body has been replaced.

In this universe of the very small and the very big, can the human only appear lost, crying out with Pascal, "The eternal silence of those infinite spaces terrifies me!"?[41] Or is it a universe in which it makes sense to speak of values, of life and death, good and evil, as meaningful distinctions within which we can hope for a "better world"? Is it a universe with which we can commune, as heart to heart, thought to thought, as I and Thou?

As humans stand peering down through their instruments into the subatomic realm and outward into the galaxies, it cannot but be evident that, for us, the human remains the "mean" or mediator between the worlds. This is so because what we perceive can only be known and evaluated from the context of our own standpoints. But also because we are faced with the recognition that humans alone, amid all the earth creatures and on all the planets of these vast galaxies, are capable of reflective consciousness. We are, in that sense, the "mind" of the universe, the place where the universe becomes conscious of itself.

Reflective consciousness is both our privilege and our danger. At least for the last several thousand years of cultural history, male ruling-class humans have used this privilege of mind to set themselves apart from nature and over dominated women and men. Thereby they denied the web of relationships that bind us all together, and within which these males themselves are an utterly dependent part. The urgent task of ecological culture is to convert human consciousness to the earth, so that we can use our minds to understand the web of life and to live in that web of life as sustainers, rather than destroyers, of it.

But also, as Teilhardian and Process thought have argued, reflective consciousness, while it distinguishes the human from animals, plants, cellular bacteria and nonbiotic aggregates of molecules, it does so only relatively, not absolutely. The capacity to be conscious is itself the experience of the interiority of our organism, made possible by the highly organized living cells of our brains and nervous systems that constitute the material "base" of our experience of awareness.

Consciousness is one type of highly intense experience of life, but there are other forms present in other species, sometimes with capacities that humans lack, as in fish that can hear ranges of sound or animals that can see ranges of light not possible to our ears and eyes. Nor can we simply draw a line between us, together with large-brained mammals, and other beings, as a distinction of "living persons" and "dead bodies." For plants too are living organic beings that respond to heat, light, water, and sound as organisms, and even chemical aggregates are dancing centers of energy.

Human consciousness, then, should not be what utterly separates us from the rest of "nature." Rather, consciousness is where this dance of energy organizes itself in increasingly unified ways, until it reflects back on itself in self-awareness. Consciousness is and must be where we recognize our kinship with all other beings. The dancing void from which the tiniest energy events of atomic structures flicker in and out of existence and self-aware thought are kin along a continuum of organized life-energy.

Our capacity for consciousness, which allows us to roam through space and time, remembering past ages, exploring the inner workings of all other existing beings on earth or on distant planets, also makes us aware of the ephemeral nature of our "self." Our capacity for consciousness is sustained by a complex but fragile organism. Cut that organism at its vital centers, in the brain or in the heart, and the light of consciousness goes out, and with it our "self."

It is this juxtaposition of the capacity of consciousness to roam through space and time, and its utter transience in its dependence on our mortal organisms, that has generated much of the energy of what has been called "religion" in the past. Much of this religious quest has sought to resolve this contradiction by denying it, imagining that consciousness was not really dependent on the mortal organism. The mental self could survive, and even be "purified" and strengthened, by the demise of the body. This concept of the "immortal self," survivable apart from our particular transient organism, must be recognized, not only as untenable, but as the source of much destructive behavior toward the earth and other humans.

An ecological spirituality needs to be built on three premises: the transience of selves, the living interdependency of all things, and the value of the personal in communion. Many spiritual traditions have emphasized the need to "let go of the ego," but in ways that diminished the value of the person, undercutting particularly those, like women, who scarcely have been allowed individuated personhood at all. We need to "let go of the ego" in a different sense. We are called to affirm the integrity of our personal center of being, in mutuality with the personal centers of all other beings across species and, at the same time, accept the transience of these personal selves.

As we accept both the value and the transience of the self, we can also be awakened to a new sense of kinship with all other organisms. Like humans, the animals and the plants are living centers of organic life who exist for a season. Then each of our roots shrivels, the organic structures that sustain our life fail, and we die. The cutting of the life center also means that our bodies disintegrate into organic matter, to enter the cycle of decomposition and recomposition as other entities.

The material substances of our bodies live on in plants and animals, just as our own bodies are composed from minute to minute of substances that once were parts of other animals and plants, stretching back through time to prehistoric ferns and reptiles, to ancient biota that floated in the primal seas of earth. Our kinship with all earth creatures is global, linking us to the whole living Gaia today. It also spans the ages, linking our material substance with all the beings that have gone before us on earth and even to the dust of exploding stars. We need new psalms and meditations to make this kinship vivid in our communal and personal devotions.

But, even as we take into our spirituality and ethical practice the transience of selves, relinquishing the illusion of permanence, and accepting the dissolution of our physical substance into primal energy, to become matter for new organisms, we also come to value again the personal center of each being. My eye catches the eye of a bird as it turns its head toward me on the side of the tree, and then continues its tasks. Brendan spies me coming up the path, and with flashing red fur is at the door, leaping in circles with unfeigned delight. My body, stretching in the sun, notices a tiny flower pushing up through the soil to greet the same sun. And we know our kinship as I and Thou, saluting one another as fellow persons.

Compassion for all living things fills our spirits, breaking down the illusion of otherness. At this moment we can encounter the matrix of energy of the universe that sustains the dissolution and recomposition of matter as also a heart that knows us even as we are known. Is there also a consciousness that remembers and envisions and reconciles all things, as the Process theologians believe? Surely, if we are kin to all things and offspring of the universe, then what has flowered in us as consciousness must also be reflected in that universe as well, in the ongoing creative Matrix of the whole.

As we gaze into the void of our future extinguished self and dissolving substance, we encounter there the wellspring of life and creativity from which all things have sprung and into which they return, only to well up again in new forms. But we also know this as the great Thou, the personal center of the universal process, with which all the small centers of personal being dialogue in the conversation that continually creates and recreates the world. The small selves and the Great Self are finally one, for as She bodies forth in us, all the beings respond in the bodying forth of their diverse creative work that makes the world.

The dialogue can become truncated. We can seek to grasp our ego centers of being in negation of others, proliferating our existence by diminishing that of others, and finally poisoning the wellspring of the life process itself. Or we can dance gracefully with our fellow beings, spinning out our creative work in such a way as to affirm theirs and they ours as well.

Then, like bread tossed on the water, we can be confident that our creative work will be nourishing to the community of life, even as we relinquish our small self back into the great Self. Our final gesture, as we surrender ourself into the Matrix of life, then can become a prayer of ultimate trust: "Mother, into your hands I commend my spirit. Use me as you will in your infinite creativity."

10

Creating a Healed World: Spirituality and Politics

In these two traditions, covenantal and sacramental, we hear two voices of divinity from nature. One speaks from the mountaintops in the thunderous masculine tones of "thou shalt" and "thou shalt not." It is the voice of power and law, but speaking (at its most authentic) on behalf of the weak, as a mandate to protect the powerless and to restrain the power of the mighty. There is another voice, one that speaks from the intimate heart of matter. It has long been silenced by the masculine voice, but today is finding again her own voice. This is the voice of Gaia. Her voice does not translate into laws or intellectual knowledge, but beckons us into communion.

Both of these voices, of God and of Gaia, are our own voices. We need to claim them as our own, not in the sense that there is "nothing" out there, but in the sense that what is "out there" can only be experienced by us through the lenses of human existence. We are not the source of life, but are latecomers to the planet. Our minds didn't fall from the skies, but are the flowering of organic body and its capacities to know itself. We can touch our fellow beings, and intuit the source of all life and thought that lies behind the whole. This contact, though humanly imaged, can be true. Its truth lies in the test of relationships; do our metaphors bear the fruits of compassion or of enmity?

We need both of these holy voices. We cannot depend on volunteerism alone to save rain forests and endangered species, set limits to the exploitation of animals and sanction abusers. We need organized systems and norms of ecological relations. Otherwise, not only will most people not comply, but will not be able to comply, because they have no way of fulfilling their daily needs except through the exigencies of the present system. But, without the second voice, our laws have no heart, no roots in compassion and fellow feeling. They fail to foster a motivating desire for biophilic living.

To begin to define an ethic for ecological living, we need to revisit the questions of good and evil, sin and fallenness, discussed in Section Three of this book. That we have a "problem" is unquestionable, but how we define the nature of that problem will determine our solutions. Christians and their secular heirs inherit two definitions of the problem of evil. For the Hebraic tradition, the problem lies in the will to disobey. The commandments of God disclose the way of justice, but we choose injustice. Yet we remain free. We can choose the path of obedience and hence of abundant living. The solution does not lie outside history, but is to be worked out within the bounds of historical existence.

For the Greek tradition, the fault is metaphysical. We are a dualism of eternal mind and mortal body. The solution lies in withdrawing into the mind and controlling the body. Ultimately the solution lies beyond death, in the discarding of the body. Yet the power to do so lies with us. What we truly know, we can do. Christianity fused these two views and hence compounded the understanding of sin. Sin is both historical and metaphysical, both something for which we are totally guilty and yet which we are powerless to resolve by ourselves.

There is much in this combined sense of guilt and helplessness that has spoken and continues to speak to our experience, perhaps even more today, as the cumulative effects of human violence mount and we feel trapped in them. Yet it can lead to many perversions that reinforce the problem: passivity, contempt for what is possible to us here and now, the desire to flee to imagined perfections outside of embodied and historical existence, and finally the scapegoating of victims as the cause of the evils we seek to repudiate and to guard ourselves against.

We need a foundation for ethical theory that is not based on a dualistic negation of the "other," whether woman or animal or body, pagans, gentiles, or barbarians (or the countercultural reversals of these projections) as the bearers of our "shadow." This does not mean that there is no such thing as evil, or that ethical distinctions as such should be repudiated for an acceptance of all that is as good or, at least, necessary. The difference between starving a child or torturing a prisoner, and nurturing their lives, is real, and reflect decisions made by actual people.

But the reality of evil does not lie is some "thing" out there. It cannot be escaped, and indeed is exacerbated by efforts to avoid it by cutting ourselves off from that "thing." Rather, evil lies in "wrong relationship." All beings live in community, both with members of their own species and with others for which they depend for food, breath, materials for construction, and affective feedback. Yet there is a tendency in the life drive itself in each species to maximize its own existence and hence to proliferate in a cancerous way that destroys its own biotic support.

This is not just a human tendency. As Lynn Margulis has pointed out, even ancient bacteria tended toward this proliferating growth, in which the consuming of others finally threatens to destroy both the environment and the species.[1] The life force itself is not unequivocally good, but becomes "evil" when it is maximized at the expense of others. In this sense "good" lies in limits, a balancing of our own drive for life with the life drives of all the others in which we are in community, so that the whole remains in life-sustaining harmony. The wisdom of nature lies in the development of built-in limits through a diversity of beings in interrelation, so that none outruns its own "niche."

Humans, particularly since the development of agriculture, have been able to develop the food base to escape the built-in limits of other species, and even of their own species in the hunter-gatherer mode. They have been able to grow their own food base and thus maximize their own lives, using land, plants, and animals as objects of control and manipulation. In the process some humans (dominant males) also have learned to maximize their own lives, both for leisure and consumption, over against other humans. The human community itself was fissured into controlling "subjects" and exploited "objects."

It is more misleading than helpful to speak about this development of systems of domination as a "fall." It might be called a "loss of innocence" and the beginning of deceit. But we need to be clear that all was not idyllic before, nor did there enter into history at that time a totally new capacity for evil not present before. Rather, a possibility in nature, the maximizing of some against others, was appropriated in a new way, organized in such a way that self-correcting limits could be avoided by those who profited. The price of exploitation was borne by the exploited.

Only as the system of exploitation reaches its maximal stage does it begin to undermine the quality of life of those at the "top," and thus force them to recognize that the whole house of cards is about to topple. Their first instinct is to stave off this demise by accelerating the exploitation of those they dominate, while seeking to maintain their own comfortable life-style with the dwindling resources of the whole. The rich try to stay rich while the poor get poorer, and the destruction of the environment increases.

Eventually the whole system collapses. This has happened before, as in the disappearance of "lost civilizations," and in a more extensive way, in the "fall" of Rome. The difference today is that the system of exploitation is global, and the possibility of destruction correspondingly global. There are not the same spaces to retreat from the collapse. Thus we face a cancerous proliferation of our species that could not only bring it to extinction, but pull much of the planetary life system down with it.

However, civilizations have not only created domination and cultures of deceit that justified domination. They have also created critical cultures designed to unmask deceit and spiritualities that awakened compassion for others, thus rebuilding culturally the balances of self-limitation and respect for the lives of others that make for good community. We inherit in our Christian tradition (as do others in their traditions) both cultures of domination and deceit and cultures of critique and compassion. We need to build on and develop the second culture to unmask and check the power of the first culture.

ENVISIONING A GOOD SOCIETY

Let us begin by envisioning something of the goal that we seek, not in the sense of a static "once-for-all" future perfection, but in the sense of healthy societies that can be sustained from season to season, which are no longer building up toxicities of destruction. This vision must start with a principle of equity: equity between men and women; between human groups living within regions; equity across human communities globally; equity between the human species and all other members to the biotic community of which we are a part; and finally equity between generations of living things, between the needs of those alive now and those who are to come.

Rebuilding human society for a sustainable earth will require far more than a plethora of technological "fixes" within the present paradigm of relations of domination. It will demand a fundamental restructuring of all these relations from systems of domination/exploitation to ones of biophilic mutuality. New technologies may well have their place, although there may also be a need to rediscover old techniques of agriculture, architecture, artisanry, and community-building as well. But technique cannot be divorced from its social and psychic contexts. A new technique or a recovery of an old one will not "take" without transformed political relations and cultural consciousness.

A healed earth is one in which all the patterns of destruction that we outlined in chapter 4 have been deeply transformed, the patterns that are resulting in proliferating population, deepening poverty, famine, soil erosion, deforestation, the extinction of species, air and water pollution, energy crises, and militarism. Just as the patterns that are producing this vast reign of death are interrelated, so a new life-sustaining community of humans as part of the biosphere of Gaia are interrelated. This does not mean that there are not many incremental steps toward this new pattern, but these incremental steps have to be guided by a holistic vision.

Let us start by looking at some of these incremental shifts, envisioning, at each point, some of the interrelated transformations that would be involved. Let us start with the need to phase out petroleum and other fossil fuels as the primary energy sources of production, transportation, and home heating. The alternative energy sources are solar, wind, water, thermal, and biomass energies, as well as human and animal activity. There are many incremental steps along the way to this shift to renewable energy sources, to accommodate, not only the dwindling supplies of fossil fuels, but also the unacceptable price of polluting the atmosphere with their emissions.

Greatly increased efficiency of the machinery is one such step, getting much more work for the same amount of fuel. Another is control of the emissions. But finally one has to look at the organization of the system itself. In the case of transportation, the private automobile becomes an unacceptable mode of transportation. Phasing it out will require a whole new system of transportation that will combine much less polluting technologies of mass transit between centers, together with walking, biking, and small electric cars locally. But this also means reorganizing the locations of living, working, recreation, and marketing units, so that much less transportation is required to connect the segments of daily life.[2]

A new transportation system is an adjunct to rebuilding organic local communities no longer fragmented across distances that are only bridgeable by the private auto. Very quickly we move from the realm of technologies to the realm of political ordering of relations. Who profits from the present system of fuel-inefficient private autos, centralized workplaces separated from living places, and the class-ethnic segmentation of neighborhoods? To locate those who profit from this system is also to name those who will mobilize their political and economic power to prevent change.

Greatly improved insulation, including environmental designs such as homes built partly into the earth, together with solar and wind technologies for generating electricity, and biomass fuels, such as wood, can dramatically lessen the costs of heating and cooling houses, cooking, and lighting. Mass development of these sustainable home technologies demands political mobilization, locally and regionally. Subsidies must be put behind ecologically sound technologies, while subsidies are withdrawn from polluting and wasteful energy companies and builders, revealing the true costs of their methods.

The questions of local and regional control and decision making, over against the power of multinational corporations, is central to this political struggle. Oil is shipped to us from halfway around the world. Wood is locally produced. Solar energy for homes comes from panels on roofs possessed by the owners of the building. Electricity from windmills also could be owned by home units or organized in small local companies.[3] The age of mega-corporations is put in question, its inefficiency and true costs exposed. The state and its ownership also is revealed. The people seek to take control of the political systems for the commonweal of all, rather than the subsidization of the profits of the rich.

The question of raising and distributing food adequate to nourish the human population (and the animals they own), without depleting the fertility of the land from which it grows, also raises a host of interrelated issues. A shift toward sustainable food production and distribution calls for a phasing out of the long transportation chains that deliver great varieties of foods from all over the globe in all seasons to elites, while the majority of humans barely survive on a poor and limited diet. We need to return to seasonal patterns of food, produced and distributed in one or several contiguous bioregions.[4]

Another shift is toward eating lower on the food chain, greatly reducing meat-eating in favor of vegetable proteins. This not only releases a vast amount of grain, presently fed to animals destined for the dinner tables of the affluent, for human consumption, but also greatly reduces the ecological impact of cattle grazing and feedlots. Saving rain forests and preventing desertification of fragile grasslands is interdependent with great reduction of domesticated animal herds.

By withdrawing the subsidies from agribusiness methods of food production, its actual inefficiency is revealed. At the same time, the small farm using organic methods should be promoted. Then many traditional forms of agriculture can be recovered in more sophisticated forms. The organic farm reclaims the traditional integration of animals and crops. Animals provide a part of the farm work force, their excrement is returned as the natural fertilizer of soils, and they are fed with agricultural wastes and grasses. Organic pest control and integrated gardening, in which various types of plants renew soils for each other, are rediscovered and refined. These are elements of an agriculture that sustains the land for the generations to come.[5]

The concern to sustain the soil for the next generation also demands more rooted communities. Farmers sustain the land to be handed down to their children; corporations are uninterested in the next generation. They pillage the environment and then flee the scene. Creating rooted farming communities also demands reversing the five-hundred-year trend of land confiscation. This trend has left most of the families of the world landless, while a few corporate landowners, the contemporary *latifundistas*, own, neglect, or deplete much of the agricultural land. Better agricultural methods that sustain the land go hand in hand with land reform that returns much of the land to local farmers in families and cooperative groups.[6]

Land reform also suggests an eventual reversal of the trends to urbanization, decentralizing the mega-urban centers and creating regional configurations in which business, educational, political, and cultural centers are integrated with their agricultural base. More hand labor and less mechanized labor would also mean more people working on and living directly from the land.

Return to the land means recovering something of the biorhythms of the body, the day, and the seasons from the world of clocks, computers, and artificial lighting that have almost entirely alienated us from these biorhythms.[7] This does not mean there is not a place for high-tech instruments of information processing and communication. But these need to become more accessible to all and organized in relation to the biotic base of life, rather than creating the delusion that this base of life has been replaced altogether.

Greatly reducing fossil fuels as the main source of energy, drastic reduction of grain-fed cattle in feedlots, shifting to organic pest control and fertilizers: these would greatly reduce major sources of air, soil and water pollution. But an ecologically sustainable society must also terminate as much as possible all forms of disposable waste. "Unnatural" toxic wastes, such as nuclear wastes and fluorocarbons, need to be phased out altogether, because these cannot be safely recycled.

Human and animal body wastes need to be treated so they can be returned to rebuild soils. Agricultural and food wastes need to be part of composting systems, both on farms and in local communities. Packaging needs to be greatly reduced, and wastes from consumer goods of all kinds recycled. Finally all human artifacts should be made to be reused many times, rather than quickly discarded.[8] These shifts too will involve deep value changes, as well as political struggles with the forces that promote the "disposable society."

The real cost of throwing away twenty-five plastic wrappings and bags after each shopping, rather than reusing several sturdy cloth bags, needs to be made evident. One way of doing this would be to have the shopper pay for the actual costs of the plastic wrappings, costs that would be avoided by those who brought their own bags, rather than hiding these costs in the costs of the food. The costs of the plastic wrapping must also include the costs of breaking them down and recycling them, as well as their initial production. Only when the true environmental costs are paid for by the producers and consumers, rather than passed on to the general public, will it be evident that the ecological society is the only truly "economical" society.

Although greatly reducing the environmental impact of human production, transportation, consumption, and waste is critical for a sustainable society, and must demand the greatest changes from the most affluent societies, a significant curbing and eventual reduction of human population itself is also necessary. If human population is allowed to double once again in forty years or less, and hits 8 billion to 10 billion in the first third of the twenty-first century, all the measures we have just discussed will go for naught. Humanity has no real alternative to population control. The question is, do we want population control to happen voluntarily, before conception, or violently by war, famine, and disease?

The promotion of effective birth control on a widespread basis sufficient to halt and reduce the world population explosion is only secondarily a matter of developing and distributing technologies, although this is not unimportant. It is, above all, a matter of how women and their bodies are socially and culturally appropriated. Many cultural, social, and economic forces impede the empowerment of women as moral agents of their own reproductive powers: poverty, demographic war, and the whole complex of attitudes that spring from patriarchy.[9]

Poor families, without adequate food or medicine for their children, but who also invest little in their children's future, will not cease to have many children as long as they fear that many of them will die, but also see that those who live can participate in the farming or scavenging that sustains the family unit. Communities under demographic threat from occupying peoples, such as the Palestinians in Israel, will not cease to have large families as long as this is the only way they have to assure the survival of their people.

Patriarchy has multiple impacts on reproductive patterns. Its valuing of the male over the female means that families cannot rest content with having produced two children, if both of these children are female. Often two males are desired to assure the patrilineage. Patriarchy also denies women control over their own sexuality and reproduction, and values women only to produce children, sharply curtailing other ways in which women can live satisfying lives and be held in esteem by their communities.

The empowerment of women as moral agents of their own sexuality and reproduction is thus an integral part of any authentic population policy. The female child needs to be valued equally with the male. This is only possible if the adult female is also seen as an autonomous person who will be an active cultural and economic agent in her own right, and not just an adjunct to a male-centered society. Only when women can no longer be beaten by men, raped by men, and traded between men as commodities, can they cease to be treated or to see themselves as passive bodies to be acted upon by men.

Women need a sense of their own integrity and to have that integrity affirmed by males. They need to have a full range of life opportunities for their many creative roles, of which reproduction is only one. They need to have the knowledge and technology of birth control and the right to enforce these in sexual relations with men. They need to have a sense that their daughters, as much as their sons, will have these many options and will be given education for them. Finally they need to see themselves as responsible agents for a just and sustainable society in their communities.

Although the empowerment of women as moral, economic, and cultural agents in their own right is crucial for effective "family planning," it also lies at the base of all the value changes that will lead from cultures of domination to cultures of biophilic mutuality. The "liberation of women" cannot be seen simply as the incorporation of women into alienated male styles of life, although with far fewer benefits, for this simply adds women to the patterns of alienated life created by and for men. In fact, it is impossible to fully add women to this alienated life of males, since the male alienated life-style is only possible by the exploitation of women who remain tied to "nature."

Rather, what is necessary is a double transformation of both women and men in their relation to each other and to "nature." Women certainly need to gain some of the individuality that has been traditionally purchased by men at their expense. But this individuation should not be based on exploitative domination (of other women or subjugated men), but needs to remain in sustaining relation to primary communities of life. The ways of being a person for others and of being a person for oneself need to come together as reciprocal, rather than being split between female and male styles of life.

It is the male rather than the female life-style that needs, however, the deeper transformation. Males need to overcome the illusion of autonomous individualism, with its extension into
egocentric power over others, starting with the women with
whom they relate. Men need to integrate themselves into life-
sustaining relations with women as lovers, parents, and co-
workers. They need to do regularly what they have hardly ever
done, even in preagricultural societies: feed, clothe, wash, and
hug children from infancy, cook food, and clean up wastes.

Only when men are fully integrated into the culture of daily
sustenance of life can men and women together begin to reshape
the larger systems of economic, social, and political life. They can
begin to envision new cultural consciousness and organizational
structures that would connect these larger systems to their roots
in the earth and to sustaining the earth from day to day and from
generation to generation.

Both the "liberation" of women into male styles of alienated
pseudoautonomy and the domestication of men into women's
dependency are equally false compensations, if they function
within the present pattern of distortion, and are not part of a
larger transformation. The domestic-public split itself must yield
to a new sense of a holistic culture that recognizes both men and
women as individuated persons in mutual interdependency with
each other and with the earth.[10]

From this familial base of relationships we turn to the largest
system of dominating power: militarism. I have suggested that
the isolated male ego that demands invulnerable and dominating
power over others is shaped developmentally through negation
of interdependency with women, in the context of woman-
exploited childraising. But this type of masculine ego finds its
most global manifestation in militarism, including the militarized
economy and national security state.

As we saw in chapter 4, since 1950 the military state, with its
appendages in professional armies and in rapacious business

corporations, which produce military equipment as a major part of international trade, have taken over more and more of the wealth of the world. In a vast enclosure of the world commons, much of the land, sea, and even air space of the earth has been expropriated for the militarized corporate economy.[11] The poorest countries are forced into increasing debt and dependency within this system.

This military state operates out of a polarized, totalitarian worldview of absolute good against absolute evil. "Good" means our invulnerability and total power over other peoples and world resources. "Evil" is anything that challenges this invulnerability and control. The earth is reduced to "resources" to be used, and interdependency with nature or with other people is denied. In any situation of conflict, the other human community is demonized, justifying their annihilation, together with the entire infrastructure of their society. Ecological weapons are stock-in-trade of modern war, craterizing and poisoning cropland and forests. Although there is a pretense of hitting only "military targets," in fact everything is a military target. Modern war is total war.

When the former Soviet Union began to collapse in disarray, as a result of its efforts to keep up in the arms race, there was talk of a "new world order" in which conversion to a peacetime economy could happen around the world. But the national security state, with its military corporations and armies, refused to consider the reduction of their power. The United States oligarchies particularly received the end of the Cold War, not as a chance to convert to an ecologically sustainable, peacetime economy, but as a victory for "our side," to be used to consolidate their global hegemony.

Immediately they began to search for new enemies to demonize, and thereby to justify new generations of weapons. They found one such enemy in Saddam Hussein, the leader of a middle-sized Arab country, who challenged their control over oil. And they proceeded to pulverize Iraq in a six-week air war in which they threw down upon it 50 percent more tonnage of bombs than were thrown on Vietnam over ten years.[12] They then declared with satisfaction that the "Vietnam Syndrome" is over; by which they meant that any disposition to question the righteousness of the military way of "solving" international disputes had been silenced.

Genuine demilitarization across the board, including the demilitarization of the United States and of Israel,[13] are the *sine qua non* of any genuine, ecologically sustainable, biospheric economy. It is not difficult to imagine the technological aspect of such conversion of the war industries to alternative production.[14] The cry that military production is necessary for economic prosperity can be refuted many times over, for such production employs far fewer people than any peacetime economy and employs them for purely destructive purposes.

The real resistance to conversion of the military industry lies, not in technology or genuine economic "sense," but in the power drives of the interlocking corporate elites of government, business, and professional military. It is their system of power that is the true "enemy of humanity" and of the earth. But the dismantling of this system of destructive power demands real "conversion," a *metanoia,* or change of heart and consciousness. This change of consciousness is one that recognizes that real "security" lies, not in dominating power and the impossible quest for total invulnerability, but rather in the acceptance of vulnerability, limits, and interdependency with others, with other humans and with the earth.

BUILDING COMMUNITIES OF CELEBRATION AND RESISTANCE

How do we carry on a struggle to heal the world and to build a new biospheric community in the face of this intransigent system of death? It is my belief that those who want to carry on this struggle in a sustained way must build strong base communities of celebration and resistance. By "base communities" I mean local face-to-face groups with which one lives, works, and prays. I do not mean that all these functions would necessarily come together for most people in one base community. Most people will find these different forms of support in a variety of groups and networks, although it is important that these many groups recognize their interconnections in one unified struggle.

There are three interrelated aspects of the work of such local communities. One is shaping the personal therapies, spiritualities, and corporate liturgies by which we nurture and symbolize a new biophilic consciousness. Second, there is the utilization of local institutions over which we have some control, our homes, schools, churches, farms, and locally controlled businesses, as pilot projects of ecological living. Third, there is the building of organizational networks that reach out, regionally, nationally, and internationally, in a struggle to change the power structures that keep the present death system in place.

We must start by recognizing that *metanoia*, or change of consciousness, begins with us. This does not happen all at once, but is an ongoing process. We all have been shaped to misname evil, to seek invulnerable power, or else to capitulate to such power demands in the hands of male authorities. We are tied to present systems of consumption and can hardly imagine alternatives to them that might give us greater peace and wholeness, even though the scramble to "keep up" in the present systems leaves us ever more insecure, anxious, and exhausted.

We need healing therapies and spiritualities of inner growth to let go of fears and open up to each other and to the world around us, to learn how to *be*, rather than to *strive*. The struggle to change the death system must be deeply rooted in joy in the goodness of life. Making healing and inner growth available to us all means unhooking them from professionalized "help," which comes with credentials and high price tags. Although there is a place for skilled people, most of what we need is fairly simple and "free."

We can survey ideas from a few good books, gather a group on a regular basis to discuss the ideas from "experts," and then begin to open up to each other and learn to become good "ears" for hearing each other's story. We also need to recover our body-psyche-spirit nexus, to learn to breathe again, to feel our life energy. Small groups can learn, perhaps with initial expert advice, and teach each other techniques of breathing, biofeedback, meditation, and massage.

We need to take the time to sit under trees, look at water, and at the sky, observe small biotic communities of plants and animals with close attention, get back in touch with the living earth. We can start to release the stifled intuitive and creative powers of our organism, to draw and to write poetry, and to know that we stand on holy ground.

In addition to personal therapies and spirituality, we need corporate liturgies as well, to symbolize and express our altered consciousness. Unfortunately most of our institutional forums of worship are tied to alienated, patriarchal consciousness. Much of their worship is literally "deadly," although some are open to partial transformation. Thus communities of new being and consciousness need to become their own liturgists. They need to learn to shape corporate liturgies to mourn together for violated lives, to midwife healing and new birth, and to taste a new creation already present.

Such communities can also learn to carry liturgy to the streets, in protest marches and demonstrations that cry out against the death system and visualize renewed life in ways that can catch the imagination of others who participate with them or watch them. We can call on all the arts—song and music, dance and mime, posters and banners, costumes and puppetry—to shape the public liturgies of biospheric politics. The Vermont-based

Bread and Puppet Theatre is a model for such public liturgies of transformed consciousness.[15]

Another essential work of local communities is to begin to live now an ecologically healthful life. We can see our own homes and other institutions over which we have some control, such as schools or churches, as "pilot projects." We can form a local committee and study a basic manual of ecological living, such as Jeremy Rifkin's *Green Lifestyle Handbook: 1001 Ways You Can Heal the Earth*.[16] We can systematically check different aspects of our lives in this structure, our energy use in heating, cooling, and lighting, toxic cleaners, waste products, land use and transportation, and begin to implement some changes that bring our home or other institutions up to ecological "code."

Such efforts can only be pilot projects and will function as learning and consciousness-raising processes. As we try to implement some changes, it will become quickly evident that our church, school, and workplace, and even our home, are not autonomous. They are dependent parts of larger systems that operate, to a large extent, to tie them to present wasteful ways of functioning. As we try, for example, to implement recycling of household wastes, we run into city waste-disposal systems and resistance to new forms of trash collection that are integrated into recycling industries. We begin to recognize these systems in their local and regional expressions, and even beyond, and to put names to those who control the decisions.

This leads us to the third role of local communities, to become political bases of organizing and action. Here again it is useful to start locally, where we can be concrete and where there is often some possibilities of real change. When our group has formulated some clear policy changes, for example, toward a recycling center coordinated with city waste collection, we can network with other groups in the city. We can form a larger organizational base, attend town council meetings, eventually run candidates for local office.

We can find ways to pressure local business, both negatively through boycotts and positively through petitions and discussion.

Such local organizing efforts will also reveal the extent to which local government and business really have local control and the extent to which they too are dependent parts of national and international political and economic systems. This is a part of a learning process in which we put names to links in the chains of control, and imagine ways to put pressure for change on the weak links in those chains. Local "green committees" begin to link up with one another across the country.[17]

We ultimately have to think and also act globally, as well as locally. We need to become knowledgeable about parallel movements in Western and Eastern Europe, Asia, Africa, and Latin America, and also the distinct problems of different regions and their interconnection with our own lives. This global consciousness plays two roles. It makes us constantly aware that our local efforts are part of a global struggle, and we are all interdependent in that struggle. It also allows us, at times, to link up with movements internationally that have political forums through the United Nations and other international organizations.[18]

We need to amend the famous slogan of René Dubos: "Think globally and act locally."[19] We need to think both locally and globally and act both locally and globally. The struggle for local changes will lack depth unless it understands itself as an integral part of a global new consciousness. This needs to be more than an abstraction. We need to read about, and sometimes visit, groups who are organizing in other parts of the world and learn from what they are doing. We need to find ways to link up concretely in international forums where the defense of the global commons of forests, oceans, and atmosphere is being carried out against their corporate abusers.

The time is short for major changes, if we are to save much of the biotic system of the earth that is in danger. The Worldwatch

Institute estimates that we have about forty years for major global shifts to be carried out voluntarily (until 2030).[20] After that time major disasters of famine and collapse of life systems, under the pressures of exploitative use, will take place, and there could well be very dangerous militarist and totalitarian responses from threatened elites, as indeed is already happening.

In speaking about the urgency of the situation before audiences, I am often asked if I am "optimistic" about the possibilities for change. The assumption behind this question seems to be that we have two ideational stances toward these crises: optimism or pessimism. But I am inclined to think that both these stances get us off the hook. If we are "optimistic," it suggests that change is inevitable and will happen in the "natural" course of things, and so we need not make much effort ourselves. Someone else will take care of it. If we are "pessimistic," change is impossible, and therefore it is useless to try. In either case we have the luxury, as critical but comfortable elites in the United States, to question the present system without being responsible for it.

What we need is neither optimism nor pessimism, in these terms, but committed love. This means that we remain committed to a vision and to concrete communities of life no matter what the "trends" may be. Whether we are immediately "winning" or "losing" cannot shake our rooted understandings of what biophilic life is and should be, although we need to adapt our strategies to the changing fortunes of the struggle. We also remain clear that life is not made whole "once and for all," in some static millennium of the future. It is made whole again and again, in the renewed day born from night and in the new spring that rises from each winter.

Being rooted in love for our real communities of life and for our common mother, Gaia, can teach us patient passion, a passion that is not burnt out in a season, but can be renewed season after season. Our revolution is not just for us, but for our children, for the generations of living beings to come. What we can do is to plant a seed, nurture a seed-bearing plant here and there, and hope for a harvest that goes beyond the limits of our powers and the span of our lives.

Notes

INTRODUCTION

1. For example, Paul R. Ehrlich, *et al., Human Ecology: Problems and Solutions* (San Francisco: W. H. Freeman, 1973).
2. For example, Bill Devall and George Sessions, *Deep Ecology: Living as if Nature Mattered* (Salt Lake City: Peregrine Smith Books, 1985).
3. Two examples of collections of ecofeminist writings are: Judith Plant, *Healing the Wounds: The Promise of Ecofeminism* (Philadelphia: New Society Publishers, 1989); and Irene Diamond and Gloria F. Orenstein, *Reweaving the World: The Emergence of Ecofeminism* (San Francisco: Sierra Club Books, 1990).
4. James Lovelock, *Gaia: A New Look at Life on Earth* (Oxford: Oxford University Press, 1979); also his *The Ages of Gaia: A Biography of Our Living Earth* (New York: Norton, 1988). Lynn Margulis and Dorian Sagan, *Microcosmos: Four Billion Years of Evolution from Our Microbian Ancestors* (New York: Summit Books), 1987). See also William Irwin Thompson, *Gaia: A Way of Knowing: Political Implications of the New Biology* (Great Barrington, MA: Lindisfarne Press, 1987).
5. See Charlene Spretnak, *The Politics of Women's Spirituality: Essays on the Rise of Spiritual Power within the Feminist Movement* (Garden City, NY: Anchor Press, 1982).
6. Matthew Fox, *The Coming of the Cosmic Christ* (San Francisco: Harper & Row, 1988), 92, 235–39.
7. For example, Chung Hyun Kyung, *Struggle to Be the Sun Again: Introducing Asian Women's Theology* (Maryknoll, NY: Orbis Press, 1990).
8. Jeremy Rifkin, *Biosphere Politics: A New Consciousness for a New Society* (New York: Crown Publishers, 1991).
9. Susan Thistlethwaite and Mary Potter Engel, eds., *Lift Every Voice: Constructing Christian Theologies from the Underside* (San Francisco: Harper & Row, 1990). In using this phrase, I go beyond the

concept of class, gender, and cultural pluralism within Christian contexts of this book, and I invite an ecofeminist dialogue across all human spiritualities.

CHAPTER 1: THREE CLASSICAL CREATION STORIES

1. Although Christians received the whole canon of the Hebrew Bible (in two versions) as their Old Testament, Pauline Christianity particularly assumed that much of the Levitical codes were no longer normative revelation. Since the New Testament is built on this selective use of Hebrew scripture, Christianity, by its very nature, cannot claim to use the entire Bible in both Testaments as equally inspired, despite fundamentalist claims to do this.

2. For the date of the *Enuma Elish,* see Isaac Mendelsohn, *Religions of the Ancient Near East: Sumero-Akkadian Religious Texts and Ugaritic Epics* (New York: Liberal Arts Press, 1955), 17–18.

3. See Elmer W. K. Mould, *Essentials of Bible History* (New York: Ronald Press, 1951), 376–77.

4. Plato's *Timaeus* stands behind the interpretations of Genesis in many church fathers. For example, see Justin Martyr, *First Apology,* chapter 60. Origen's treatise, *de Principiis,* assumes the world picture of the *Timaeus.*

5. Irrigation was essential to the agriculture of ancient Sumeria and Babylonia, and is often seen as a major source of early urbanization and social cooperation. Irrigation practices, however, also caused soil salinization in antiquity; see Thorkild Jacobsen, *Salinity and Irrigation Agriculture in Antiquity* (Malibu, CA: Undena Publications, 1982).

6. See Patrick D. Miller, *The Divine Warrior in Early Israel* (Cambridge: Harvard University Press, 1973).

7. Deuteronomy 5:12–14 includes sons and daughters, male and female slaves and oxen, and donkeys and livestock in the mandate for sabbatical rest from labor; also Exodus 20:10.

8. The concept of the "divine image" in Genesis 1:27 does not suggest that humans "look like" God, but rather refers to the royal image that is carried by the king's representative. Thus Adam as bearer of the divine image is established as representative of God's royal power or sovereignty over creation. See Odil Hannes Steck, *World and Environment* (Nashville: Abingdon Press, 1980), 103–8.

9. Leviticus 25:39–46.

10. Leviticus 25:39–46; see William Swartley, *Slavery, Sabbath, War and Women: Case Issues in Biblical Interpretation* (Scottdale, PA: Herald Press, 1983).

11. Phyllis Bird, "Male and Female, He Created Them: Genesis 1:27b in the Context of the Priestly Account of Creation," *Harvard Theological Review* 74, no. 2 (1981): 129–59. An expanded version of this article appears in a volume on the idea of *imago dei* in the Christian theological tradition, Kari Borresen, ed., *Image of God and Gender Models* (Oslo: Solum Forlag, 1992), 11–34.

12. Phyllis Trible, "Depatriarchalizing in Biblical Interpretation," in *Journal of the American Academy of Religion* XLI/1 (March 1973): 30–48. Trible argues that the helpmeet designation of Eve indicates a relationship of mutuality, but this ignores the design of the story, which is intended to define this helpmeet status in a one-sided, auxiliary way. The rabbinic interpretations of the passage make clear this intention by worsening it; see Rosemary Ruether, *Womenguides: Readings Toward a Feminist Theology* (Boston: Beacon, 1985), 71–72.

13. Lynn White, "The Historical Roots of our Ecologic Crisis," *Science* 155 (March 10, 1967): 1203–1207, reprinted in David and Eileen Spring, *Ecology and Religion in History* (New York: Harper & Row, 1974), 15–31.

14. See reply by James Barr, "Man and Nature: The Ecological Controversy and the Old Testament," in David and Spring, *Ecology and Religion in History,* 48–75.

15. See Judah Schochet, *Animal Life in Jewish Tradition: Attitudes and Relationships* (New York: KTAV, 1984).

16. Although Israel's view of God as Lord of creation precluded identifying God with storms or seeing God as dying in drought, yet the experience of divine presence in such events was preserved by seeing God as acting through these natural events, expressing his will, as in Isaiah 25; see Steck, *World and Environment,* 174–87.

17. Plato, *Timaeus,* 49–50.

18. Thus the Athanasian Creed distinguished the three "persons" in God, between each other and over against creation, by saying: "The Father is made of none; neither created, nor begotten. The Son is of the Father alone: not made, not created, but begotten. The Holy Ghost is of the Father and of the Son: neither made, nor created, nor begotten, but proceeding."

19. Gnostic texts on the pleroma of God regularly speak of both begetting and gestation between male-female principles in the divine world; see Ptolemaeus's account of the pleroma in *Gnosticism: A Source Book,* edited by Robert Grant (New York: Harper and Brothers, 1961), 163–64. Orthodox trinitarian texts eliminate a female principle in God, but sometimes talk as if God the "Father" is androgynous; for example, the Eleventh Council of Toledo, 675 C.E., speaks of the divine Word as coming forth "from the womb of the Father" (*de utero Patris*). See C. M. Lacugna, "Re-conceiving

the Trinity as the Mystery of Salvation," *Scottish Journal of Theology,* (1975): 38:21.

20. The Greek word for soul, *psyche,* is feminine, but the translator, B. Jowett, uses the masculine article for it throughout.

21. Plato, *Republic,* IV, 443.

22. Plato, *Republic,* V, 455–56.

23. See Norman K. Gottwald, *The Tribes of Yahweh: A Sociology of the Religion of Liberated Israel, 1250–1050 B.C.E.* (Maryknoll, NY: Orbis Press, 1970), 210–20.

24. The classical Christian problematics of the doctrine of creation are explored in Augustine, *The City of God,* books 11–14.

25. For the roots of the Christian doctrine of the Trinity in Hellenistic and Jewish Hellenistic religious philosophies, see Harry A. Wolfson, *The Philosophy of the Church Fathers,* 2d ed. (Cambridge: Harvard University Press, 1964); also his *Philo: Foundations of Religious Philosophy in Judaism, Christianity and Islam* (Cambridge: Harvard University Press, 1947).

26. Androgynous concepts of God were developed particularly in Gnostic theologies, but are also found in more conservative forms in mystical Judaism and in Syriac Christianity. See Rosemary R. Ruether, *Womenguides: Readings toward a Feminist Theology* (Boston: Beacon Press, 1985), 20–35.

27. See William G. Rusch, *The Trinitarian Controversy* (Philadelphia: Fortress Press, 1980), 17–24 and *passim.*

28. For Augustine's belief in original immortality, see page 137 of this volume.

29. The ambiguity between spiritual equality and social-physical subordination of women to men is laid out in Eleanor McLaughlin, "Equality of Souls: Inequality of Sexes: Women in Medieval Theology," in *Religion and Sexism: Images of Women in the Jewish and Christian Traditions,* edited by Rosemary R. Ruether (New York: Simon and Schuster, 1974), 213–66. See also Kari Borresen, *Subordination and Equivalence: The Nature and Role of Women in Augustine and Thomas Aquinas,* translation from French original (Washington, D.C.: University Press of America, 1981).

CHAPTER 2: DOES SCIENCE HAVE A NEW CREATION STORY?

1. Copernicus, *De Revolutionibus Orbium Coelestium,* preface by Andreas Osiander (Nuremburg: 1543). See Dorothy Stimson, *The Gradual Acceptance of the Copernican Theory of the Universe* (New York: Baker and Taylor, 1917).

2. *Dialogo de Due Massimi Sistemi del Mundo* (1632). For a recent reappraisal of this conflict between Galilio and the Vatican, see *The Galileo Affair: A Meeting of Faith and Science* (Città Vaticano: 1985).

3. For the concept of the "spiritual body" in Paul, see 1 Corinthians 15:35–54. For the Patristic development of this idea, see Origen, *De Principiis* III.2; and Gregory Nyssa, "On the Soul and the Resurrection," in *Nicene and Post-Nicene Fathers,* 2d series, vol. 5 (London: Parker, 1893), 464–65.

4. See Gertrude Himmelfarb, *Darwin and the Darwinian Revolution* (New York: Norton, 1968).

5. Archbishop James Ussher of Armagh, Ireland (1581–1656), calculated the date of creation from the biblical account: *Annales Veteris et Novi Testamenti* (1650–54). This was the source for the dating of creation from 4004 B.C. inserted in the margin notes of Authorized Versions of the Bible from 1701.

6. See Langdon Gilkey, *Creationism on Trial: Evolution and God in Little Rock* (Minneapolis: Winston Press, 1985).

7. The separation of fact and value was based on the Kantian distinction between empirical knowledge and practical or ethical knowledge. It was particularly developed by Albrecht Ritschl (1822–89) and the Ritschlean school of theology.

8. For a classical expression of liberal faith in scientific and technological progress as an expression of the development of virtue, see Antoine-Nicholas de Condorcet, *Sketch for a Historical Picture of the Progress of the Human Mind,* translated by June Barraclough (London: George Weidenfeld and Nicolson, 1955), 196–202.

9. See David E. Powell, *Anti-Religious Propaganda in the Soviet Union* (Cambridge: MIT Press, 1975); also Eugene B. Shirley and Michael Rowe, eds., *Candle in the Wind: Religion in the Soviet Union* (Washington, D.C.: Ethics and Public Policy Center, 1989).

10. On Newtonian physics as mechanical philosophy, see Carolyn Merchant, *The Death of Nature: Women, Ecology and the Scientific Revolution* (San Francisco: Harper & Row, 1980), 275–79.

11. See Fritjof Capra, *The Turning Point: Science, Society and the Rising Culture* (New York: Simon and Schuster, 1982).

12. Fritjof Capra, *The Tao of Physics: An Exploration of the Parallels between Modern Physics and Eastern Mysticism* (New York: Bantam, 1977).

13. Nigal Calder, *The Key to the Universe: A Report on the New Physics* (New York: Viking, 1977), 181–85; also Steven Weinberg, *The First Three Minutes* (New York: Basic Books, 1977); and John Boslough, *Stephen Hawking's Universe* (New York: Avon, 1985).

14. Calder, *The Key to the Universe,* 172–73.

15. Calder, *The Key to the Universe,* 173–74.
16. Calder, *The Key to the Universe,* 175–77; also John Wheeler, *Mind in Nature* (San Francisco: Harper & Row, 1982).
17. Anne H. Ehrlich and Paul R. Ehrlich, *Earth* (New York: Franklin Watts, 1987), 15–19.
18. Ehrlich and Ehrlich, *Earth,* 20–26.
19. Ehrlich and Ehrlich, *Earth,* 30–33.
20. For the female discovery of agriculture as an extension of female gathering activities, see M. Kay Martin and Barbara Voorhies, *Female of the Species* (New York: Columbia University Press, 1975), 216.
21. Ehrlich and Ehrlich, *Earth,* 62–71.
22. World population is projected to be 6.251 billion by 2000 C.E. See United Nations, Department of International and Economic Affairs, *World Population Prospects* (New York: UNIPUB, 1989).
23. Anne H. Ehrlich and Paul R. Ehrlich, *Extinction: The Causes and Consequences of the Disappearance of Species* (New York: Random House, 1981).
24. Proven reserves of petroleum that can be extracted easily totaled 650 billion barrels in 1982. If the world continued to use petroleum at the rate of 20 billion barrels a year (the average for the first three years of the 1980s), this supply would be depleted in less than thirty-three years, or by 2014. See Lester R. Brown, *Population Policies for a New Economic Era,* Worldwatch Paper no. 53 (Washington, D.C.: Worldwatch Institute, 1983), 15.
25. See Thomas Berry, *The Dream of Earth* (San Francisco: Sierra Club Books, 1988).
26. Ehrlich and Ehrlich, *Earth,* 22.
27. Ehrlich and Ehrlich, *Earth,* 24.
28. Anne H. Ehrlich, Paul R. Ehrlich, and John P. Holdren, *Human Ecology: Problems and Solutions* (San Francisco: W. H. Freeman and Company, 1973), 154–55.
29. Ehrlich and Ehrlich, *Earth,* 48–49.
30. Ehrlich and Ehrlich, *Earth,* 36; also *Water: Rethinking Management in an Age of Scarcity,* Worldwatch Paper no. 62 (Washington, D.C.: Worldwatch Institute, 1984), 6–11.
31. Paul R. Ehrlich, *The Machinery of Nature* (New York: Simon and Schuster, 1986), 239–87.
32. Sally Slocum, "Woman the Gatherer: Male Bias in Anthropology" in Rayna R. Reiter, ed., *Toward an Anthropology of Women* (New York: Monthly Review Press, 1975), 36–50.
33. Carol Adams, *The Sexual Politics of Meat* (New York: Continuum, 1990), 26–38, 157.
34. Ehrlich and Ehrlich, *Earth,* 25–26.

35. Arthur Ferrill, *The Origins of War: From the Stone Age to Alexander the Great* (London: Thames and Hudson, 1985).

36. Ferrill, *The Origins of War,* 14–16.

37. Kathleen Newland, *Women and Population Growth: Choice Beyond Childbearing,* Worldwatch Report, no. 16 (Washington, D.C.: Worldwatch Institute, 1977).

38. See Brian Swimme, "How to Heal a Lobotomy," in Irene Diamond and Gloria Orenstein, eds., *Reweaving the World: The Emergence of Ecofeminism* (San Francisco: Sierra Club Books, 1989), 15–22; also his *The Universe Is a Green Dragon: A Cosmic Creation Story* (Santa Fe, NM: Bear and Company, 1985).

CHAPTER 3: RELIGIOUS NARRATIVES OF WORLD DESTRUCTION

1. The story of the flood goes back before Sumerian times and was current in oral form from early Sumerian times (3500 B.C.E.). The tablets on which the extant version was written come from the Sumerian library discovered in the excavations of Nippur, 1750 B.C.E. See Samuel Noah Kramer, *History Begins at Sumer* (New York: Doubleday, 1959), 150–54.

2. Kramer, *History Begins at Sumer,* 153.

3. See "The Descent of Inanna" in Diana Wolkstein and Samuel Noah Kramer, *Inanna: Queen of Heaven and Earth: Her Stories and Hymns from Sumer* (New York: Harper & Row, 1983), 52–71.

4. See Wolkstein and Kramer, *Inanna,* 85–89, for the story of Dumuzi's descent into the underworld.

5. "Hymn to Demeter," in *The Homeric Hymns: A New Prose Translation, and Essays, Literary and Mythological,* by Andrew Lang (Freeport, NY: Books for Libraries Press, 1899; reprint, 1972), 183–210; also N. J. Richardson, ed., *The Homeric Hymn to Demeter* (Oxford: Clarendon Press, 1974).

6. E. A. Wallis Budge, *Osiris: Egyptian Religion of Resurrection* (New York: University Books, 1961). Also Plutarch, *De Iside et Osiride,* edited by Gwyn Griffiths (Cardiff: University of Wales Press, 1970).

7. "Poems about Anath and Baal," in *Religions of the Ancient Near East,* edited by Isaac Mendelsohn (New York: Liberal Arts Press, 1955), 224–26.

8. Mendelsohn, *Religions of the Ancient Near East,* 256. "Wadies flowing with honey" was a metaphor for "sweet" or non-salty rainwater flowing in the ravines.

9. Contrast Zechariah 14:12–20, depicting the punishment of the enemies of Israel, with Isaiah 2:2–4, in which the nations are called to come up to Zion and "learn war no more."

10. *The Bundahis,* in *The Sacred Books of the East: Pahlavi Texts,* edited by Edward W. West (Oxford: Clarendon Press, 1897; reprint, Delhi, India: Motilal Banarsidass, 1965), vol. 5, 1–151.

11. Origen, *On First Principles,* edited by G. W. Butterworth (New York: Harper & Row, 1966), 52–58.

12. Daniel 7:13–14.

13. Daniel 12:2–3.

14. Isaiah 65:20; see also Rachel Z. Dulin, *Old Age in the Hebrew Scripture.* Ph.D. Diss. (Joint Program, Garrett-Northwestern University, 1982).

15. Hans von Campenhausen, *The Formation of the Christian Bible,* translated by J. A. Baker (Philadelphia: Fortress Press, 1972).

16. Sheila McGinn-Moorer, *The New Prophecy of Asia Minor and the Rise of Ecclesiastical Patriarchy in Second Century Pauline Traditions.* Ph.D. Diss. (Joint Program, Garrett-Northwestern University, 1989), 276–96.

17. W. H. C. Frend, *The Donatist Church: A Movement of Protest in Roman North Africa* (Oxford: Clarendon Press, 1985).

18. Augustine, *The City of God,* books 20–22. Also Norman Cohn, *The Pursuit of the Millennium* (New York: Harper and Brothers, 1961).

19. Christopher Hill, *The World Turned Upside Down: Radical Ideas during the English Revolution* (New York: Viking Press, 1975).

20. Cary's tracts are found on microfilm in the Thomason Tracts, British Museum.

21. It is not clear whether Cary is referring to two actual people or to collective groups. She assumes the reference is known to her readers.

22. For example, the Social Creed adopted by the Methodist Church in 1908, later taken as the social platform of the U.S. Council of Churches; see Rosemary Ruether, *The Radical Kingdom: The Western Experience of Messianic Hope* (New York: Paulist Press, 1970), 90.

23. See "The Kingdom of God," in *Walter Rauschenbusch, Selected Writings,* edited by Winthrop S. Hudson (New York: Paulist Press, 1984), 76–79.

24. Catherine Albanese, *America: Religions and Religion* (Belmont, CA: Wadsworth, 1981), 145–46; also Edwin Scott Gaustad, ed., *The Rise of Adventism* (New York: Harper & Row, 1974).

25. Ronald L. Numbers, *Prophetess of Health: A Study of Ellen G. White* (New York: Harper & Row, 1976).

26. Ellen White, *The Great Controversy* (1880) (Jemison, AL: Inspiration Books East, 1988), 411–30.

27. Regina Sharif, *Non-Jewish Zionism: Its Roots in Western History* (London: Zed Press, 1983).

28. Rosemary Ruether, *Faith and Fratricide: The Theological Roots of Anti-Semitism* (New York: Seabury Press, 1974), 147.

29. Hal Lindsay, *The Late Great Planet Earth* (Grand Rapids, MI: Zondervan, 1970); *The 1980s, Countdown to Armageddon* (New York: Bantam, 1981); also John F. Walvoord, *Armageddon, Oil and the Middle East Crisis* (Grand Rapids, MI: Zondervan, 1974, 1990).

30. For apocalypticism in the mind of Ronald Reagan, see Lawrence Jones, "Reagan's Religion," *Journal of American Culture,* 8 (1985): 59–70. Also Sara Diamond, *Spiritual Warfare: The Politics of the Christian Right* (Boston: South End Press, 1989).

31. See the comparative study of fundamentalism across world religions, *Fundamentalisms Observed,* edited by Martin E. Marty and R. Scott Appleby (Chicago: Chicago University Press, 1991).

32. Christopher Manes, *Green Rage: Radical Environmentalism and the Unmaking of Civilization* (Boston: Little, Brown and Company, 1990), 225–42.

CHAPTER 4: NEW NARRATIVES OF WORLD DESTRUCTION

1. The *Worldwatch Papers* and the annual *State of the World* report are available from the Worldwatch Institute, 1776 Massachusetts Avenue N.W., Washington, D.C. 20036. Between 1977 and 1991, 102 Worldwatch Papers have been issued by the Institute. *State of the World* reports have been issued annually since 1984.

2. See Paul R. Ehrlich, Anne H. Ehrlich, and John P. Holdren, *Human Ecology: Problems and Solutions* (San Francisco: W. H. Freeman, 1973), 12–13, 206–7.

3. See "US Called Major Cause of Damage to Earth," *Chicago Tribune* (April 4, 1990); also *Basta: National Journal of the Chicago Religious Task Force on Central America,* 59 E. Van Buren Street, Chicago, IL 60605 (July 1990): 4.

4. Eduardo Galeano, *Open Veins of Latin America: Five Centuries of the Pillage of a Continent* (London: Monthly Review Press, 1973), 21–70.

5. Tevetan Todorov, *The Conquest of America: The Question of the Other* (New York: Harper & Row, 1984), 133. Galeano, *Open Veins,* 50, gives the figures of 90 million reduced to 3.5 million over the first 150 years of colonization.

6. According to Carolyn Merchant, of the 65,000 indigenous people in Northern New England, 10,000 remained by 1674. Their numbers were reduced by wars and disease brought by the colonists. In *Ecological Revolutions: Nature, Science and Gender in New England* (Chapel Hill, NC: University of North Carolina Press, 1989), 90.

7. According to Eric Williams, between 1492, with the arrival of Columbus, and 1572, the indigenous population of between 200,000 and 300,000 on the island of Hispanola had been virtually exterminated. In *From Columbus to Castro: The History of the Caribbean, 1492–1969* (New York: Harper & Row, 1970), 33. Tasmania, an island south of Australia, was brought under British control in 1803 and made a penal colony. Its entire indigenous population was exterminated.

8. United Nations, Department of International Economic and Social Affairs, *World Population Prospects 1988* (New York: 1989).

9. Lester Brown, *et al., State of the World, 1990* (New York: Norton, 1990), 11. For the causes and current trends in infant mortality, see Kathleen Newland, *Infant Mortality and the Health of Societies,* Worldwatch Paper no. 47 (Washington, D.C.: Worldwatch Institute, 1981).

10. In 1920 in the United States, average life expectancy for white males was 54.4 and white females 55.6, for nonwhite males 45.5 and nonwhite females 45.2. In 1985 it was 71.8 for white males and 78.7 for white females, 67.2 for nonwhite males and 75.2 for nonwhite females. In Sweden in 1986 it was 73.1 for males and 79.1 for females, while in Bangladesh it was 49.2 for males and 48.2 for females: *World Almanac* (New York: 1988), 825, 721, 655.

11. Lester Brown, *et al., Twenty-two Dimensions of the Population Problem,* Worldwatch Paper no. 5 (Washington, D.C.: Worldwatch Institute, 1976), 30.

12. See Kathleen Newland, *Women and Population Growth: Choice Beyond Childbearing,* Worldwatch Paper no. 16 (Washington, D.C.: Worldwatch Institute, 1977).

13. Brown, *Twenty-Two Dimensions,* 42–45, 61–63, 67–69.

14. Brown, *Twenty-Two Dimensions,* 9–10.

15. Brown, *State of the World, 1990,* 59; also Lester Brown, *Changing the World Food Prospect: The Nineties and Beyond,* Worldwatch Paper no. 85 (Washington, D.C.: Worldwatch Institute, 1986), 8–9.

16. Edward C. Wolf, *Beyond the Green Revolution: New Approaches for Third World Agriculture,* Worldwatch Paper no. 73 (Washington, D.C.: Worldwatch Institute, 1986), 9.

17. Brown, *State of the World, 1990,* 60–61; also Lester Brown and Edward C. Wolf, *Soil Erosion: Quiet Crisis in the World Economy,* Worldwatch Paper no. 60 (Washington, D.C.: Worldwatch Institute, 1984).

18. Lester Brown, *Worldwide Loss of Cropland,* Worldwatch Paper no. 24 (Washington, D.C.: Worldwatch Institute, 1978), p. 11.

19. For example, in Central America the poorer half of the population eats only ten pounds of meat a year, compared with a per capita meat consumption of 175 pounds a year in the United States. In

Central America, among other impoverished areas of the world, land is cleared for cattle ranches whose produce goes almost entirely to the United States and local elites, reducing the land for grain crops that feed the poor: see Tom Barry and Deb Preusch, *The Central American Fact Book* (New York: Grove Press, 1986), 153–55. Eating high off the food chain through meat consumption can be termed a "food swindle," since it takes roughly ten pounds of grain to produce one pound of beef cattle. In American feedlot production of beef, it takes 20,000 calories of fossil fuel energy to produce 500 food calories in a one-pound steak: see Frances Moore Lappe, "Choose to Eat Low on the Food Chain," in *The Green Lifestyle Handbook*, edited by Jeremy Rifkin (New York: Henry Holt, 1990), 60.

20. In Guatemala the pacification plan of the military government (PAAC) had as one of its major components the replacement of the Indian culture of corn with a new agricultural base that focused on nontraditional crops for export. This project has been supervised by consultants from the United States, Israel, and Taiwan: Barry and Preusch, *The Central American Fact Book*, 236–37.

21. In 1967 the U.S. President's Advisory Committee Panel on the World Food Supply estimated that 20 percent of the people in underdeveloped countries were undernourished (not receiving enough food per day): Paul R. Ehrlich, *et al., Human Ecology: Problems and Solutions* (San Francisco: W. H. Freeman, 1973), 70. In the 1980s the gap between rich and poor had widened in most of the world. In 1989, 62 percent of sub-Saharan Africans were living at the destitution level, 25 percent of Asians, 35 percent of Latin Americans. In Brown, *State of the World, 1990*, 139.

22. *State of the World*, 55; Lester Brown estimates that at present rate of use (1983), the more easily available supplies of petroleum will be consumed in thirty-five years: see Brown, *Population Policies for a New Economic Era*, Worldwatch Paper no. 53 (Washington, D.C.: Worldwatch Institute, 1983), 14–15. See also Christopher Flavin, *World Oil: Coping with the Dangers of Success*, Worldwatch Paper no. 66 (Washington, D.C.: Worldwatch Institute, 1985).

23. Sandra Postel, *Air Pollution, Acid Rain and the Future of Forests*, Worldwatch Paper no. 58 (Washington, D.C.: Worldwatch Institute, 1984); also Brown, *State of the World 1990*, 108.

24. Brown, *State of the World 1990*, 103.

25. Denis Hayes, *Pollution: Neglected Dimensions*, Worldwatch Paper no. 27 (Washington, D.C.: Worldwatch Institute, 1979), 17–22.

26. See Paul and Anne Ehrlich, *Extinction: The Causes and Consequences of the Disappearance of Species* (New York: Random House, 1981). Also Edward C. Wolf, *On the Brink of Extinction:*

Conserving the Diversity of Life, Worldwatch Paper no. 78 (Washington, D.C: Worldwatch Institute, 1987).

27. This has been a major emphasis in the writings of Thomas Berry. See his book with Thomas Clarke, *Befriending the Earth* (Mystic, CT: Twenty-Third Publications, 1990), 11–13.

28. Gil Elliot, *Twentieth Century Book of the Dead* (London: Penguin, 1972), 23. Also *World Almanac* (New York: 1988), 338.

29. *World Military Expenditures and Arms Transfers 1988,* U.S. Arms Control and Disarmament Agency (Washington, D.C.: The Agency, 1989).

30. *World Armaments, 1963–1973,* U.S. Arms Control and Disarmament Agency (Washington, D.C.: The Agency, 1974).

31. Seymour Melman, *The Permanent War Economy: American Capitalism in Decline* (New York: Simon and Schuster, 1974), 18–19; also "The New Military Budget," in *Peace and Justice Journal,* a publication of the American Friends Service Committee (April/May 1990).

32. *World Military Expenditures 1988,* 3–12.

33. Patrick G. Coy, "Wars of the World Leave Little to Celebrate," *National Catholic Reporter* 26, no. 38 (August 24, 1990); also Michael Klare, ed., *Low-Intensity Warfare* (New York: Pantheon, 1988).

34. *World Military Expenditures 1988,* iii, 21–23.

35. See Stephen Schlesinger and Stephen Kinzer, *Bitter Fruit: The Untold Story of the American Coup in Guatemala* (Garden City, NY: Doubleday and Company, 1982).

36. On environmental damage in Guatemala, see *OSGUA* (Organization in Solidarity with the People of Guatemala) *Newsletter* (Spring 1989).

37. *World Almanac, 1988,* 340.

38. See Fabrizio Tonello, "Lobbing One into the Kremlim," *The Nation* (October 23, 1989): 445–46.

39. Israel's nuclear weapons program was developed in secret. When an Israeli nuclear technician, Mordechai Venunu, revealed its existence, he was kidnapped by the Mossad (Israel's CIA), tried, and imprisoned for treason. See James M. Wall, "Nuclear Arms and the Missing Man," *Christian Century* 103 (November 19, 1986): 1019–1020; the estimate of Israel's nuclear strength in 1991 is found in Seymour M. Hersh, *The Sampson Option* (New York: Random House, 1991).

40. Howard Hiatt, "The Medical Consequences of Nuclear War: A Case for Prevention," in *Waging Peace: A Handbook for the Struggle to Abolish Nuclear Weapons* (San Francisco: Harper & Row, 1982), 82–83.

41. Taken from a 1977 study of the Defense Department's Civil Preparedness Agency, Jonathan Schell, *The Fate of the Earth* (New York: Avon Books, 1982), 17–18.
42. Schell, *The Fate of the Earth,* 18–20; also A. Cohen and S. Lee, eds., *Nuclear Weapons: The Future of Humanity* (Totowa, NJ: Rouman and Allanheld, 1980).
43. Michael Renner, "Assessing the Military's War on the Environment," in Lester Brown, et al., *State of the World, 1991* (New York: Norton, 1991), 132–52.
44. See UNICEF report on *Children War Victims* (March 1991), The U.S. Committee for UNICEF, 540 North Michigan Avenue, Chicago, Illinois, 60611. The effect of the pinpoint bombing of the Iraqi military-industrial infrastructure was to release an ongoing plague of diseases caused by famine, polluted water, and lack of electricity and medicines, killing tens of thousands of the most vulnerable Iraqis, especially small children. This has been further aggravated by the embargo that continues after the war, preventing Iraq from selling oil and importing food and medicines: See James Fine, "Iraq Now: Relief Held Hostage," in *Christianity and Crisis,* 51, no. 15 (October 21, 1991): 336–38.
45. Fine, "Iraq Now: Relief Held Hostage," note 32.
46. For postwar Pentagon plans in Kuwait, see "Pentagon Plans to Run Kuwait after the War," in the *National Catholic Reporter* (March 8, 1991): 13. For a general assessment of U.S. plans for hegemony in the Gulf region after the Gulf War, see Michael Moushabeck and Phyllis Bennis, eds., *Beyond the Storm: A Gulf Crisis Reader* (New York: Olive Branch Press, 1991).
47. See the report on Pentagon plans for future wars, *National Catholic Reporter,* vol. 28, no. 17 (February 28, 1992): 3.

CHAPTER 5: CLASSICAL NARRATIVES OF SIN AND EVIL

1. George Foote Moore, *Judaism in the First Centuries of the Christian Era* (New York: Schocken Books, 1971), vol. 1, 283–88.
2. See the Community Rule of the Qumran Community, in *The Dead Sea Scrolls in English,* edited by G. Vermes (Baltimore: Penguin, 1962), 76–77.
3. The scriptural locus for this concept of "zeal for the law" is Numbers 25:6–13. For a critical evaluation of this concept as the origin of the Zealot movement, see Richard A. Horsley, *Jesus and the Spiral of Violence: Popular Jewish Resistance in Roman Palestine* (San Francisco: Harper & Row, 1987), 121–29.

4. Judith Plaskow, *Standing Again at Sinai: Judaism from a Feminist Perspective* (San Francisco: Harper & Row, 1990), 178–85.

5. Plaskow, *Standing Again at Sinai*, 100–7.

6. Exodus 10:14–15.

7. Bernadette Brooten, *Women Leaders in the Ancient Synagogue: Inscriptional Evidence and Background Issues* (Chico, CA: Scholars Press, 1982).

8. Joshua 24:13.

9. See Albrecht Alt, "The Settlement of the Israelites in Palestine," in *Essays in Old Testament History and Religion* (Oxford: Blackwell, 1966), 173–222.

10. See Cotton Mather's *Soldiers Counselled and Comforted* (Boston: Samuel Green, 1689), where the American Indians are compared with the Amalekites, which the Israelites are mandated by God to slay.

11. Martin Prozesky, Religious Studies Department, University of Natal in Pietermarizburg, South Africa, recalled that in his youth he frequently heard the Zulus compared to Amalekites in sermons (interview: September 1989). For Afrikaner ideology of religious nationalism, see Leonard Thompson, *The Political Mythology of Apartheid* (New Haven: Yale University Press, 1985).

12. For the comparison of Palestinians to Amalekites in rabbinic pronouncements, see Uriel Tal, "The Land and the State of Israel in Israeli Religious Life," *Proceedings of the Rabbinic Assembly of the 76th Annual Convention* (Grossinger, NY: Rabbinic Assembly, 1977), 9 ff. For the Gush Emunim movement, see Ian Lustick, *For the Land and the Lord: Jewish Fundamentalism in Israel* (New York: Council on Foreign Relations, 1988).

13. Plato, *Phaedrus*, 247.

14. Plato, *Phaedrus*, 248.

15. From the account of Ptolemaeus's system in Irenaeus, *Adversus Haereses*, Book 1; translation from *Gnosticism: A Source Book of Heretical Writings from the Early Christian Period*, edited by Robert M. Grant (New York: Harper and Brothers, 1961), 163–64.

16. "The Poimandres of Hermes Trismegistus," in Hans Jonas, *The Gnostic Religion: The Message of the Alien God and the Beginning of Christianity* (Boston: Beacon, 1963), 152–53.

17. Irenaeus, *Adversus Haereses*, Book V, in *Early Christian Fathers*, edited by Cyril Richardson (Philadelphia: Westminster Press, 1953), 461–67.

18. Origen, *On First Principles* II, 2, 2 (New York: Harper & Row, 1966), 81–82.

19. For example, Gregory Nazianzus, Oration 38.12, where "Man" is described as acquiring a mortal body after the Fall: *Nicene and*

Post-Nicene Fathers, 2d series, edited by Philip Schaff and Henry Wace (London: Parker, 1894), vol. 7, 348.

20. Gregory Nyssa, "On the Soul and the Resurrection" in *Nicene and Post-Nicene Fathers,* 2d series, edited by Philip Schaff and Henry Wace (London: Parker, 1893), vol. 5, 464–65.

21. Augustine, *Confessions,* Book 7, sec. 16.

22. Pelagius, "Letter to Demetrias," in *Theological Anthropology,* edited by J. Patout Burns (Philadelphia: Fortress, 1981), 39–55.

23. Paul, Romans 7:23.

24. Augustine, "On the Grace of Christ" XXV:26: in *Theological Anthropology,* 79.

25. Augustine, "De Praedestinatione Sanctorum" and "De Dono Perseverantiae," *Patrologia Latina,* vol. 44, cols. 959–90, and vol. 45, cols. 993–1034 (Paris: Migne, 1861).

26. Augustine, *The City of God,* XIV, 26.

27. Augustine, "De Nuptiis et Concupiscentia," *Corpus Scriptorum Ecclesiasticorum Latinorum,* edited by Caroli F. Urba and Josephi Zycha (Prague and Vindobonae: F. Tempsky, 1902), vol. 42, 210–319.

28. Augustine, *Confessions* Book 8, secs. 8–12.

CHAPTER 6: PARADISE LOST AND THE FALL INTO PATRIARCHY

1. Hesiod, *Work and Days,* edited by M. L. West (Oxford: Clarendon Press, 1978), chapters 5–6.

2. For an exploration of the lost paradise motif and the preservation of childhood narcissism, see Erich Fromm, *Man for Himself* (New York: Rinehart and Company, 1947), 38–42, and his *You Shall Be as Gods: A Radical Reinterpretation of the Old Testament and Its Tradition* (New York: Rinehart and Winston, 1966), 71.

3. See Joan Bamberger, "The Myth of Matriarchy: Why Men Rule in Primitive Society," in *Women, Culture and Society,* edited by Michelle Zimbalist Rosaldo and Louise Lamphere (Stanford: Stanford University Press, 1974), 263–80.

4. Particularly J. J. Bachofen, *Das Mutterrecht* (Stuttgart: Krais and Hoffman, 1861). It has never been translated into English in its entirety. An abridged English translation appeared as *Myth, Religion and Motherright,* translated by Ralph Manheim, Introduction by Joseph Campbell (London: Routledge and Kegan Paul, 1967).

5. Friedrich Engels, *The Origin of the Family, Private Property and the State* (1885; reprint, New York: International Publishers, 1942).

6. Sir Arthur Evans (1851–1941) was the chief archaeologist for the excavation of the Palace of Knossos on Crete. Influenced by

matriarchal theory, he described his findings in Crete in that inter-
pretive framework. An important interpreter of pre-Classical Greek
culture, from the matriarchal perspective, was Jane Ellen Harrison
(1850–1928), *Themis: A Study of the Social Origins of Greek Religion* (Cambridge: The University Press, 1921) and *Prolegomena to
the Study of Greek Religion* (Cambridge: The University Press,
1922). A popularizer of the matriarchal thesis is poet and classical
scholar Robert Graves, *The White Goddess: A Historical Grammar
of Poetic Myth* (New York: Creative Age Press, 1948).

7. This was Bachofen's view of matriarchy, and is the standard one
found in interpretations of the development of Greek culture. See,
for example, Gilbert Murray, *Five Stages of Greek Religion* (Garden
City, NY: Doubleday and Company, 1955), and Walter Otto, *The
Homeric Gods: The Spiritual Significance of Greek Religion* (London: Thames and Hudson, 1954).

8. Marxist interpretations of women's status in primitive communism
and future communism are August Bebel, *Women Under Socialism*
(1883), translated by Daniel de Leon (New York: Schocken Books,
1971), and Evelyn Reed, *Problems of Women's Liberation: A Marxist Approach* (New York: Pathfinder Press, 1971).

9. Matilda Joslyn Gage, *Woman, Church and State* (1893); reprint
(Watertown, MA: Persephone Press, 1980).

10. Frank Boas (1858–1942) turned anthropology away from comparative studies and schemes of universal evolution of culture and
sought to make it an exact science studying particular elements of
culture in specific social contexts.

11. For example, Merlin Stone, *When God Was a Woman* (New York:
Dial Press, 1976), and Elizabeth Gould Davis, *The First Sex* (Baltimore: Penguin Books, 1971).

12. Matthew Fox, *Original Blessing: A Primer in Creation Spirituality*
(Santa Fe, NM: Bear and Co., 1983).

13. Fox, *Original Blessing*, 46.

14. Fox, *Original Blessing*, 270–76.

15. Christopher Manes, *Green Rage: Radical Environmentalism and
the Unmaking of Civilization* (Boston: Little, Brown and Company,
1990), 225–48.

16. See Jim Cheney, "Ecofeminism and Deep Ecology," *Environmental
Ethics* 9 (Summer 1987): 115–46. Also Marti Kheel, "Ecofeminism
and Deep Ecology: Reflections on Identity and Difference," in
Covenant for a New Creation: Ethics, Religion and Public Policy,
edited by Carl S. Robb and Carl Casebolt (Maryknoll, NY: Orbis
Books, 1991), 141–64.

17. Mary Daly, *The Church and the Second Sex* (New York: Harper &
Row, 1968); *Beyond God the Father* (Boston: Beacon, 1973); her

Gyn/ecology (Boston: Beacon, 1978); and her *Pure Lust* (Boston: Beacon, 1984).

18. Mary Daly, *Webster's First Intergalactic Wickedary of the English Language* (Boston: Beacon, 1987), 136.

19. Daly, *Webster's First*, 198; also Daly, *Pure Lust*, 93.

20. Carol Christ, "Rethinking Theology and Nature," in *Weaving the Visions: New Patterns in Feminist Spirituality*, edited by Carol Christ and Judith Plaskow (San Francisco: Harper & Row, 1989), 314–25.

21. Carol Christ, *The Laughter of Aphrodite: Reflections on a Journey to the Goddess* (San Francisco: Harper & Row, 1987), 117–31.

22. "Reflections on the Initiation of an American Woman Scholar into the Symbols and Rituals of the Ancient Goddess," in *Journal of Feminist Studies in Religion* 3, no. 1 (1987).

23. James Mellaart, *Catal Hüyük: A Neolithic Town in Anatolia* (London: Thames and Hudson, 1967). Also his *The Neolithic Near East* (London: McGraw-Hill, 1975).

24. See Marija Gimbutas, "Women and Culture in Goddess-oriented Old Europe," in Plaskow and Christ, *Weaving the Visions*, 63–71.

25. Marija Gimbutas, *Goddesses and Gods of Old Europe: Myths and Cult Images* (Berkeley: University of California Press, 1989); and her *The Language of the Goddess: Unearthing the Hidden Symbols in Western Civilization* (San Francisco: Harper & Row, 1989).

26. Gimbutas, "Women and Culture," in Plaskow and Christ, *Weaving the Visions*, 63–71.

27. Riane Eisler, *The Chalice and the Blade: Our History, Our Future* (San Francisco: Harper & Row, 1987), 42–58.

28. Mellaart, *Neolithic Near East*, 13: "As things are we can deduce relatively little about social structure, the nature of authority, law and customs, etc." See also his *Catal Hüyük*, 225–26. Anne L. Barstow, I believe, goes beyond the evidence in assuming that a decentralized social structure means shared political power between men and women. See her "The Uses of Archaeology for Women's History: James Mellaart's Work on the Neolithic Goddess at Catal Hüyük," *Feminist Studies* 4, no. 3 (October 1978): 7–18.

29. Summarized in James Mellaart, *The Archaeology of Ancient Turkey* (London: The Bodley Head, 1978), 44–48, 419–23.

30. See Carol Christ, "Lady of the Animals," in *Encyclopedia of Religion*, vol. 8 (New York: Macmillan, 1987): 419–23.

31. Richard E. Leakey, *The Making of Mankind* (New York: E. P. Dutton, 1981), 55–76.

32. Mark Cohen, *The Food Crisis in Prehistory: Overpopulation and the Origins of Agriculture* (New Haven: Yale University Press, 1977).

33. Nancy M. Tanner, *Becoming Human* (Cambridge: Cambridge University Press, 1981), 83–106.
34. Tanner, *Becoming Human,* 222.
35. Margaret Ehrenberg, *Women in Prehistory* (London: British Museum Publications, 1989).
36. Peggy Reeves Sanday, *Female Power and Male Dominance: On the Origins of Sexual Inequality* (Cambridge: Cambridge University Press, 1981), 24–28. Sanday's comparative study of societies is limited by her dependence on a great variety of accounts done by others.
37. See Gerda Lerner, *The Creation of Patriarchy* (New York: Oxford University Press, 1986), 46–52.
38. Leakey, *Making of Mankind,* 98–109.
39. See Richard Lee and I. De Vore, eds. *Kalahari Hunter-Gatherers: Studies of the !Kung-San and Their Neighbors* (Cambridge: Harvard University Press, 1976); and Richard Lee, *The !Kung-San: Men, Women and Work in a Foraging Society* (London: Cambridge University Press, 1979).
40. Ehrenberg, *Women in Prehistory,* 77–99.
41. For matricentric Indian culture, see Pupul Jayakar, *The Earth Mother* (San Francisco: HarperCollins, 1990).
42. Arthur Ferrill, *The Origins of War: From the Stone Age to Alexander the Great* (London: Thames and Hudson, 1985).
43. Ehrenberg, *Women in Prehistory,* 99–107.
44. See Ruby Rohrlich, "State Formation in Sumer and the Subjugation of Women," in *Feminist Studies* 6, no. 1 (Spring 1980): 76–102; also Sarah Pomeroy, *Goddesses, Whores, Wives and Slaves: Women in Classical Antiquity* (New York: Schocken, 1976), 57.
45. Ehrenberg, *Women in Prehistory,* 109–18, also Ruby Rohrlich-Leavitt, "Women in Transition: Crete and Sumer," in *Becoming Visible: Women in European History,* edited by Renate Bredenthal and Claudia Koonz (Boston: Houghton Mifflin Company, 1977), 36–59.
46. Sanday, *Female Power and Male Dominance.*
47. See also Yolanda Murphy and Robert F. Murphy, *Women of the Forest* (New York: Columbia University Press, 1974), for a study of the Mundurucu Indians of Brazil as an example of a gender conflictual society.
48. This problem of the effect of female parenting on female and male development has been studied by Dorothy Dinnerstein, *The Mermaid and the Minotaur: Sexual Arrangements and Human Malaise* (New York: Harper & Row, 1976); also Nancy Chodorow, *The Reproduction of Mothering* (Berkeley: University of California Press, 1978). Chodorow and Dinnerstein have been criticized for basing their critique of female parenting and its reproduction of gender stereotypes on a middle-class division of labor in which

women do the domestic work and childcare, while men provide the means of living from "outside." See "Gender in the Context of Class and Race: Notes on Chodorow's *Reproduction of Mothering*," in Elizabeth V. Spelman, *Inessential Woman: Problems of Exclusion In Feminist Thought* (Boston: Beacon Press, 1988), 80–133; also the discussion in *Signs: Journal of Women in Culture and Society* 6, no. 3 (Spring 1981): 482–514. The suggestions in this chapter, however, do not derive from this middle-class context, but rather from studies of societies that are either deprived (poor African-Americans or South African blacks), or Asian Indians, where women do both the childcare and a major proportion of the work that sustains the household, and yet where this "power" of women is countered by a high level of active and passive violence (see note 53, below).

49. Sanday, *Female Power and Male Dominance*, 21–24.
50. Sanday, *Female Power and Male Dominance*, 16–19.
51. Sanday, *Female Power and Male Dominance*, 91–108.
52. Sanday, *Female Power and Male Dominance*, 184–211.
53. For examples of the patterns of disrupted patriarchy among black South African women, see Jane Barrett *et al.*, eds., *Vukani Makhosikazi: South African Women Speak* (London: Third World Publications, 1985), 125–76.

CHAPTER 7: CONSTRUCTING THE SYSTEMS OF DOMINATION

1. For the connection of the myth of overthrow of matriarchy and male puberty drama, see Joan Bamberger, "The Myth of Matriarchy: Why Men Rule in Primitive Society," in Michelle Zimbardo Rosaldo and Louise Lamphere, *Woman, Culture and Society* (Stanford: Stanford University Press, 1974), 263–80.
2. For Sumerian history and early documents, see Thorkild Jacobsen, *The Treasures of Darkness* (New Haven: Yale University Press, 1972); also Samuel Noah Kramer, *History Begins at Sumer* (Garden City, NY: Anchor Books, 1959) and *The Sumerians: Their History, Culture and Character* (Chicago, IL: Chicago University Press, 1963); and Denise Schmandt-Besserat, ed., *The Legacy of Sumer* (Malibu, CA: Biblioteca Mesopotamia, 1979).
3. See M. A. Dandamaev, *Slavery in Babylonia* (Dekalb, IL: University of Northern Illinois Press, 1984).
4. There was a significant difference between temple slaves, who could not be sold and had a regular family life, as indicated by patronymics, and domestic slaves, who could be sold and were sexually available to the owning males: see Amelie Kuhrt, "Non-Royal Women in the

Late Babylonian Period: a Survey," in *Women's Earliest Records from Ancient Egypt and Western Asia: Proceedings of the Conference on Women in the Ancient Near East, Brown University, Providence, Rhode Island, November 5–7, 1987,* edited by Barbara S. Lesko (Atlanta, GA: Scholars Press, 1989), 230–33.

5. An Akkadian version of this myth as part of the flood story, with the Sumerian prototype, is found in W. G. Lambert and A. R. Millard, eds., *Atra-Hasis: The Babylonian Story of the Flood* (Oxford: Clarendon Press, 1970), 43–59, also 15.

6. *Enuma Elish,* Tablet VI, 1.8, also 1.34; *Religions of the Ancient Near East: Sumero-Akkadian Religious Texts and Ugaritic Epics,* edited by Isaac Mendelsohn (New York: Liberal Arts Press, 1955), 36, 37.

7. See Thorkild Jacobsen, *Sumerian King List* ASII (Chicago: University of Chicago Press, 1939), 104, vs. 35–42; also Jerrold S. Cooper, "Third Millennium Mesopotamia" and Marc Van de Mieroop, "Women in the Economy of Sumer," in Lesko, *Women's Earliest Records,* 47–70. Also Bernard F. Batto, *The Study of the Roles of Royal Women at Mari* (Baltimore: John Hopkins University Press, 1974).

8. Katarzyna Grosz, "Some Aspects of the Postion of Women in Nuzi," and Martha T. Roth, "Marriage and Matrimonial Prestations in First Millennium Babylonia," in Lesko, *Women's Earliest Records,* 171–73 and 245–55.

9. Grosz, "Some Aspects," in Lesko, *Women's Earliest Records,* 173–77.

10. Rivkah Harris, "Independent Women in Ancient Mesopotamia," in Lesko, *Women's Earliest Records,* 145–56.

11. For preliminary efforts to assess women's declining status in Mesopotamian society over three millennia, see Ruby Rohrlich Leavitt, "Women in Transition: Crete and Sumer," in *Becoming Visible: Women in European History,* edited by Renate Bridenthal and Claudia Koonz (Boston: Houghton Mifflin Company, 1977), 50–57. Also Barbara Lesko, "Women of Egypt and the Ancient Near East," in Bridenthal and Koonz, *Becoming Visible* (2d ed., 1987), 41–77. Assyrian law in the late second millennium reflects a strict patriarchal system: see Claudio Saporetti, *The Status of Women in the Middle Assyrian Period* (Malibu, CA: Undena Publications, 1979).

12. For the thesis that Israel began as a revolt of hill tribes against the class hierarchical cities of Canaan, and thus had from its origins a strong motive of egalitarianism between covenanting males, see Norman K. Gottwald, *The Tribes of Yahweh: A Sociology of the Religion of Liberated Israel, 1250–1050 B.C.* (Maryknoll, NY: Orbis Press, 1979).

13. This ideal of reclaiming equality between male householders by returning alienated land and freeing Hebrew slaves is expressed in the Jubilee vision of Leviticus 25 and also in the vision of redemption as land redistribution, with each householder able to sit "under their own vine and fig tree," that is, Isaiah 65:17–25.

14. Exodus 19:14–15.

15. For a summary of women's status in Mosaic law, see Phyllis Bird, "Images of Women in the Old Testament," in *Religion and Sexism: Images of Woman in the Jewish and Christian Traditions,* edited by Rosemary R. Ruether (New York: Simon and Schuster, 1974), 48–57.

16. The connection of the story of Eve's creation from Adam's "rib" and the male puberty rite was suggested by Theodor Reik, *The Creation of Woman: A Psychoanalytical Inquiry into the Myth of Eve* (New York: McGraw Hill, 1960).

17. Carol Ochs sees in the story of Abraham's attempted sacrifice of Isaac an expression of the patriarchal negation of the power of the mother, the supersession of the ethics of blood kinship of matricentry with a primary obligation to an abstract moral principle, represented by the Voice of God, *Behind the Sex of God* (Boston: Beacon, 1977), 45. Fanchon Shur, a Jewish feminist dancer, has composed a dance *midrash* on the sacrifice of Isaac, in which Sarah's mounting rage against both Abraham and God finally issues in the intervening "angel" who stops the sacrifice; for information contact Fanchon Shur, Director, Growth in Motion, 4019 Red Bud Avenue, Cincinnati, Ohio 45229.

18. A considerable literature exists exploring the relationship between kingship rites in the Ancient Near East and in Israel: see S. H. Hooke, ed., *Myth, Ritual and Kingship: Essays on the Theory and Practice of Kingship in the Ancient Near East and in Israel* (Oxford: Clarendon Press, 1958). For the presence of the Goddess in the Solomonic temple, see Raphael Patai, *The Hebrew Goddess* (Philadelphia: Ktav, 1967), 29–100.

19. *The Hebrew Goddess,* 137–205.

20. On the metaphor of the whore in Hebrew thought, see Phyllis Bird, "'To Play the Harlot': An Inquiry into an Old Testament Metaphor," in *Gender and Difference,* edited by Peggy L. Day (Minneapolis, MN: Fortress Press, 1989), 75–94; also her "The Harlot as Heroine in Biblical Texts: Narrative Art and Social Presupposition," in *Semeia* 46 (1989): 119–39.

21. Rohrlich-Leavitt, "Women in Transition: Crete and Sumer," 42–50. However, the very existence of large palace centers with vast storehouses indicates a ruling-class pattern of accumulation that testifies against the claims of Rohrlich-Leavitt that there was no significant class hierarchy in Minoan Crete.

22. See Sarah B. Pomeroy, *Goddesses, Whores, Wives and Slaves: Women in Classical Antiquity* (New York: Schocken Books, 1975), 57–78.

23. See Philip Slater, *The Glory of Hera: Greek Mythology and the Greek Family* (Boston: Beacon Press, 1968).

24. Hesiod, *Works and Days,* chapters 5–6.

25. Aeschylus, *Eumenides,* lines 234–242; from *The Complete Greek Drama,* edited by Whitney J. Oates and Eugene O'Neill, vol. 1 (New York: Random House, 1938), 297.

26. Page DuBois, *Centaurs and Amazons: Women and the Pre-History of the Great Chain of Being* (Ann Arbor, MI: University of Michigan Press, 1982), 49–77.

27. DuBois, *Centaurs and Amazons,* 129–49.

28. Aristotle, *Generation of Animals,* 729–75, and *Politics,* 1254.

29. Elaine Pagels, *The Gnostic Gospels* (New York: Random House, 1979), 48–69.

30. See Rosemary Ruether, "Misogynism and Virginal Feminism in the Fathers of the Church," in *Religion and Sexism: Images of Women in the Jewish and Christian Traditions* (New York: Simon and Schuster, 1974), 156–68. For Augustine's justification of slavery and the coercive role of the state in disciplining heretics, see *City of God* XIX, 14–16 and Epistle 185, *ad Bonifacium,* VII, 24.

31. J. B. Bury, *The Idea of Progress* (New York: Macmillan Co., 1932).

32. Thorkild Jacobsen, *Salinity and Irrigation Agriculture in Antiquity* (Malibu, CA: Undena Publications, 1982).

33. J. Donald Hughes, *Ecology in Ancient Civilization* (Albuquerque: University of New Mexico Press, 1975).

34. "The Rule of Saint Benedict," sec. 48, in *Western Asceticism,* Owen Chadwick, editor (Philadelphia: Westminster Press, 1958), 321–22; for the relationship of monasticism and farming, see Marie Dominique Chenu, *Nature, Man and Society in the Twelfth Century* (Chicago: University of Chicago Press, 1968); also Jacques Leclercq, *Bernard of Clairvaux and the Cistercian Spirit* (Kalamazoo, MI: Cistercian Publications, 1976).

35. See Charles Avila, *Ownership: Early Christian Teachings* (Maryknoll, NY: Orbis Press, 1983).

36. William Short, *Saints in the World of Nature: The Animal Story as Spiritual Parable in Medieval Hagiography, 900–1200 A.D.* (Rome: Franciscan Publications, 1983).

37. See René Dubos, "Franciscan Conservation versus Benedictine Stewardship," in *A God Within* (New York: Charles Scribner, 1972), 153–74.

38. The second-century *Acts of Paul and Thecla* is one example of an early Christian perspective where celibacy is seen as freeing women from subjugation to the family and state and opening up the freedom

to act as a traveling evangelist. See Rosemary Ruether, "Asceticism and Feminism: Strange Bedfellows?" in *Sex and God: Some Varieties of Women's Religious Experience* (London: Routledge and Kegan Paul, 1987), 229–50,

39. See Kari Vogt, "Becoming Male: A Gnostic and Early Christian Metaphor," in Kari Borresen, ed., *Image of God and Gender Models in Judaeo-Christian Tradition* (Oslo: Solum Forlag, 1991), 172–87.

40. See the discussion on the ambivalence of Christian views of birth as "sin and death" in Rosemary Ruether, *Sexism and God-Talk: Toward a Feminist Theology* (Boston: Beacon Press, 1983), 240–49.

41. While the literature of the apocryphal Acts, such as the *Acts of Paul and Thecla*, seems to be written from a female ascetic point of view and affirms women's ministry, the Pseudo-Clementine literature of the second to third centuries C.E. seems to reflect a male ascetic viewpoint. Its major emphasis is on the need of the monk to avoid all contact with women, even with nuns: see especially "Two Epistles Concerning Virginity," in *Ante-Nicene Fathers*, Alexander Roberts and James Donaldson, eds. (New York: Scribners, 1899), vol. 8, 51–66.

42. See Susan Wemple, *Women in Frankish Society: Marriage and the Cloister, 500–900 A.D.* (University of Pennsylvania Press, 1983).

43. Carolyn Merchant, *The Death of Nature: Women, Ecology and the Scientific Revolution* (San Francisco: Harper & Row, 1980), especially chapters 1 and 4.

44. For example, Plato's *Republic* IV, 434–35, where the self is hierarchically ordered into mind, will, and appetites, corresponding to the three social classes of the philosopher kings, the warriors, and the workers.

45. Bonaventure, *The Mind's Road to God* (New York: Liberal Arts Press, 1953), 9.

46. The term "Prince of this World" (*ho archon tou kosmou*) appears primarily in the Gospel of John (12:31; 14:30; 16:11). A related idea, "the Prince of the power of the air," appears in Ephesians 2:2.

47. *Malleus Maleficarum*, translated by Montague Summers (London: J. Rodker, 1928).

48. John Calvin, *Institutes*, in *On the Christian Faith* (New York: Liberal Arts Press, 1957), 3–40.

49. If one visits medieval churches in the regions of Switzerland, Holland, or England taken over by Calvinists, the stripping of interior statuary, destruction of the medieval stained glass, and smashed heads of the figures on the lower levels of the exterior are still quite evident. The popular violence generated by the Reformation particularly offended the humanist Erasmus. In his work on concord in the church (1533), he defended the use of images with the words:

"He who takes the imagery out of life deprives it of its highest pleasure: we often discern more in images than we conceive from the
written word." From Johan Huizinga, *Erasmus and the Age of the
Reformation* (New York: Harper Brothers, 1957), 167–68.

50. Zwingli particularly represented the symbolic view of the Eucharist
in his *Commentary on True and False Religion* (1525), against
Luther's insistence on the physical presence. The Colloquy of Mar-
burg was convened in 1529 to solve this dispute, but ended in a
parting of the ways between the Lutheran and Reformed traditions
on eucharistic theology.

51. Rosemary S. Keller, "New England Women: Ideology and Experience in First Generation Puritanism, 1630–1650," in *Women and
Religion in America: The Colonial and Revolutionary Periods,*
edited by Rosemary R. Ruether and Rosemary S. Keller (San Francisco: Harper & Row, 1983), 135, 152–56.

52. On the changing economic opportunities for working women, see
Alice Clark, *The Working Life of Women in the Seventeenth Century* (London: G. Routledge and Sons, 1919; reprint, 1968). On the
struggle between midwives and male surgery, see Jean Donnison,
Midwives and Medical Men (New York: Schocken, 1977). On
women's status see Katherine Rogers, *Feminism in Eighteenth Century England* (Urbana, IL: University of Illinois Press, 1982); and
Janelle Greenberg, "The Legal Status of English Women in Early
Eighteenth Century Law and Equity," *Studies in Eighteenth Century Culture* 4 (1975): 171–81.

53. See particularly, Brian Easlea, *Witch Hunting, Magic and the New
Philosophy* (New Jersey: Humanities Press, 1980; also Morris
Berman, *The Reenchantment of the World* (Ithaca: Cornell Univer-
sity Press, 1981), 28–31, and Carolyn Merchant, *The Death of
Nature,* 163–91.

54. James I, *Daemonologie,* 3 books (London: A. Hatfield, 1603).

55. See particularly William Leiss, *The Domination of Nature* (New
York: Braziller, 1972), 55.

56. See Francis Bacon, "*Novum Organum,*" Part 2, in *Works,* edited by
James Spedding (London: Longmans, 1887–1901), vol. 4, 247; and
the "Masculine Birth of Time," in Benjamin Farrington, *Francis
Bacon: Philosopher of Industrial Science* (New York: H. Schu-
mann, 1949), 62.

57. René Descartes, *Discourse on Method and Selected Writings,* translated by John Veitch (New York: Open Court, 1951).

58. Descartes, *Discourse on Method and Selected Writings,* part V.

59. See Berman, *Reenchantment,* 106–13, on the role of churchmen in
the promotion of a split between religion and science.

60. Isaac Newton, *Mathematical Principles of Natural Philosophy*
(1687), translated by Andrew Motte (London: Dawsons of Pall

Mall, 1968). Newton also explored theological ideas in his *Two Notable Corruptions of Scripture* and *Observations on the Prophecies of Daniel and the Apocalypse of St. John* (posthumous, 1733), Introduction by William Whitla (London: J. Murray, 1922).

61. See Merchant, *Death of Nature*, 80–126; also Frances A. Yales, *Giordano Bruno and the Hermetic Tradition* (Chicago: University of Chicago Press, 1964).

62. Berman, *Reenchantment*, 59–65.

63. See Eduardo Galeano, *The Open Veins of Latin America: Five Centuries of the Pillage of a Continent* (New York: Monthly Review Pres, 1973); also Alfred Crosby, *Ecological Imperialism: The Biological Expansion of Europe, 900–1900* (London: Cambridge University Press, 1986).

64. For a third-world feminist critique of the negative effects of Western "development" on women, the poor, and the land, see Vandana Shiva, *Staying Alive: Women, Ecology and Development* (London: Zed Books, 1988).

CHAPTER 8: HEALING THE WORLD: THE COVENANTAL TRADITION

1. See the discussion of the nature-history split in recent European Protestant theology in H. Paul Santmire, *The Travail of Nature: The Ambiguous Ecological Promise of Christian Theology* (Philadelphia: Fortress Press, 1985), chapter 9.

2. Santmire, *The Travail of Nature,* chapter 10.

3. This is the view taken by Old Testament scholars, such as Gerhard von Rad, "The Theological Problem of the Old Testament Doctrine of Creation," in *The Problem of the Hexateuch and Other Essays* (New York: McGraw-Hill, 1966), 131–43.

4. For feminist interpretations of the Hagar story, see Phyllis Trible, *Texts of Terror: Literary Feminist Readings of Biblical Narratives* (Philadelphia: Fortress Press, 1984), 9–35.

5. These attributions of personlike qualities to nature are often dismissed as either meaningless "poetry" or as survivals of Baalism in Hebrew scripture. Either way, they can be ignored as a serious part of the theology of the biblical God. Although they may be survivals of Baalism, I see that neither as bad nor as incompatible with Yahwism. Clearly the Old Testament writers who used such language did not either. It is important to understand that "animism" does not mean deification of nature, but simply the recognition of personlike life in nature. The denial of this is distinctly peculiar to the modern West.

6. The condemnation of the biblical doctrine of human dominion as the key source of the ecological crisis is found particularly in Lynn White's widely read essay, "The Historical Roots of our Ecologic Crisis," which appeared originally in *Science* (March 10, 1967): 1203–1207. It has been a key justification of an absolutistic rejection of the Jewish and Christian traditions in much of the American ecological movement, although the ultimate reason why this essay was used in this way is that it coincided with a predisposition to such hostility that was already present.

7. See James Barr, "Man and Nature: The Ecological Controversy and the Old Testament," in *Ecology and Religion in History,* edited by David and Eileen Spring (San Francisco: Harper & Row, 1974), 48–75.

8. For one of the major explorations of the relation of peoplehood and land in biblical thought, see W. D. Davies, *The Gospel and the Land: Early Christianity and the Jewish Territorial Doctrine* (Berkeley: University of California Press, 1974).

9. See particularly Richard C. Austin, *Hope for the Land: Nature in the Bible* (Atlanta: John Knox Press, 1988), 97–114.

10. Austin, *Hope for the Land,* 115–26. Also John Howard Yoder, *The Politics of Jesus* (Grand Rapids: William B. Eerdmans Press, 1972), 64–78.

11. Yoder, *The Politics of Jesus,* 64–78.

12. Although most of the text in Luke 4:18–19, which Jesus purportedly read in his synagogue in Nazareth, is taken from Isaiah 61:1–2, there are some discrepancies. Luke read from the Septuagint version of Isaiah 61:1 a mistranslation of "opening of the prisons to those who are bound" as "opening the eyes of those who are blind," and he also added a phrase from Isaiah 58:6, "to set at liberty those who are oppressed."

13. Winstanley laid down the basic principles of the Digger movement in his 1649 manifesto, *The True Levellers Standard Advanced.* For a discussion of this movement, see Christopher Hill, *The World Turned Upside Down: Radical Ideas During the English Revolution* (New York: Penguin, 1975), 107–50.

14. See Conrad Cherry, *God's New Israel: Religious Interpretations of American Destiny* (Englewood Cliffs, NJ: Prentice-Hall, 1971), 42–43.

15. Cherry, *God's New Israel,* 42–43.

16. Cherry, *God's New Israel,* 42–43.

17. See Wolfgang Roth and Rosemary Ruether, *The Liberating Bond: Covenants, Biblical and Contemporary* (New York: Friendship Press, 1978), 67–83.

18. For outbreaks of anti-Arab and anti-Muslim hate in the United States during the 1991 Persian Gulf War, see *ADC Times,* the

newsletter of the American-Arab Anti-Discrimination Committee (January 1991).

19. For an overview of this issue, see Roderick F. Nash, *The Rights of Nature: A History of Environmental Ethics* (Madison: University of Wisconsin Press, 1989).

20. This is my own interpretation. For histories of anticruelty and its connection with English relations to pets, see Keith Thomas, *Man and the Natural World: Changing Attitudes in England, 1500–1800* (New York: Penguin, 1984). Also James Serpell, *In the Company of Animals: A Study of Human-Animal Relationships* (London: Basil Blackwell, 1986).

21. See particularly Peter Singer, *Animal Liberation*, 2d ed. (New York: The New York Review of Books, 1990).

22. Tom Regan, *The Case for Animal Rights* (Berkeley: University of California Press, 1983).

23. Regan, *The Case for Animal Rights*, 294–97.

24. Regan, *The Case for Animal Rights*, 359–63.

25. Paul and Anne Ehrlich, *Extinction: The Causes and Consequences of the Disappearance of Species* (New York: Random House, 1981).

26. Daniel B. Botkin, in a paper delivered at the Fifth Annual Casassa Conference, "Ecological Prospects: Theory and Practice," March 14–15, 1991, Loyola Marymount University, Los Angeles, California, titled "Ecological Theory and Natural Resource Management: Scientific Principle or Cultural Heritage," showed how sentimental attachment to elephants resulted in a proliferation of these animals that virtually destroyed the huge area of the Kenyan Wildlife Park as a life-bearing habitat for elephants or any other life.

27. Certain parts of the Deep Ecology movement also share a *laissez-faire* principle that imagines that undisturbed habitats for wild animals can be restored by withdrawal of human interference, but some of these writers also idealize the hunter as model of human communion with wild nature. See Paul Shepard, *Nature and Madness* (San Francisco: Sierra Club Books, 1982); also his *The Tender Carnivore and the Sacred Game* (New York: Scribners, 1973).

28. See discussion in John Cobb, *Matters of Life and Death* (Louisville, KY: Westminster/John Knox Press, 1991), 33–43.

29. See David C. Coats, *Old MacDonald's Factory Farm* (New York: Continuum, 1989).

30. Regan, *The Case for Animal Rights*, 349.

31. Christopher Stone, *Should Trees Have Standing? Toward Legal Rights for Natural Objects* (Los Altos, CA: Sierra Club Books, 1974).

32. Christopher Stone, *Earth and Other Essays: The Case for Moral Pluralism* (New York: Harper & Row, 1987).

33. David Rothenberg, in his paper "The Individual and the Community: Two Approaches to Ecophilosophy in Practice," in the Casassa
Conference (see note 26, above), contrasted the American individu-
alist approach, which is operative even in the success of the Endangered Species Act, and the Norwegian national plan for management
of environmental resources, which stresses a series of interrelated
communal principles of relation of the Norwegian people and its
land.
34. Richard C. Austin, in his *Reclaiming America: Restoring Nature to
Culture* (Abingdon, VA; Creekside Press, 1990), suggests a Constitutional amendment that would give civil rights to the (American)
earth. This amendment does not focus on individual animals, but
on the three areas of endangered species, natural life-support systems, and sites of particular aesthetic beauty (156–69).
35. For the insight into the encounter with nature as person without
anthropomorphism, I am indebted to the book by Erazim Kohak,
*The Embers and the Stars: A Philosophical Inquiry into the Moral
Sense of Nature* (Chicago: The University of Chicago Press, 1984).
36. Martin Buber's development of the philosophy of I-Thou relationship as the primary encounter with God, in and through, not only
other human beings, but trees and other living things, remains the
source of this insight: see his *I and Thou* (New York: Charles Scribner, 1958).

CHAPTER 9: HEALING THE WORLD:
THE SACRAMENTAL TRADITION

1. The idea that Plato was indebted to Moses is a commonplace in
Hellenistic Jewish thinkers, such as Philo: Richard Baer, *Philo's Use
of the Categories of Male and Female* (Leiden: Brill, 1970), 6. It also
is taken for granted in Patristic writings; see Justin Martyr, *1st Apology, 59*, and *Hortatory Address to the Greeks, 25–26, 31*.
2. See Philip Merlan, *From Platonism to Neoplatonism,* 3d ed. (The
Hague: Martinus Nijhoff, 1975).
3. *The Chaldean Oracles,* edited by Sapere Aude (London: Theosoph-
ical Publishing Society, 1895); also Hans Lewy, *Chaldean Oracles
and Theurgy: Mysticism, Magic and Platonism in the Later Roman
Empire* (Paris: Etudes Augustinienne, 1978) and Garth Fowden,
*The Egyptian Hermes: A Historical Approach to the Late Pagan
Mind* (Cambridge: Cambridge University Press, 1986).
4. R. E. de Witt, *Albinus and the History of Middle Platonism* (Cambridge: Cambridge University Press, 1937); also Plotinus, *Enneads,*
translated by Stephen MacKenna (London: Faber, 1969).

5. *Corpus Hermeticus*, text and French translation by A. D. Nock and A.-J. Festugiere (Paris: Société d'édition "Les Belles Lettres," 1960), 2 vols.

6. Proverbs 8; and Wisdom of Solomon 6–8.

7. See E. R. Goodenough, *By Light, Light: The Mystic Gospel of Hellenistic Judaism* (New Haven: Yale University Press, 1935).

8. See Sigmund Mowinckel, *He That Cometh: The Messiah Concept in the Old Testament and Later Judaism* (New York: Abingdon Press, 1955), 324–25.

9. Patrick Rogers, *Colossians* (Wilmington: Michael Glazier, 1980), 13–17.

10. For an analysis of the terms in the New Testament and their pre-Christian roots, see Walter Wink, *Naming the Powers: The Language of Power in the New Testament* (Philadelphia: Fortress Press, 1984).

11. One hundred years was seen as the fullness of human life: see Isaiah 65:20.

12. The heresy of docetism haunted the struggle in the first five centuries of Christianity to define the "two natures" in Christ. The view that Jesus only appeared to take on a body, but did not have a real material body, was most explicitly stated in Gnostic Christianity, such as Valentinianism. In the fourth century, the Neoplatonic philosopher turned Christian bishop, Synesius of Cyrene, openly declared his inability to believe in the bodily resurrection: see Jay Bregman, *Synesius of Cyrene: Philosopher-Bishop* (Berkeley: University of California Press, 1982), 120.

13. See D. S. Wallace-Hadrill, *The Greek Patristic View of Nature* (New York: Barnes and Noble, 1968), 66.

14. *Ad Haer.* V.2.2.

15. *Ad Haer.* V.34.2, 3.

16. *Ad Haer.* V.36.3.

17. This is Augustine's view, passed on as the dominant view for the Latin medieval church: *City of God* 20.7.

18. For example, Chrysostom, *Commentary on Romans*, 14: see Wallace-Hadrill, *The Greek Patristic View of Nature*, 115–20.

19. C. E. Rolt, *Dionysius the Aeropagite on the Divine Names and the Mystical Theology* (London: SPCK, 1940).

20. See particularly Heiko Oberman, *The Harvest of Medieval Theology: Gabriel Biel and Late Medieval Nominalism* (Cambridge: Harvard University Press, 1963), 30–46.

21. Frances A. Yates, *Giordano Bruno and the Hermetic Tradition* (New York: Random House, 1969), 12–13.

22. The antiquity of Hermes Trismegistus is attested to in the church fathers, and thus the Renaissance thinkers believed they had it on the best authority: for example, Augustine, *City of God* 18:29.

23. See particularly William Huffman, *Robert Fludd and the End of the Renaissance* (London: Routledge, 1988).

24. Henry More, *Manual of Metaphysics* (1671); see C. A. Patrides, ed., *The Cambridge Platonists* (Cambridge, MA: Harvard University Press, 1970).

25. See excerpts from Spinoza's *Ethics* in *The Age of Reason: Seventeenth Century Philosophers,* edited by Stuart Hampshire (New York: New American Library, 1956), 99–141. Also R. G. Collingwood, *The Idea of Nature* (New York: Oxford University Press, 1970), 103–12.

26. Wordsworth returned to more orthodox Christianity in his later years, becoming an admirer of the Oxford movement, while Coleridge came to be seen as a founder of the "Broad Church Movement": Basil Willey, *Nineteenth Century Studies: Coleridge to Matthew Arnold* (New York: Harper & Row, 1949), 1–50.

27. For Hegel's view and the transition to the modern view of nature, see Collingwood, *The Idea of Nature,* 121–32.

28. See Matthew Fox, *Original Blessing* (Santa Fe, NM: Bear and Co., 1983), 117, 157, 229.

29. Matthew Fox, *The Coming of the Cosmic Christ* (San Francisco: Harper & Row, 1988), 129–55.

30. Fox, *The Coming of the Cosmic Christ,* 235–39.

31. See Rosemary Ruether, "Matthew Fox and Creation Spirituality," in *The Catholic World* (July/August, 1990): 168–72.

32. Barbara Newman, author of *Sister of Wisdom: St. Hildegard's Theology of the Feminine* (Berkeley: University of California Press, 1987), has conveyed to me her critique of Fox's mistranslations and misinterpretations of the writings of Hildegard of Bingen. See her review in *Mystics Quarterly* XV.4 (December 1989): 190–94.

33. Pierre Teilhard de Chardin, *The Phenomenon of Man* (New York: Harper and Brothers, 1959).

34. See James Lovelock, *Gaia: A New Look at Life on Earth* (New York: Oxford University Press, 1979); also *The Ages of Gaia: Biography of our Living Earth* (New York: Norton, 1988).

35. See Teilhard de Chardin, *Phenomenon of Man,* 285–90; also his *The Divine Milieu* (New York: Harper & Row, 1960), 133–39.

36. See John Cobb and David Ray Griffin, *Process Theology: An Introductory Exposition* (Philadelphia: Westminster Press, 1976); also Marjorie Suchocki, *God-Christ-Church: A Practical Guide To Process Theology* (New York: Crossroads, 1989).

37. Alfred North Whitehead, *Process and Reality: An Essay in Cosmology* (New York: Macmillan, 1929), 519–33.

38. See particularly Marjorie Suchocki, *The End of Evil: Process Eschatology in Historical Context* (Albany: State University of New York Press, 1988), 97–114; also her *God-Christ-Church,* 183–216.

39. See Jasper Hopkins, *A Concise Introduction to the Philosophy of Nicholas of Cusa* (Minneapolis: University of Minnesota Press, 1978), 7–43; also Pauline M. Watts, *Nicolaus Cusanus: A Fifteenth-Century Vision of Man* (Leiden: Brill, 1982), 33–74.
40. The analogy comes from Fritjof Capra, *The Tao of Physics* (New York: Bantam Books, 1976), 54.
41. Blaise Pascal, *The Pensées,* edited by J. M. Cohen (Baltimore: Penguin Books, 1961), 57.

CHAPTER 10: CREATING A HEALED WORLD: SPIRITUALITY AND POLITICS

1. This analysis appeared in a talk by Lynn Margulis, "Gaia Minus Man," at the conference "Ecological Prospects: Theory and Practice," at Loyola Marymount University, Los Angeles, California, March 15, 1991. Margulis is one of the major theoreticians of the Gaia Hypothesis.
2. Marcia D. Lowe, "Rethinking Urban Transport," in *State of the World, 1991* (New York: Norton, 1991), 56–73.
3. See Christopher Flavin and Nicolas Lenssen, "Designing a Sustainable Energy System," Lester Brown et al., editors, *State of the World, 1991* (New York: Norton), 21–38; also Amory B. Lovins, *Soft Energy Paths: Toward a Durable Peace* (Cambridge, MA: Ballinger Publishing Company, 1977).
4. Jeremy Rifkin, *Biosphere Politics: A New Consciousness for a New Century* (New York: Crown Publishers, 1991), 287–92; also Kirkpatrick Sale, *Dwellers in the Land: The Bioregional Vision* (San Francisco: Sierra Club Books, 1985).
5. Wes Jackson, *New Roots for Agriculture* (Lincoln: University of Nebraska Press, 1985).
6. For example, the Spanish conquerors in the Americas created huge plantations, and this still shapes landholding patterns in these regions. Land reform remains the most central issue of social justice; see the pastoral letter by the Guatemalan bishops, *Clamor for Land,* published in *Reflections: The Guatemalan Church in Exile* (Managua, Nicaragua: May 1988).
7. Jeremy Rifkin, *Time Wars: The Primary Conflict in Human History* (New York: Simon and Schuster, 1989).
8. John E. Young, "Reducing Waste, Saving Materials," in *State of the World, 1991,* 39–55.
9. Kathleen Newland, *Women and Population Growth: The Choice Beyond Childbearing,* Worldwatch Report no. 16 (Washington, D.C.: Worldwatch Institute, 1977).

10. Rifkin, *Biosphere Politics*, 319–26.

11. Rifkin, *Biosphere Politics*, 11–91.

12. See March 20, 1991, United Nations Report on the damage done by United States bombing of Iraq: *International Socialist Review* (April 1991): 1–4.

13. Israel is usually ranked as the fourth largest military power, despite its small size, and has both nuclear and chemical weapons; see Jane Hunter, *Israel's Foreign Policy: South Africa and Central America* (Boston: South End Press, 1988).

14. See Michael Renner, "Converting to a Peaceful Economy," in *State of the World, 1990,* 154–72; also Kevin Cassidy, "Arms Control and the Home Front: Planning for the Conversion of Military Production Facilities to Civilian Manufacturing," in *Peace and Change* 14, no. 1 (January 1989): 46–64.

15. For more information write, The Bread and Puppet Theatre, Rural Delivery, Glover, VT 05839.

16. Jeremy Rifkin, *Green Lifestyle Handbook: 1001 Ways You Can Heal the Earth* (New York: Henry Holt and Company, 1990).

17. In the United States, the Green political movement has taken the form of Green Committees of Correspondence, Clearinghouse, P.O. Box 30208, Kansas City, MO 64112.

18. For example, the World Conference on Environment and Development: see Lester R. Brown, *State of the World* (New York: Norton 1990), 12–16.

19. Cited in Rifkin, *Green Lifestyle Handbook,* 286.

20. *State of the World, 1990,* 172–90.

Index

Philo, 231

Physics, and Christian creation story, 37–40

Plaskow, Judith, 117

Plato, 183, 184, 185, 230; creation story of, 22–26; view of evil of, 122–24

Poimandres, 125–26, 134

Pollution, and world destruction, 99–100

Population: escalating, 54–55; food for, 92–96; and poverty, 88–92

Population control, 55, 91–92, 263–64

Poverty, and population, 88–92

Process theology, 246–47

Puritanism: and apocalypticism, 75–77; and covenantal tradition, 216–18; and scientific revolution, 194

Reagan administration, apocalyptic thinking of, 81

Regan, Tom, 219–21, 223, 225

Republic (Plato), 24

"Resurrection of the Witnesses" (Cary), 75, 76

Revelation, Book of, apocalyptic stories of, 71–73

Rifkin, Jeremy, 11, 271

Ritschl, Albrecht, 36

Roman empire, fall of, 186–87

Sacramental tradition, 229; and cosmic Christology, 231–37; and cosmo-logical theology, 237–40; and ecofeminist theocosmology, 247–53; and ecological theology, 240–47; Hellenistic roots of, 230–31

Sanday, Peggy Reeves, 165–69

Schelling, Friedrich Wilhelm, 239

Science: and Christian creation story, 32–40; creation story from, 40–47

Scientific revolution, 194–97

Scopes, John, 35

Seventh Day Adventists. *See* Adventists

Sin, and evil, 115–16, 139–42

Single Integrated Operating Plan (SIOP), 107

Slavery: in Athens, 183–84; in Babylo-nian creation story, 18–19; in Greek creation story, 25; in Hebrew cre-ation story, 20; in Mesopotamia, 174–75

Spinoza, Benedictus de, 239

Spirituality: ecological, 205–7, 251–53; new, 4

Sprenger, Jacob, 191

State of the World report (Worldwatch Institute), 87

Stone, Christopher, 225–26

Suchocki, Marjorie, 246

Sumeria, flood story from, 61–62

Swimme, Brian, 57

Tanner, Nancy, 157

Tao of Physics, The (Capra), 39

Technology, and ecological life-style, 258–59

Teilhard de Chardin, Pierre, 240, 242–45

Theology: cosmological, 237–40; ecological, 240–47

Tiamat (ancient Mother Goddess), 17–22, 175–77, 200

Timaeus (Plato), 16, 22, 24, 26, 122, 123, 125

Transportation, 259–60

Urbanization, 95, 164, 262

U.S. Arms Control and Disarmament Agency: armaments expenditures estimate from, 103; nuclear bomb effects estimate from, 107–8

Vegetarianism, 224–25, 261. *See also* Food

Walvoord, John, 81

War: and colonialism, 198; and world destruction, 103, 104–6, 109–10, 111. *See also* Militarism

Western culture, classical, and domina-tion, 3

White, Ellen, 78–79

Whitehead, Alfred North, 240, 246–47

Winstanley, Gerrard, 215

Winthrop, John, 216–17

Witchcraft, 191, 193–94

Women: in Athens, 181–84; and Christian asceticism, 188–89, 191; in Israel, 178–81; in Mesopotamia, 174–78; and new life-style, 264–66. *See also* Gender; Matriarchy

"Word in Season to the Kingdom of England, A" (Cary), 75–76

Wordsworth, William, 240

Worldwatch Institute, 87, 272–73

Worldwatch Papers (Worldwatch Institute), 87